i

To my family and friends who listened to my stories, encouraged me to write them down, proof read the numerous drafts and then insisted that I publish - my thanks.

PROLOGUE

War is not all heroic deeds and daring-do, even for the Special Forces the glory only occupies a very small part of any conflict. For commanders, much of the time is spent in detailed preparation and planning but for the men it is largely taken up in moving from A to B and then on to C or perhaps back to A again. "On the bus, off the bus," and every one spends a lot of time just sitting around waiting for someone somewhere to make a decision, any decision. There are brief moments of frenzied activity when it is realized that all the training was not a waste of time but they are relatively rare.

The majority of books written about conflicts tend to concentrate on the moments of glory or the political machinations that wrought the conflict in the first place. This is history as the history books depict it. However, 'ordinary' life fills the gaps that surround these momentous events but is generally omitted from the record. Nevertheless, I believe a record of this 'social history' is just as important for, without it, future generations will have a poorer understanding of what life was really like.

This is by no means an official history. It is a diary of the observations of one individual - me - and how the Gulf War of 1991 affected me at a personal level. I did not perform any great heroic deeds and my name will not be recorded in the annals of history as a brilliant commander. In fact my claim to fame is only an assumed glory because fate chose to deposit me into the select company of the British Special Forces; the SAS. My job as 'quartermaster' to the Chinook helicopter flight that supported these gallant soldiers was unusual and fascinating but not the stuff of which epic sagas are made. Nevertheless, it gave me the opportunity to observe, at close quarters, the daily life of these people; their hopes, fears and humorous interludes.

Having originally recounted my adventures orally to friends and family, I have subsequently written this account as a narrative in an attempt to capture the original story telling atmosphere. It is, therefore, best read aloud but you must choose your audience carefully. Many of the words and expressions used, although common parlance in military circles, may be unfamiliar to the 'civilian' ear. They derive from the centuries of British military service in 'foreign' parts where they have become the lingua franca. Likewise, I have written much of the dialogue in 'English as she is spoke', but, where possible points of confusion or misunderstanding occur, have offered explanations which I hope make the matters clearer.

I hope you will find this as absorbing to read as I have found it to write. By the way, names and places have been changed to protect the innocent (?).

ABBREVIATIONS and EXPLANATIONS
A4 - paper sheet size (21 x 29.69 cm)

A-10 - Fairchild Republic battlefield close support aircraft (also known as the 'Warthog').

AAA (Triple A) - Anti Aircraft Artillery

ACO - The Admiralty Compass Observatory, now part of the Defence Research Agency.

ADMIN - Administration

AMEX- American Express credit card.

AM/FM - Amplitude Modulation and Frequency Modulation.

ALs - Amendment List.

AP - Air Publication.

APU - Auxiliary Power Unit

ASAP - As soon as possible.

AVRO - AV.Roe and sons. Aircraft manufactures, now part of British Aerospace.

AWACS - Airborne Warning and Control System (a modified Boeing 707 transport aircraft fitted with large 'mushroom radome)

BA - British Airways

BFPO - British Forces Post Office.

Brylcream - A hair cream much favoured by RAF Aircrew during the 1940s/50s

C-130 - The Lockheed Hercules military transport aircraft

CASEVAC - Casualty Evacuation.

Chinook - A twin rotor heavy lift helicopter made by Boeing Vertol.

CNN - American news broadcasting network

CO - Commanding Officer.

COMMS - Communications.

COMPO - Composite rations

C/T - Chief Technician

DAC - Dangerous Air Cargo.

dB - decibel.

DDSF - Deputy Director of Special Forces

DFC - Distinguished Flying Cross

DMS -Directly Moulded Sole.

Drm - Dirham - UAE unit of currency

DSO - Distinguished Service Order.

DZ - Drop Zone.

EEC - European Economic Community.

EVC -Evasion Chart.

expat (ex-patriot) - an exile, self imposed.

ft - feet

Flt Lt- Flight Lieutenant

GCs - Ground Crew.

GD Aerosystems Course - An RAF post-graduate course.

G & T - Gin and Tonic.

'George' - Aircraft's automatic pilot.

GLIM s - Small battery powered lights to mark the edges of runways. taxiways. obstructions etc. So called because they just glimmer.

GMT - Greenwich Mean Time

GPO - General Post Office.

GPS - Global Positioning by Satellite (navigation system).

GSM - General Service MedaL

HE - High Explosive.

HQ - Headquarters.

HUD - Head Up Display

IBM - International Business Machines (computer manufacturing company).
ID - Identification
INTO - Intelligence Officer.
INTSUM - Intelligence Sunmiazy.
IR - InfraRed.
JP233 - An airfield denial weapon containing many bomblets dropped at very low level.

KFS - Knife, Fork and Spoon.
KHz - Kilohertz (cycles per second X 10_3)
Kit Kat - A milk chocolate covered biscuit
KKIA - King Kahlid International Aiiport
KKMC - King Kahlid Military City
KLM - Dutch Royal Airways
Kts - Knots (nautical miles per hour).
LCD - Liquid Crystal Display.
LGB - Laser Guided Bomb.
LLTV - Low Light Television.
m - metres
MET - Meteorological.
MHz - Megahertz (cycles per second X 10_6)
MiD - Mention in Despatches.
MoD - Ministry of Defence.
MRE - Meals, Ready to Eat (USA version of COMPO)
MT - Motor Transpoit
NAAFI - Navy, Army and Air Force Institutes
NAPS - Nerve Agent Pe-treatment Set (anti-nerve agent pills)
NBC - Nuclear, Biological and Chemical.

NVGs - Night Vision Goggles.
'O' Group (Orders Group) - Daily gathering of senior officers for the promulgation of orders.
Ops - Operations
ORBAT - Order of Battle (make up of army).
Pan - Area on an airfield where aircraft are parked. Known by the Americana as a Ramp.
PhD - Doctor of Philosophy.
Puma - Medium lift helicopter made by Aerospatiale
PVC - Poly Vinyl Chloride.
R & R - Rest and Relaxation.
RAF - Royal Air Force.
Reynard Mr - A Fox.
Round Robin - Military transport engaged in picking up and dropping off passengers/freight as required on a 'circular
3
route.
SAM - Surface to Air Missile.
SAS - Special Air Service.
SBS - Special Boat Squadron.
SCUD - Russian surface to surface missile.
SENGO - Senior Engineering Officer.
SF - Special Forces.

SH - Support Helicopters.
SNCO - Senior Non-Commissioned Officer.
'Spectre' - A C-130 gun ship.
Sqn Ldr - Squadron Leader.
STOL - Short Take Off and Landing
TELEX - Teleprinter Exchange (typed messages sent via telephone lines)

bing", and life would resume its idyllic pattern. The strange thing
ne else wanted the job. Perhaps it had something to do with the
lways emphasised the tedium and said little of the freedom. Thus
Autumn of 1990 when Iraq invaded Kuwait and the build up to
declared to all and sundry, including my wife, Janet, that there
n God's earth I would be involved. I mean, who would want a
in the middle of a desert war? Silly me!

came and went and I still basked in this delusion that the
flict would pass me by, and then on the 9th of January I received
phone call.

ing in the middle of the compass base at Royal Naval Air Yard,
r Gosport in Hampshire. It was quite a mild day for January and,
small base, Norrie and I had decided to go and play 9 holes at
club in the afternoon. It was about mid-day and we were about
h the survey when a Land Rover was seen to approach. The
the wheel informed me that I was to 'phone my desk officer as
. I left Norrie to continue with the survey and accompanied the
e Air Traffic Control Tower.

cer was at RAF Innsworth, Gloucestershire, and usually only
en I was due for posting. I was not due to be posted for another
uld not think why he should want to speak to me. To say that
y enquiry came as a surprise is an understatement. All he said
bags, you're off to the Gulf the day after tomorrow. Report
Strike Command as soon as you can and contact Squadron
I will confirm this by signal." He then gave me a telephone
ch to call this squadron leader, whose name seemed vaguely
g up.

was say "Yes sir!", and put the 'phone down. On the way back
se my mind started to race. Where was I going? What was
here was I going to get all my kit from? I had handed it all
my current ground tour. Most important of all, what was I

ilarly nonplussed but responded with, "Go on then, bugger
clear up." So I did just that. His parting shot was, "Hey,
computer in the office?"

you some notes," I said, and drove off.

TriStar - A three engined, wide body, passenger jet aircraft made by the Lockheed corporation.
Tri-wall - A three layered, cardboard board.
TV - Television.
UAE - United Arab Emirates
UK - United Kingdom.
UN - United Nations
USA - United States of America.
UTC - Co-ordinated Universal Time
VC 10 - A British Aerospace jet passenger aircraft
Wg Cdr - Wing Commander.
WWI- World War 1.
WWII - World War 2.
ZSU 23/4 - A Russian built, four barrelled, 23mm, anti aircraft artillery tank.

1 - THE CALL TO ARMS - 9/10 JAN 1991

By this time you probably will have read the official factual accounts of the conflict by such notables as Generals "Stormin' Norman" Schwarzkopf and Sir Peter De La Billiere. Likewise you may have thrilled to the exciting narratives of SAS exploits behind enemy lines in books such as Bravo Two Zero. Now it is time for you to hear another side of the story; a side built around the exploits of an "average serviceman" who just got caught up in it. A story of comradeship, frustration, difficult times, but above all the 'trench' humour which is synonymous with war.

In the autumn of 1990 I was a Flight Lieutenant Navigator of 19 years service in the RAF. Of those 19 years I had spent the first five in the back of an AVRO Shackleton, watching a radar screen and directing Lightnings and Phantoms on to Russian Tupelov TU-20 "Bears" in the Iceland/Faroes gap. The next ten years saw an association with the SH (support helicopter) world. I say 'association' because, in the early days, navigators were rarely found on support helicopter squadrons, and those that were had to qualify as Crewmen/ Loadmasters. They were usually placed in charge of the map store and expected to plan, though not necessarily take part in, any overseas sortie which fell to the squadron. Nevertheless, having duly qualified as a Puma Crewman, I embarked upon a career which included three years on a UK based squadron, two years in Northern Ireland, and four years on a tactics and trials unit. It was during this latter period that I had occasion to work in conjunction with elements of the SAS, trying out some strange items of equipment and even stranger techniques that they wished to employ. It was this "special forces" work that was ultimately to lead me into the Gulf War, but more of that in a moment.

All good things come to an end and, although most aircrew join the Air Force to fly, inevitably one is subject to the rigours of a ground tour. In my case the prospects did not look too bleak. Not for me the long grey days at the controls of an ebony bomber (a desk) in some MoD cupboard at St Giles Court. (By the way, St Giles is the patron saint of beggars and cripples) Instead, I had managed to secure a twelve month sabbatical at the RAF College, Cranwell (the "College of Knowledge"), attending the GD Aerosystems Course and thereby increasing my usefulness to the RAF with the promise of a good chance of a flying tour to follow.

The GD Aerosystems Course (GD stands for general duties and therefore is the get out clause when the good chance of a flying tour turns out to be a

ground tour after all) is an attempt to tea
radar theory, among other things, in ord
establishments such as Farnborough and
content is of a classified nature and bef
"positively vetted", that is, interviewed
any kind of security risk. It does not d
this vetting interview as I found to my
question, "Do you enjoy normal sex?"
'normal', it took a further 40 minutes
really wanted to know was if I had ho

Part of the GD Aerosystems Cou
word thesis on a given subject. Min
particular bomb sight would functio
calculations showed that it would, b
paper. Clearly I had to fluff it out a
applications of the sight. After mu
discrepancy in the planned and act
my thesis was stamped Top Secret
of the course. I must have really u
of being posted to one of the afor
was sent to the Admiralty Compa
where I became "Mr Compass Ba

My job at the ACO was to ca
bases. A compass base is a magi
their compasses checked and ca
most part involves standing for
swept and rain soaked airfields
compass readings within an are
However, what made the job b
service life, I was, to all intent
small unit of about 250 civilia
the only RAF person there. Ir
total. I did not have to wear a
perform, I was not called upo
of my time on the road, trave
civilian, on expenses! The
taught me to play golf and s
airfield itinerary as possible
complain about the weather
member of the team would

people are d
was that no
fact that we
it was, in the
war started, I
was no way o
compass base

Christmas
impending co
the fateful tele

I was stand
Fleetlands, nea
as it was only a
Hindhead golf
half way throug
Naval rating at
soon as possibl
rating back to t

My desk off
made contact w
two years and c
his response to
was, "Pack your
to Headquarters
Leader Sanders.
extension on whi
familiar, and hun

All I could do
to the compass ba
I going to do? W
in when I took up
going to tell Janet

Norrie was sin
off and leave me t
how do you use th

"I'll try to leave

Movement Signal

On the way to Strike Command at High Wycombe, I stopped at a phone box to ring Janet. "I've no idea at the moment," I said in answer to her inevitable questions, "I'll let you know when I get back, when ever that will be." As you can imagine, I was not really conscious of the remainder of that journey. I was trying to work out what, in the name of God, they wanted me for.

The car park at HQ Strike Command was unusually full and there was an increased security state in force. I managed to find a parking space and joined the queue at the temporary security check post. I stated my business, and was relieved to discover that I was expected. I was directed to an inner "fortress", built into the chalk of the Chiltern Hills, where I had to queue for yet another security check. Told to wait in a small side office, I sat and studied the faces of the other occupants. Some were, like me, in civilian dress, others wore uniforms, and of all services and ranks, but apart from the odd pleasantry nothing was said; all eyes fixed on a middle distance. For me, the call to arms was still very new but from these faces, many of whom had been involved with the preparation for war since the first hint of the invasion of Kuwait, I began to get the feeling that this whole issue might be serious.

My reverie was broken by a familiar voice which said, "Hello Roger, glad you could make it." I looked up and saw 'Sandy' standing there. I am dreadful at remembering names but I don't forget faces and here was one I instantly recognised, perhaps the ears, like forward pointing radar scanners, helped with the recognition. I had last seen Don Sanders six or seven years earlier when we had shared an office on the Tactics and Trials flight and he valiantly tried to teach me to fly the Chinook helicopter. Actually he hadn't done a bad job, but we had parted company shortly after and I had lost track of him.

"Did I have a choice then sir?" He had been promoted to squadron leader since our last meeting.

"Not really," was his reply, "You were at the head of a cast of one. This job came up and I thought, who can do this? Your name came immediately to mind and, as your security clearance was still intact, you were nominated, proposed and elected."

"Thanks." I said as sarcastically as one can to a squadron leader, "But what is the job?"

"Can't talk here," was his reply, "But come with me and all will be revealed."

This turned out to be far from the truth but off he went through the security turnstile which, to my surprise, let me in as well. After several minutes of twisting and turning through the labyrinth of corridors we ended up at a door covered in security and combination locks. The door finally yielded to his ministrations to reveal a small and untidy office the walls of which were covered with maps of all kinds of the Gulf. There were two other people in the office who studiously ignored us and carried on with what ever it was they were doing. Presumably anyone who could get through the plethora of combination locks on the door obviously had a right to be there and did not warrant a second look.

Sandy lodged himself on the edge of a desk and, in his inimitable fashion, launched straight in.

"You know the Special Forces (SF) flight attached to 7 Sqn?" (7 Sqn was a squadron of Chinooks at RAF Odiham, Hampshire.).

"Ye-es, I know of them," I replied, " And I know the rumours that they support the SAS, but what they actually do I have no idea."

"Good." he said, "That's as it should be. Well, when I left Tactics and Trials flight I went to work for them." No wonder I had lost track of him.

TriStar - A three engined, wide body, passenger jet aircraft made by the Lockheed corporation.

Tri-wall - A three layered, cardboard board.

TV - Television.

UAE - United Arab Emirates

UK - United Kingdom.

UN - United Nations

USA - United States of America.

UTC - Co-ordinated Universal Time

VC 10 - A British Aerospace jet passenger aircraft

Wg Cdr - Wing Commander.

WWI- World War 1.

WWII - World War 2.

ZSU 23/4 - A Russian built, four barrelled, 23mm, anti aircraft artillery tank.

1 - THE CALL TO ARMS - 9/10 JAN 1991

By this time you probably will have read the official factual accounts of the conflict by such notables as Generals "Stormin' Norman" Schwarzkopf and Sir Peter De La Billiere. Likewise you may have thrilled to the exciting narratives of SAS exploits behind enemy lines in books such as Bravo Two Zero. Now it is time for you to hear another side of the story; a side built around the exploits of an "average serviceman" who just got caught up in it. A story of comradeship, frustration, difficult times, but above all the 'trench' humour which is synonymous with war.

In the autumn of 1990 I was a Flight Lieutenant Navigator of 19 years service in the RAF. Of those 19 years I had spent the first five in the back of an AVRO Shackleton, watching a radar screen and directing Lightnings and Phantoms on to Russian Tupelov TU-20 "Bears" in the Iceland/Faroes gap. The next ten years saw an association with the SH (support helicopter) world. I say 'association' because, in the early days, navigators were rarely found on support helicopter squadrons, and those that were had to qualify as Crewmen/ Loadmasters. They were usually placed in charge of the map store and expected to plan, though not necessarily take part in, any overseas sortie which fell to the squadron. Nevertheless, having duly qualified as a Puma Crewman, I embarked upon a career which included three years on a UK based squadron, two years in Northern Ireland, and four years on a tactics and trials unit. It was during this latter period that I had occasion to work in conjunction with elements of the SAS, trying out some strange items of equipment and even stranger techniques that they wished to employ. It was this "special forces" work that was ultimately to lead me into the Gulf War, but more of that in a moment.

All good things come to an end and, although most aircrew join the Air Force to fly, inevitably one is subject to the rigours of a ground tour. In my case the prospects did not look too bleak. Not for me the long grey days at the controls of an ebony bomber (a desk) in some MoD cupboard at St Giles Court. (By the way, St Giles is the patron saint of beggars and cripples) Instead, I had managed to secure a twelve month sabbatical at the RAF College, Cranwell (the "College of Knowledge"), attending the GD Aerosystems Course and thereby increasing my usefulness to the RAF with the promise of a good chance of a flying tour to follow.

The GD Aerosystems Course (GD stands for general duties and therefore is the get out clause when the good chance of a flying tour turns out to be a ground tour after all) is an attempt to teach aircrew difficult sums, statistics and radar theory, among other things, in order to fit them for research work at establishments such as Farnborough and Boscombe Down. Much of the course content is of a classified nature and before embarking upon it one has to be "positively vetted", that is, interviewed by security personnel to see if you pose any kind of security risk. It does not do to stray from the "yes/no" answers in this vetting interview as I found to my cost for when, in response to the question, "Do you enjoy normal sex?" I asked for a qualification of the word 'normal', it took a further 40 minutes to determine that what my inquisitor really wanted to know was if I had homosexual tendencies. But I digress.

Part of the GD Aerosystems Course also involves the writing of a 10,000 word thesis on a given subject. Mine was to determine whether or not a particular bomb sight would function at heights of below 100 feet. My calculations showed that it would, but I had achieved this in half a side of A4 paper. Clearly I had to fluff it out a little and so decided to look at the proposed applications of the sight. After much diligent searching I discovered a serious discrepancy in the planned and actual usage rates but when I pointed this out my thesis was stamped Top Secret and I was not allowed to present it at the end of the course. I must have really upset someone for upon graduation, instead of being posted to one of the aforementioned flying research establishments I was sent to the Admiralty Compass Observatory (ACO), just outside Slough where I became "Mr Compass Base".

My job at the ACO was to carry out magnetic surveys of aircraft compass bases. A compass base is a magnetically clean area where aircraft are taken and their compasses checked and calibrated. The job itself is tedious and for the most part involves standing for up to five hours at a time in the middle of wind swept and rain soaked airfields taking and recording upwards of one hundred compass readings within an area usually no bigger than a football pitch. However, what made the job bearable was the fact that, for the first time in my service life, I was, to all intents and purposes, a free agent. The ACO was a small unit of about 250 civilian personnel set in 38 acres of park land. I was the only RAF person there. In fact there were only five military personnel in total. I did not have to wear a uniform, there were no secondary duties to perform, I was not called upon to be duty officer. But best of all, I spent most of my time on the road, travelling from airfield to airfield, both military and civilian, on expenses! The other member of the team, 'Norrie', a golfing nut, taught me to play golf and so we introduced as many golf courses into our airfield itinerary as possible. On the odd occasion that either of us saw fit to complain about the weather or a particularly grumpy landlady, the other member of the team would utter the words, "Yes, but think what the poor people are doing", and life would resume its idyllic pattern. The strange thing was that no one else wanted the job. Perhaps it had something to do with the fact that we always emphasised the tedium and said little of the freedom. Thus it was, in the Autumn of 1990 when Iraq invaded Kuwait and the build up to war started, I declared to all and sundry, including my wife, Janet, that there was no way on God's earth I would be involved. I mean, who would want a compass base in the middle of a desert war? Silly me!

Christmas came and went and I still basked in this delusion that the impending conflict would pass me by, and then on the 9th of January I received the fateful telephone call.

I was standing in the middle of the compass base at Royal Naval Air Yard, Fleetlands, near Gosport in Hampshire. It was quite a mild day for January and, as it was only a small base, Norrie and I had decided to go and play 9 holes at Hindhead golf club in the afternoon. It was about mid-day and we were about half way through the survey when a Land Rover was seen to approach. The Naval rating at the wheel informed me that I was to 'phone my desk officer as soon as possible. I left Norrie to continue with the survey and accompanied the rating back to the Air Traffic Control Tower.

My desk officer was at RAF Innsworth, Gloucestershire, and usually only made contact when I was due for posting. I was not due to be posted for another two years and could not think why he should want to speak to me. To say that his response to my enquiry came as a surprise is an understatement. All he said was, "Pack your bags, you're off to the Gulf the day after tomorrow. Report to Headquarters Strike Command as soon as you can and contact Squadron Leader Sanders. I will confirm this by signal." He then gave me a telephone extension on which to call this squadron leader, whose name seemed vaguely familiar, and hung up.

All I could do was say "Yes sir!", and put the 'phone down. On the way back to the compass base my mind started to race. Where was I going? What was I going to do? Where was I going to get all my kit from? I had handed it all in when I took up my current ground tour. Most important of all, what was I going to tell Janet?

Norrie was similarly nonplussed but responded with, "Go on then, bugger off and leave me to clear up." So I did just that. His parting shot was, "Hey, how do you use the computer in the office?"

"I'll try to leave you some notes," I said, and drove off.

Movement Signal

On the way to Strike Command at High Wycombe, I stopped at a phone box to ring Janet. "I've no idea at the moment," I said in answer to her inevitable questions, "I'll let you know when I get back, when ever that will be." As you can imagine, I was not really conscious of the remainder of that journey. I was trying to work out what, in the name of God, they wanted me for.

The car park at HQ Strike Command was unusually full and there was an increased security state in force. I managed to find a parking space and joined the queue at the temporary security check post. I stated my business, and was relieved to discover that I was expected. I was directed to an inner "fortress", built into the chalk of the Chiltern Hills, where I had to queue for yet another security check. Told to wait in a small side office, I sat and studied the faces of the other occupants. Some were, like me, in civilian dress, others wore uniforms, and of all services and ranks, but apart from the odd pleasantry nothing was said; all eyes fixed on a middle distance. For me, the call to arms was still very new but from these faces, many of whom had been involved with the preparation for war since the first hint of the invasion of Kuwait, I began to get the feeling that this whole issue might be serious.

My reverie was broken by a familiar voice which said, "Hello Roger, glad you could make it." I looked up and saw 'Sandy' standing there. I am dreadful at remembering names but I don't forget faces and here was one I instantly recognised, perhaps the ears, like forward pointing radar scanners, helped with the recognition. I had last seen Don Sanders six or seven years earlier when we had shared an office on the Tactics and Trials flight and he valiantly tried to teach me to fly the Chinook helicopter. Actually he hadn't done a bad job, but we had parted company shortly after and I had lost track of him.

"Did I have a choice then sir?" He had been promoted to squadron leader since our last meeting.

"Not really," was his reply, "You were at the head of a cast of one. This job came up and I thought, who can do this? Your name came immediately to mind and, as your security clearance was still intact, you were nominated, proposed and elected."

"Thanks." I said as sarcastically as one can to a squadron leader, "But what is the job?"

"Can't talk here," was his reply, "But come with me and all will be revealed."

This turned out to be far from the truth but off he went through the security turnstile which, to my surprise, let me in as well. After several minutes of twisting and turning through the labyrinth of corridors we ended up at a door covered in security and combination locks. The door finally yielded to his ministrations to reveal a small and untidy office the walls of which were covered with maps of all kinds of the Gulf. There were two other people in the office who studiously ignored us and carried on with what ever it was they were doing. Presumably anyone who could get through the plethora of combination locks on the door obviously had a right to be there and did not warrant a second look.

Sandy lodged himself on the edge of a desk and, in his inimitable fashion, launched straight in.

"You know the Special Forces (SF) flight attached to 7 Sqn?" (7 Sqn was a squadron of Chinooks at RAF Odiham, Hampshire.).

"Ye-es, I know of them," I replied, " And I know the rumours that they support the SAS, but what they actually do I have no idea."

"Good." he said, "That's as it should be. Well, when I left Tactics and Trials flight I went to work for them." No wonder I had lost track of him.

Throughout the SH (support helicopter) world the SF flight were known by reputation for being 'Secret Squirrels' but that was all that was known by those who did not need to know any more. "Now that all this lot's blown up I'm acting as the UK co-ordinator for their operations out in the Gulf."

"What are they doing?" I asked, knowing it was a silly question as soon as I had uttered it.

"Can't tell you that, it's secret," he replied, " but they need an Ops (operations) officer and that's where you come in. You're booked on a TriStar out of RAF Brize Norton the day after tomorrow. Any questions?"

"Yes! Where am I going?" I asked hopefully.

"Can't tell you that either." he said, "but when you arrive at Riyadh tell them you're for Operation 'JEMMY' and they'll put you on the right plane. All will be revealed."

"But I thought this war was called Operation GRANBY." I said.

"The general action is," he replied, "but your little outfit wishes to remain as incognito as possible, so JEMMY it is."

"How long is all this planned to last?" I asked, hardly expecting a sensible answer.

"Nominally six months," came the reply, "then you will be replaced."

Oh yes, I thought, and if I head a cast of one who is going to replace me? But I said nothing and just nodded sagely. "I see. So what now?"

"Go to RAF Odiham first thing tomorrow and they will kit you out. They are expecting you."

This was fortunate. I lived in married quarters at Odiham, and had done for the previous six years, so at least I knew the people and my way round the station. The briefing over, I took my leave of Sqn Ldr Sanders, he wished me luck and I drove out of the car park hardly any wiser than when I had entered it. It was now about half past three and time was short, I had to get my mind into gear and try to form some plan of action. Human beings are great at making plans but we seldom include in those plans contingencies for our sudden removal from the scene. Oh, some of us make wills but few of us actually plan for death and the consequences of our disappearance from the scene and its effect on other people. Not that I was going to die, hopefully, but I was going to disappear for six months, at least. There were many loose ends to be tidied up and all I could hope to do was tie some knots in the ends of just a few of them. I needed a very short list of priorities.

Firstly, I had to go back to the ACO. Norrie genuinely did not know how to get our compass base information out of the computer, he could, and occasionally did type the odd report, but up till now I had always set the thing up, stored the files and generally saw to the admin. Fortunately the ACO was only a minor deviation from my journey home.

All the way to the ACO I was trying to make this list of priorities. I had one of those note pads with a suction pad that you can fix to your windscreen and I scribbled away as I drove. More than once I looked up just in time to avoid driving into the kerb, pedestrians and other road users. I defy any ordinary person to be single minded in situations like this. Apart from the obvious things I was going to need like uniform, equipment, knife, fork and spoon, etc. I decided I would also take one or two items which would make life just a little more comfortable. Baden Powell, in his book Scouting for Boys, said that only the tenderfoot 'roughs' it in camp. There is no point in proving you can bleed if you don't have to. So what luxuries could I afford to take in what was obviously going to be a limited space?

By the time I had arrived at the ACO I had decided on two things, firstly a personal stereo tape player with radio capable of receiving the BBC World Service and secondly, I would take my sand wedge and a couple of golf balls. The radio/tape player would keep me in touch with reality and, as the desert was just one big bunker and I certainly needed to practice my bunker shots, the sand wedge was almost an essential. My golf pro would be proud of me. The first of these items I did not possess, my two children did, but up to this point I had never had the need for one. However, their's did not have radios so I would have to go and buy one. On second thoughts though, it was my birthday in 9 days time, I would suggest this as an ideal present. The sand wedge, on the other hand was no problem. I would just take the one from my golf bag.

I arrived at the ACO just before four o'clock and explained to the section supervisor what had happened. I 'phoned Janet and updated her with as much as I knew, which was not a lot and said I would be home about six o'clock. Janet, who is an executive secretary at IBM had informed her boss that she would not be in for the next couple of days and explained why. The immediate reaction was to tell her to go as soon as she wanted to and not to return until everything had been sorted. Indeed, throughout the whole time I was away, IBM gave her unfailing support for which I wish to record my thanks.

Norrie had not yet returned from Fleetlands so I set about typing out a skeleton idiots guide to the hidden mysteries and science of the computer, at least I set out a step by step guide on how to switch it on, extract the desired file, save it, print it and, most important, how to get out of the program and switch off. Have you noticed this is the instruction most often missing from computer manuals. They go into great detail on how to start up but almost invariably fail to tell you how to get out. With this finished I went home.

When I arrived home Janet was understandably apprehensive but had lost none of her secretarial efficiency. She had started to collect together those personal things that she thought I would want to take with me. She had also telephoned our youngest son (Matthew 17) at Bedford School and his housemaster had immediately despatched him home by train with the instructions not to return until he was ready. We had not always seen eye to eye with this man, but his support for Matthew during the next few months while I was away was impeccable. Jonathan (20), our eldest had left Bedford after 'A' levels and elected to find a job. He had left home but was living with his girlfriend, Lara, in a small house on the far side of Basingstoke, about seven miles away, and was, therefore, also on tap. By nine o'clock I had my family around me.

To say it was an odd evening is a serious understatement. I 'phoned my parents and various friends and relations with the news but could not answer any of their questions. Firstly because I did not know the answer to most of them myself and secondly because the security implications prohibited me from answering those I did know. I continued to collect together personal kit and made a list of jobs to be done the next day. The atmosphere was subdued. Obviously I had been away on exercise before but exercises are always of a finite time and you know when you will return. This was different. It was open ended. Despite the assurances that I would be relieved after six months I could not help thinking of the servicemen in the second world war, who left home at short notice and didn't come back for five years, if they were lucky!

The open ended exercise scenario is one of the training techniques adopted by the SAS. On certain of the escape and evasion exercises the candidate is given a map grid reference to get to. When he gets there he is given another one, and so on. The candidate does not know when, or how, this process will end and it takes a particular type of character to deal with this continual state of uncertainty. However, not being an SAS candidate, needless to say I spent a fairly sleepless night. The next day dawned. I have no recollection if it was bright and clear, I was just conscious of the fact that I had 24 hours in which to get my act together.

I had been told to report to the RAF Regiment Flight at RAF Odiham, which I duly did. I was informed that I was not actually expected but, as I was just one of a continuous dribble of personnel re-enforcing the troops already in the Gulf, the "system" was geared up to process me. This was good news and bad news. The good news was that the 'system could deal with me. The bad news was: If I was not expected at Odiham, was any one else expecting me? Did I have a seat on the aircraft tomorrow? Would there be any one to meet me in Riyadh? I did not have a lot of time to ponder these things. Time was running out and my list of priorities was not as short as I would have wished.

As far as the Regiment Flight personnel were concerned, their priority was to ensure that I was 'current on my weapon'. Translated into English, that means that I had to know how to load, fire and clean the weapon appropriate to my rank and job and have practised the same within the last twelve months. I said that I had fired my obligatory 25 rounds not six months previously and was therefore 'current'. The sergeant in charge thought it would be a good idea if we ran through it again just to refresh our memories and I agreed, whereupon he handed me one of the newly introduced SA-80 assault rifles.

I protested, "This is not an officer's weapon. Officers, especially aircrew officers, have the 9mm Browning pistol."

"Not any more sir," he replied, "no use to man or beast anyway."

"Why then," I demanded, "have I wasted the last 20 years with the Browning?"

"Can't say sir, but its the SA-80 now sir." "Corporal! This officer needs the full package."

The corporal ushered me into a small side office. "Not used one of these before, sir?"

"No."

"Then we'll start with the sling."

The SA-80 is the British answer to a comprehensive re-appraisal on what the basic infantry weapon is all about and the product of a serious re-think on design. It is light and compact, much of which is achieved by incorporating the barrel in the stock, thus maintaining barrel length (which gives you accuracy) whilst considerably shortening the overall length of the weapon. All non metallic parts are made of moulded plastic, instead of wood which, again, reduces weight. The working parts are manufactured to a high standard and its action is smooth. The overall result is a light, accurate rifle. It is also capable of being fitted with a bayonet. A multi-purpose, Swiss Army knife of a bayonet but nevertheless, still a bayonet. So that, at the end of the day, despite all the sophistication of the 20th century, the modern infantryman is still armed with little more than a short stabbing spear just as his ancestors were back in the Stone Age. However, this spear was obviously designed in a laboratory by boffins and exhibits one or two curious design features which make it a less than practical infantry weapon.

Unlike its American counterpart, the Armalite, it is not particularly robust and does not take kindly to being dropped or ill treated (something which tends to happen in the field). It is too well made and, unlike, its Russian equivalent, the AK-47 Kalashnikov, the closely engineered tolerances of its mechanical parts cause it to jam in dusty conditions and only accept a very limited range of other countries' ammunition. The AK-47, on the other hand, will fire having been dropped in a silty river and take almost any bullet of approximately the same calibre. This may not be good engineering but the resulting versatility makes it extremely popular among soldiers fighting in less than ideal conditions.

The SA-80 can only be used right handed, but even so has a curious cocking system which requires you to reach over to the 'wrong' side of the rifle. Finally, it has the most complex sling ever designed to confuse the common soldier let alone air force officer. When fitted properly it provides an excellent support for accurate fire, but it is like a Christmas puzzle and, in true military fashion, is removed every time the rifle is taken into the armoury so that the next poor sod has to re-string it and try not to end up with a hammock. It is born of the same mentality that orders the sergeant to "Bugger the men about", because they are relaxing, the very conclusion I arrived at approximately 30 seconds after the corporal had started his instruction on the sling, SA-80, for the use of.

"Do I need to know all this Corporal?" I asked, "Just show me where to put the ammunition and how to take off the safety catch."

He looked pained. "The lecture on the sling usually takes up the first day of a five day course, sir." He exclaimed.

"Corporal, I am going off to war, tomorrow." I said, "I don't have five hours to spend on this let alone five days, now get real." But he did not seem to understand. The sergeant had told him to give the officer the whole package and that was what he was going to do. I had little better luck with the sergeant.

"I'm not sure you can be issued with a weapon unless you've done the full course and we've signed you up, sir." was the answer to my inquiry.

At this point I invited them to stand to attention while I held them in a one way conversation and pointed out that it would be their responsibility to explain to the Air Officer Commanding at Strike Command why they had sent me off to war without a rifle. In the end we came to a compromise. They showed me how to fire it, strip it and clean it, and I put the sling in my pocket and promised to find out how to use later. Much later it came in very handy for securing a package, but that's another story. By the time we had finished it was late morning and I still didn't have any kit.

My next port of call was the tactical clothing store where all the kit necessary for living in the field is issued.

"You'll want a set of webbing then." said the storeman, and proceeded to pile a collection of canvass belts and pouches on the counter in front of me.

The '58 pattern webbing is very close kin to the SA-80 sling. The basic idea of a belt and harness arrangement, onto which you can fit an infinite combination of pouches, pockets and bags and end up with a custom built rucksack, is good. Unfortunately, the canvass belt, to which you attach all these other items, is so stiff, even when old and worn, that it takes the hands of a blacksmith to bend and fold it to accept the clips of the pouches. I suppose there were some instructions on how to assemble the original one, laid down on tablets of stone back in '58 (does anyone know which '58?), but they have been lost in the mists of time and the ritual has to be passed down by word of mouth from generation to generation. Unluckily, as with all handed down tradition, the tale gets varied slightly; sometimes because it is misheard; sometimes because it is misunderstood. For example:

"Send reinforcements. We're going to advance."

Becomes:

"Send three and four pence. We're going to a dance." (For those who are not old enough, 'three and four pence' is a sum of pre-decimal money, three shillings and four pence, about £0.17)

Alternatively:

"Gladly the Cross I'd bear."

Becomes:

"Gladly the cross eyed bear."

Whatever happened, along the way the instructions on how to assemble the '58 (1758?) pattern webbing became garbled for no two sets ever look alike. You either end up with one pouch too many that will not fit anywhere but was made to contain your most important piece of kit or there is an ominous gap on the belt which every one else has managed to fill and leaves you wondering what you have mislaid. No matter what its final form, the '58 (1858?) pattern webbing was conceived of the idea that you may not want to carry all your kit all the time, and is so constructed to allow you to shed superfluous items at will, if you can bend the belt. A great theory. However, it breaks the first law of field craft which is, 'Never be parted from any of your kit'. So the last thing you do is leave odd little piles of pouches containing such irrelevant articles as your sleeping bag, water bottle or gas mask in remote corners of even remoter fields in the vain hope that some day you might pass that way again.

You can imagine the scene. "Stand to! Enemy fire incoming! Gas masks on!"

"But sergeant, I didn't think I'd need it. I've left it in my tent."

"All right lad. Just you go over there and die quietly."

"Thank you sergeant."

Yeah, yeah, yeah! I don't think!

However, back to the storeman. I explained my shortage of time and asked if he had a set of webbing already made up.

"No sir," came the reply, "only in kit form." And he smiled at his own pun and looked as if he expected me to do the same.

"But what happens to all those sets that are handed back?" I asked, ignoring his attempt at wit.

"Oh we take them to bits and put all the separate items into their respective storage bins."

"Why?"

"For stock taking sir. Have to do regular stock checks."

"But if you had them all made up you would only have to count each set once and just multiply by the number of items each set is supposed to have."

He paused, and I thought the logic of this argument had eluded him. "No," he said, "Wouldn't work. There's not always enough bits to make up complete sets."

That would account for the gaps! I realised I was not going to win this debate so I changed tack for my eyes had seen something at the back of one of the shelves. "Look I really don't have time to put all this together, just let me have one of those rucksacks." I said, pointing to the rather nice Berghaus.

He turned and looked, and then sucked his teeth, "Can't let you have that sir."

"Why not?"

"It's the last one, some one might want it."

I snapped. Turning, I went out of the door and slammed it. I counted to ten then opened it again and went back to the counter. The storeman had not moved. "Right!" I said, "Now I am someone else. I want that rucksack and the rest of the items on this list. I don't care who else may want it. I'm at the head of this particular queue and furthermore I don't give a toss what your scale lists say I am or am not entitled to. Do you understand?" He opened his mouth to protest. "If you say one word," I continued, "I shall charge you under Section 69."

Section 69 of the manual of Royal Air Force law, to my mind inappropriately numbered as it provides for any misdemeanour not specifically catered for under all the other acts, has the all-embracing definition of "conduct prejudicial to the good order of the service". In other words it covers everything and there is no way out of it. It is rather like the American "Catch 22" where regulation 22 states that you can be discharged from service if you can prove you are insane. The catch being that if you can understand the regulation and action the paperwork you must be sane; again, no way out. The storeman looked aggrieved but started to pile the items contained in my list on the counter. When he came to the desert camouflage jacket and trousers he became agitated.

"What's the matter?" I asked.

"Haven't got any desert cam." was the tremulous reply.

"What?" I said, incredulous.

"No, sir. Honest sir. You're not going to believe this, sir. It was all sold to Iraq as part of an arms deal about two years ago. The manufactures have only just been given the contract to start up the lines again. We've been told to issue jungle green camouflage kit instead."

It was so improbable it had to be true. Only the Brits could go to war in the desert, having sold their cam kit to the enemy, disguised as patches of verdant undergrowth.

"'Got some suede desert boots though, sir, what size?"

"They're not green are they?" I queried.

"Oh no sir." he said, genuinely affronted, "Sort of sandy colour with reinforced toe caps."

"Go on then, I'll take a pair," I said "even though I've got some of my own."

The rest of this kitting out process was uneventful and I left the stores with a large plastic bag full of useful items. It was now lunch time. My list of priorities for the afternoon included firing my newly acquired SA-80 on the range and organising transport (MT) to take me to RAF Brize Norton airfield the next day. Both these I achieved almost without mishap, indeed I got my best ever grouping with a rifle which seemed to mollify the still disgruntled RAF Regiment corporal. However, over lunch, Janet had said that she would take me to Brize Norton but when I went to tell MT I was informed that I could not take my rifle in my own car, I had to personally accompany it and civilians (including wives and other family members) could not ride in service transport if weapons were being carried. I did not argue as I had half expected it any way. It just meant that Janet and the boys would make the same journey at the same time as myself and two precious hours together would be lost. The military have a lot to learn about human relations.

Towards the middle of the afternoon I presented myself at 7 Squadron. The SF flight, to whom I had been attached, were administered by the squadron but, because of their particular role, of necessity occupied a secure part of the building. That is, they would have done if they had been at home. The squadron building was deserted except for a skeleton administration and engineering staff. I should have realised, the aircrew and their support teams had been dispatched back in October at the first sign of trouble. Such is the lot of the Support Helicopter (SH) force. It is said that since the end of the second world war there has only been one year when British forces have not been on active service somewhere in the world. In the majority of cases those forces have been supported by detachments of RAF helicopters. Theatres such as Borneo, Aden, Northern Ireland, Cyprus, Belize, Rhodesia, The Falklands and Beirut, to name just the obvious ones, have all seen them. In the last 50 years it may have been the fast jet world that has come to epitomise the RAF but it is the SH force that has won most of the campaign medals.

I found the squadron adjutant and apprised him of the situation. He wasn't expecting me either but it did not seem to bother him. He added my name to the squadron's nominal role as 'temporarily attached' and said that Janet would be included on the wives' coffee morning list. He asked if I needed anything. "Only something in which to pack all my kit." I replied.

"That's no problem." he answered, and promptly produced a large 'tri-wall' cardboard box and a roll of black 'bodge' tape.

Tri-wall, as its name suggests is a sort of cardboard plywood, ie three layers of thin card, each separated from the next by a layer of corrugated cardboard and the whole lot stuck together with glue. The result is a board of surprising strength and durability. Bodge tape is what holds the Air Force together. It is a linen tape, one side of which is coated in black shiny material which defies analysis, the other, an adhesive that will stick to anything, except the black shiny material on the other side. Armed with these I went home to pack.

At home I found that my family had also had a busy day. Jonathan and Matthew had been out and purchased a Sony Mega Bass Walkman which also incorporated an FM/AM radio and then spent the rest of the day recording tapes for me to take. It was rather like Desert Island disks except that someone else had selected what they thought were my eight favourite tunes. But they didn't do badly. I have a catholic taste in music and the library I ended up with encompassed Peter, Paul and Mary, Mozart, Billy Joel and Beethoven. The radio, however was a slight disappointment and it was my fault for not explaining myself properly. It was a classic case of 'don't assume, check!' In the hectic circumstances I had assumed their knowledge but not checked their understanding. They had, in all fairness, specifically asked for and had been given a radio that would receive BBC World Service transmissions. Unfortunately, FM transmissions are only 'line of sight' and the AM frequency band of this particular model (500 - 1600 KHz) only just makes it over the horizon. What I really wanted was a short wave receiver that would pick up the 'BEEB' in any foreign field corner. Not one that, whilst it worked perfectly well, only received UK transmissions as far away as the middle of France. However, it was too late to change anything now and I was very pleased with the tape player. Music has always been an important part of my life and I could not imagine spending long periods of time without it. In the end I did manage to buy a short wave radio, but how and when will be revealed in due course.

While I was finishing packing my rucksack and tri-wall box, Norrie and his wife, Lisa, arrived to wish me bon voyage. Norrie said that the directions I had left for unlocking the mysteries of the office computer almost worked and he would get by. They left with final instructions on how to achieve the perfect bunker shot.

Janet, meanwhile, had been preparing dinner. It was a very special meal because, not only would it be the last we would share together for a long time, but it was her birthday the next day, the day of my departure, and my birthday one week later. By half past seven the family had gathered and the party began. We opened hurriedly wrapped birthday presents and cards, blew out candles on a token cake and got slightly merry. Janet said she had packed a surprise present for me in my rucksack which I would find eventually. In fact there were three, but I will tell you about them later.

Despite everything I slept well, I think the port helped, but woke apprehensively early the next morning to face the unknown.

2 - OUTWARD BOUND - 11 Jan '91

The aircraft in which I was due to depart for Riyadh was scheduled to leave RAF Brize Norton on the 11th of January, 1991, at 1300. This, in itself, was odd. In the passenger air transport world (the shiny fleet), take off times are usually calculated so that there is minimum disruption at the destination airport, i.e. the aircraft arrives around mid-morning, is turned round and departs mid-afternoon. All nice and cosy for the staff in the far flung exotic locations who have nothing worse to contend with than how to spend their overseas allowances. However, it does mean that at the UK end departures and arrivals often occur at some bizarre times. To make sure you are actually around to get on the aeroplane at some ungodly hour, you are often asked to check in, not just one hour before take off, but six or seven. This is not quite as horrendous as it sounds, for hotel type accommodation is provided at the aptly named Gateway House. Here you can stay the night before an early departure and therefore suffer, or cause, the least amount of disturbance. In practice, however, the result is somewhat less than perfect. The bar in the Gateway does not shut until 2300, Sod's law says that you will meet at least one long lost pal whom you have not seen since Pontius was a pilot and you still have to get up at 0200 for an 0400 take off.

Invariably there are at least six wives, each with small children, going to join their husbands in some far flung part of the globe. Probably it is the first time they will have made such a journey, certainly on their own and they are fraught and harassed. Mix this with hardened squaddies who have stored a few tins for the odd 'bevy' after the bar has closed and you can guess at the mental and physical state of the majority of passengers as they board the plane in the early hours of the morning. For some reason, however, we had avoided the very early start and all its consequent hassle. War obviously had its benefits after all. Oh Yeah?

The journey to RAF Brize Norton from Odiham takes approximately 1 hour 45 minutes. With their usual efficiency the movements staff generally take two hours to process you and get you onto the aeroplane. Even so, it was with a certain amount of incredulity that I was informed that MT would pick me up at 0730 for a 1300 flight! And, considering that I had to go to the armoury first to pick up my SA-80, it meant that I still had an early start.

Nevertheless, the 11th of January began, as do most of my days, with breakfast. I cannot start the day without breakfast. It does not matter what time I get up, early or late, I must have breakfast. Not so long ago in the armed forces breakfast was a parade and as such it was compulsory to attend. There were two reasons for this, in the first place it made sure that you got up, secondly, it ensured that you were properly prepared to face the physical demands of the day; the alternative was to face the prospect of being placed on a charge. The threat of jankers (punishment for defaulters/restrictions) is now gone but I find that a cup of coffee and a cigarette do not really prepare you for the rigours of the day. For me breakfast is still a parade.

My breakfast usually comprises grapefruit juice (to sharpen the teeth) muesli and Allbran (with added dried figs), a slice of brown bread with honey and two cups of tea. I embark upon this ritual, not because I am a health freak or anything like that, I enjoy red meat and double cream as well as anyone, but it is a breakfast of minimum effort that works. If I have time, and someone else to do the washing up, I am just as likely to have a full fry, black pudding, the lot. But usually there is not enough time to prepare that sort of meal and clean up afterwards.

Breakfast complete, I donned my jungle camouflage and made my way through a bare, leafless, frosty morning to the armoury to pick up my SA-80. It was actually an exchange as I had decided to lodge my 12 bore shotgun with them whilst I was away. Normally you have to apply for permission from the Station Commander to put private weapons in the armoury but, for once, sense prevailed and it was taken in without any problems. The main reason for doing this was because my licence was due to run out at the end of the month and renewing it had not appeared on my list of priorities. It might not be strictly legal but at least it would be secure. In the end, I discovered on my return, that the police had identified the problem and allowed an amnesty for all those in a similar situation, as long as the licence was renewed within one month from the date of the owner's return from the Gulf.

After due identification, my SA-80, together with a magazine but no ammunition, was handed to me. "You'll get bullets issued to you when you need them." the armourer informed me. I acknowledge that this is probably sensible, there is nothing more dangerous than bored aircrew with loaded guns, but it did just cross my mind that it was an act of faith to rely on someone turning up with your ammunition just as the enemy hordes are charging your position. However, I signed for the weapon and went to find MT.

The reason for the early start now became apparent. The coach taking me to RAF Brize Norton was going via RAF Lyneham to drop off some stores which were to be shipped out to the Gulf by Hercules transport aircraft. We were then going on to Brize to pick up a TriStar. I boarded the bus and found it almost empty. Of the few other people on board, I was the only one dressed to go to war. For the first time I felt rather lonely. We drove to my quarter and loaded my rucksack and tri-wall box. I explained to Janet about our detour to RAF Lyneham and told her not to expect to see me at Brize until about 1030 and off we went.

The coach journey was uneventful and tedious. Military coaches are spartan and noisy and are not made for either speed or comfort. The three interminable hours it took to get to RAF Brize Norton were three hours I could have spent with my family, albeit in a car. But rules are rules. However, you would have thought that in these enlightened times even the armed forces would be alive to the needs of the camp followers. But I digress. We finally reached RAF Brize Norton and I got off the bus and joined a medium sized queue to put myself in the hands of the 'Movers' at the check-in desk.

Movers are the military version of airline desk staff and baggage handlers. The RAF Transport Fleet operates on the same lines as a civilian airline, but more so. In the first place you are issued with a ticket that any airline passenger would recognise but this is then accompanied by copious instructions on how to get to the airport by all other known means of transport. You are also informed in no uncertain terms how much luggage you can take with you and that there is no such thing as excess baggage. I had studiously ignored this and was prepared to argue the toss but in the end my bags and boxes were accepted without a second glance.

However, before I could check in my 'bags' I had to fill in several forms and labels. The labels intrigued me. In true military tradition, every rucksack, bag and box already had its owner's name writ large upon it in broad, waterproof felt tip pen; far more secure than a tie on label. No way you were ever going to pick up someone else's kit by mistake and, as there was no other flight that day, where else could the luggage go? Nevertheless, we duly filled in our labels and tied them to our possessions.

The forms were equally intriguing. One in particular, the 'Next of Kin' form is something that the serviceman becomes very familiar with. It requires you to declare such details as, the two people you would most like to be informed in case of an accident, and your religion. I am always amazed that after all these years no one has bothered to keep a record of these details. Obviously they do not because you fill in one of these forms each time you fly, go on a course or arrive at a new posting. At a conservative estimate I have personally completed this form somewhere in the region of 60 times.

On a previous occasion and with an element of seriousness, I had asked the attendant Mover, "Why religion?"

"So that it ensures the correct priest will perform the last rights in the event of your untimely demise." he replied.

"But as long as my ashes are returned to be scattered over Stonehenge, the denomination of who does it isn't really important," I said.

"You must put something in the box, sir." He insisted.

I tried to fit in 'Monotheist' but the form was designed with only enough room to accept C of E, RC or, at a pinch, 'Method', so I wrote 'Heretic' in very small letters and have continued to do so ever since and no one has ever commented. Perhaps I will end up at Stonehenge after all.

Checking in the baggage was reasonably painless but I was informed that I had to carry my rifle with me. I was then issued with a boarding card, identical to anything that BA or any other civilian operator might give out. Why?

On a civilian flight, a boarding card serves several purposes. It carries the number of the seat, smoking or non-smoking, that has been allocated to you, although for the number of times that you find someone else already sat in your seat upon your arrival it might as well not bother. What is it that removes a punter's ability to count or follow the logic of A - B - C whenever he enters a train, plane or theatre? Yes, you've seen them. In the wrong seats, in the wrong rows, possibly even in the wrong theatre. Definitely on the wrong planet. I was once on an American Airlines internal flight from Washington to West Palm Beach when, just as the aircraft had started its take off run, a man in the seat in front of me pushed the stewardess attention button, stood up and announced to the world in general in a rather bemused tone, "Hey! I shouldn't be on this flight." I don't know what his final destination was but he went via West Palm Beach.

The boarding card also acts as a form of identity. At the check-in desk you have proved yourself by presenting ticket, passport etc. and have been given this single piece of card in exchange. It is now your pass to your seat. But this is a military flight, we carry military identity cards and are subject to military rules and regulations. Surely, if we were just herded onto the plane and told to sit in the first empty seat we came to we would do as we were told.

"Odd numbers one pace forward. March! You will sit in the seats on the right, even numbers on the left."

"Is that the left as we face the nose or the tail, Sergeant?"

"Don't ask questions, there's a good officer, just follow the corporal."

And we would, and there would be no problems. We do it every day of our military lives. Why is air transport different? I have a sneaking suspicion that they are practising for privatisation or the day that they are offered a better job outside. Nevertheless, I took my boarding card and went and sat in the lounge with my family and waited to be called 'airside'. About an hour later we were informed that there was a delay, some minor problem with the aircraft, but we were to proceed through security and wait. I said my fond farewells along with a hundred others, promising to take care and be back as soon as possible, but not having a clue what was really going to happen.

At the security check the metal detector bleeped wildly.

"Have you got anything metal on you, sir?" The military policeman asked me. I waved my SA-80 at him. "No, apart from that," he said.

What was he expecting? Without exception all the passengers on this flight were armed and so were the crew members. We were going off to war. I fumbled through my pockets and came up with a few coins, some keys and my Swiss Army Penknife.

"You are not supposed to carry knives in the aircraft cabin." He said, "you should have put it in your hold baggage."

I waved my SA-80 at him again and got the distinct impression that he thought I was threatening him. "I shall remember next time." I lied.

"Alright." He said, "I shall make an exception this time," and waved me through.

The departure lounge at RAF Brize Norton was not designed for lengthy occupation. There are chairs and tables, a coffee vending machine and loos and not much else. Nevertheless, one aspect, that appears at first glance to be an advantage over most other airports, is that it is at ground level, has big picture windows and opens out directly onto the pan so that you can actually see the aeroplanes. This would be great at civilian airfields like Heathrow or Gatwick where, with an aircraft taking off or landing every minute, there is always something going on; free entertainment for you and the kids. But at most civilian airfields you are tucked away round some corner which probably only allows you a partial view of the aircraft you are about to board. However, the advantage at RAF Brize Norton is only illusory because, whilst you have an unrestricted view of the pan and the airfield, there is nothing happening. At best, RAF Brize Norton handles six movements a day. If you are really lucky you might catch a crew doing 'manders circuit bashing' (mandatory continuation training) where they spend several hours just flying in circles (oblongs with rounded ends really) and practising various approaches to the runway, landing and taking off and doing it all over and over again. But today, the only view through the square window comprised two or three TriStars, a couple of VC10s and a bleak, windswept, Oxfordshire landscape. I found a seat and took a book out of my grip. When I was packing, one of the decisions I had to make was what book or books to take. I reasoned that I did not have much room but needed something substantial. In the end I chose two, Tolkien's The Lord of the Rings and a copy of the Koran; the Muslim Holy Book.

The Lord of the Rings is a fantasy story concerning the triumph of good over evil. It is written in the style of a saga. According to the Oxford English Dictionary a saga is:

A medieval prose narrative or series of books embodying the history of a king or family; a story of heroic achievement and adventure often at great personal cost to the hero.

And that exactly describes the Lord of the Rings. It may sound old fashioned and outmoded but it is this tale that has formed the base of many similar ones and spawned numerous video cults of the 'dungeons and dragons' ilk. To my mind it is the benchmark and has no equal for depth or perception. I have read it several times but it does not get stale and every time I have discovered some new facet. In fact it has become my constant companion. It lives on the coffee table and when I have nothing better to do I pick it up and read a few pages. When I have finished it, I start again.

The Koran, on the other hand was something quite different. As you may have gathered from my problems with the next of kin forms it is not that I do not believe in "God" it is just that I find it more and more difficult to come to terms with "religion". I have no difficulty with the concept of a "Great Architect of the Universe". It seems an awful waste of time and effort if we are here just by chance and I cannot help but feel that we are all part of some great game or pattern. If this is so, then it is logical to suppose that there is a guiding force; someone to light the fuse for the big bang. Likewise it does not matter to me what you call this force, God, Allah, Mother Nature, it is unimportant. I find that in those to whom it is important it engenders dogma and from this grows fanaticism, power politics and the control of many by a few.

Nevertheless, we are all bound very closely to religion for, whether we like it or not, over the ages it has influenced the way we think and act and forms the basis of the society in which we live. And not just us. What we call different cultures are, to a great extent, the result of the influence of a particular religion on a people or country. So, if you are going, as I was, to spend some time as a guest, part of an invading force, or possibly a prisoner in an alien culture it would be a distinct advantage to at least try and understand the basic driving forces behind that culture, and one of the first steps to this understanding is to become familiar with the religion of that culture. Hence the Koran.

I had made several brief visits to Saudi Arabia during my time as a compass base surveyor and, after the first one, discovered that to know a little of what makes Arabs tick certainly pays dividends. For instance, contrary to what the vast majority of Christians are brought up to believe, Islam is not a heathen or pagan religion. It has much in common with both the Old and New Testaments, telling, in its own way, the stories of the Creation, Moses and the birth of Jesus to name but a few. However, Muslims totally reject the concept of the Trinity and that Jesus was anything other than a prophet. For them it is blasphemy of the highest degree to suggest that God is in any way divided or abased himself by taking human form in the person of Christ. Their dictum is: 'There is no other god but God'. Nevertheless, they acknowledge the common lineage shared with Jews and Christians, referring to them as 'People of the Book' but regarding them as having strayed from the true path, though not beyond redemption. This is more than can be said for Jewish and Christian regard for Muslims.

Armed with just this scant knowledge I managed to evade a lengthy delay in the Riyadh airport customs hall by asking if it was customary to treat People of the Book to the prolonged and minute inspections I had seen meted out to other arrivals. I was met with a stony stare, but my bags were duly given the magic chalk mark and we passed through six hours sooner than some other fellow travellers who did not know the pass words. I hoped that further study of the Koran might give me a deeper insight into Islamic culture and perhaps ease my stay in their lands.

Mind you, I was treading a dangerous path. The Koran is the written account of the Word of God as revealed to the Prophet Mohammed (peace be upon him) and it is blasphemy to deviate from the original. Now the original was written in Arabic, which I do not speak and cannot read. My copy was an English translation and, to compound the transgression, the chapters had been rearranged into a more logical order. If that were not bad enough, the book was published by Penguin, who had recently published Salman Rushdie's 'The Satanic Verses'. Such are the complexities of 'religion'.

The lounge slowly filled and conversations were struck. Some of the people were returning to the Gulf from Christmas leave. Some, like myself were going out for the first time. All shared a common apprehension, for Saddam Hussein was showing no signs of backing down by the 15th of January, in accordance with United Nations Resolution 678, and it looked as though conflict was inevitable.

Time dragged on. Eventually, after numerous cups of coffee and subsequent trips to the loo, at about 1545 we were invited to board the aircraft. No reasons for the delay were given, perhaps an engine had fallen off or the pilot had gone mad and bitten the navigator but we were not to know. Simply, "Your attention please. The aircraft is now ready for boarding. Will those sitting in rows ... etc. etc."

Another Mover was standing at the exit handing out leaflets printed on pink paper. These informed us that because of the war (What war? It hadn't yet started!) we were to expect a limited steward service on the flight. In normal times this seldom comprised little more than a 'butty box' with tea, coffee and squash and it made one wonder just what deprivations were in store. As it turned out, normal service had been resumed, for this flight at least, and we were not disappointed by our spam sandwiches, slice of fruit cake, Kit Kat, packet of crisps and the invariable green apple. It should be a boost to the morale of the country in general to note that tax payers' money is not being wasted on such trivia as hot meals for the troops on their way to war.

You will also be very glad to hear that there is no such thing as alcohol on Royal Air Force passenger aircraft. None is carried and the consumption of self acquired alcohol is forbidden during the flight. Two reasons are given. Firstly it is argued that the weight of the booze would reduce the carrying capacity of the aircraft and secondly that it might encourage the soldiers to fight (each other). Now I am not advocating that every military flight should be a bacchanalian orgy but can you really imagine why squaddies, under the eyes of their officers and SNCOs and the threat of the full penalty of military law, should be any more likely to resort to fisticuffs on a military transport aircraft than when unsupervised on a package flight to the south of Spain. Logic would seem to dictate the opposite result, and that a couple of lagers would send every one to sleep and ensure a totally uneventful trip. But logic was never the strong point of military planning. And by the way, just how much would all this booze actually weigh? Well, one full can of beer weighs approximately 11 ozs. A

Travel Instructions

TriStar aircraft can carry up to 400 passengers. At two cans each, that is 550 lbs or two soldiers in full kit, surely a small price to pay for a contented, self-loading cargo. It was the same perverse logic which led the Air Force to strip out the video in-flight entertainment equipment from the TriStars when they bought them from British Airways. 14 hours in the air from England to the Falklands without a drink and no video really made for popular flights.

"Wot's this? Men not 'appy? Make the aircraft a no smoking zone till morale improves."

Don't laugh, that has happened as well!

As daylight faded we made our way across the pan to our waiting aircraft. Now, suddenly it became obvious why there had been a delay. The aircrew were too embarrassed to let us see the aeroplane in the full light of day. RAF passenger transport aircraft are usually painted white with a rather tasteful dark blue lightning flash horizontally along the centre of the fuselage together with silver wings. In fact they are known by troops returning to the UK as 'the big white goeshomey bird', but this thing, as it caught the dying rays of the sun was pink! A delicate pastel shade somewhere between salmon and apricot. How can any self respecting man go to war in a pink aeroplane? But as we got closer the full travesty was revealed. The body, and tail were certainly pink but the wings were still silver and the blue lighting flash had been retained. Had there been no time to finish the job? Was the pink paint still wet? I asked the steward at the bottom of the steps.

"Camouflage, sir," was his answer.

"But what about the wings?" I enquired, "surely they stand out like dogs' balls?"

"Can't paint those sir, it would interfere with the flaps and air brakes and such like," he replied.

There was no more time to pursue this conversation as a queue was beginning to form at the bottom of the steps, but half way up a thought occurred to me. Was this why there was no booze? Had we sacrificed our beer for the weight of a coat of Dulux's best?

A 'pink' Tristar

The aircraft was fitted out for both passengers and freight. The front section of the cabin was equipped with approximately one hundred seats, set out in the familiar seating pattern of a wide bodied jet; three - five - three. The rear portion of the cabin was entirely devoid of seats. The bare floor was stacked with containers securely lashed to the floor with chains. There was no telling what was in them. Under peace time rules it was forbidden to carry passengers and 'dangerous air cargo' (DAC) together, but we were not playing under peace time rules.

At 1610, having been delayed for 3 hours, the TriStar taxied out and started to accelerate down the runway. I always take a note of the time from the start of the take off run to the moment the aircraft 'rotates' and actually leaves the ground. It gives an indication of how heavythe aircraft is; how much fuel, freight and passengers is being carried. On average this take off run lasts about 30 seconds. This evening it took 48 seconds before we lifted off into the unknown future of a January evening. God only knows what was in those crates!

After all the uncertainty and tensions of the day, the flight was uncannily relaxed. I cannot recall clearly the details of the flight but I remember that, not long after take off, a group of about 15 of us, almost exclusively RAF, migrated to the back of the 'plane where the galley and loos were situated, and there we remained, leaning up against the packing cases, just talking. It was all fairly subdued. After initial introductions the topic of conversation turned, inevitably, to the prospect of conflict. About half of the people on the aircraft were returning to the Gulf after spending Christmas/New Year in the UK. They were quizzed on what conditions were like 'out there'. The answers were somewhat surprising. The Air Force seemed to have moved en masse into hotels, and were living the life of Reilly; driving out to the airfield only when there was any flying to be done. Fighter jockeys and shiny fleet operators have a reputation for finding excuses to avoid 'field conditions', perhaps it is a hangover from the 'Brylcream' image of WWII. Whatever the reason, they end up in air conditioned hotels with en-suite everything, much to the chagrin of the rest of the armed forces, especially the support helicopter people who spend most of their time in the field playing soldiers. I enquired of the whereabouts of the SH force but few seemed to have heard of them let alone knew where the were. I was not in the least surprised.

The six hour flight seemed to pass all too quickly. In no time at all we were approaching Riyadh's King Kahlid International Airport. It was 0100 local time, Saudi Arabia being three hours in front of Greenwich Mean Time (GMT). You may or may not know but, officially there is no longer such a thing as GMT. It is now known as UTC or universal time constant. It is also referred to as 'Zulu' time. For the convenience of navigation, time keeping etc. the world has been divided up into 24 segments of 15° longitude each, this being the distance the sun travels in one hour. Each of these segments is labelled alphabetically with reference to the zone through which the Greenwich meridian (line of 0° longitude) passed. Thus, GMT +1 hour is called Alpha, GMT +2 hours is called Bravo. etc. etc. To avoid confusion (?) the GMT segment was called Zulu However, as far as the inhabitants of Riyadh were concerned it was one o'clock in the morning.

The TriStar taxied to its parking slot and the great Rolls-Royce RB.211 engines wound down to silence. I had expected a blast of hot air to meet us as we emerged from the aircraft cabin, after all we were in the desert, but it did not happen. It was certainly less cold than RAF Brize Norton but it was not what I had anticipated. We subconsciously seem to ignore the fact that deserts can be, and often are cold. At night, even in the summer time, because there is little cloud cover all the heat of the day is radiated away and the temperature can often drop below zero. Death valley in California is noted both for very high and low temperatures and holds the record for the greatest difference in temperature between night and day in a 24 hour period. Add to this the general subconscious lack of realisation that the desert, especially the area that was to become our home for the next few months, also has a winter period and you can see that it can catch you unawares. In fact it cost some of our toughest soldiers their lives.

The pan was a hive of activity under the glare of gantry mounted arc lights. As I stepped onto the concrete something else that I was not expecting caught my attention. The place was covered in kiwis. Silhouettes of kiwis were everywhere, painted on equipment, vehicles, buildings. You name it, and if it stood still for more than thirty seconds, it had a kiwi painted on it. It was not the graffiti that surprised me it was the symbol itself. I do not know why but I had not expected New Zealanders to be taking part in the conflict. In truth I had not given it much thought but had assumed that the allied forces which made up the Coalition ranged against Iraq were composed only of Saudi, American, French and British troops. Perhaps that was because they were the only ones to get a mention in news reports back home. In fact over 40 separate countries contributed men and equipment in support of the Coalition. Not all fought. The Kiwis, for instance took no aggressive role, but they provided invaluable support in handling casualties, passengers and equipment at the various airheads.

The next surprise was the airport itself. It was only partially built. The runways and air traffic facilities were obviously serviceable but the terminal building was just a shell. We were directed to a temporary steel stairway which led to the first floor where troop reception and administration had been set up. As I started up the first two or three steps of the stair I was suddenly struck with a very powerful sense of *déja vu*.

In Northern Ireland, one of the main security bases in South Armagh, is a place called Bessbrook Mill. It is an old linen mill on the outskirts of Bessbrook village, situated on a hill overlooking the town of Newry. At the height of the linen industry it was a wealthy concern and sported the first electric railway to be built in Britain to transfer the linen cloth to the markets in Newry, below. Remains of the track can still be seen and one or two of the local hen houses look remarkably like old carriages. However, with the advent of man made fibres, the linen trade declined and with it Bessbrook mill. When 'the troubles' came to a head in the late '60s it was taken over by the security forces, fortified and used as a main base from which to mount operations in the area of South Armagh that has come to be known as 'bandit country'. The facilities are cramped and spartan and there are a maze of corridors, formed by default by the myriad partitions erected, in what must have been the main weaving shed, to produce offices, messes, gymnasia and all the other things you would expect to find in a normal military base. It is a peculiar thing about the military but, wherever they find themselves, even if for only a few days, they will beaver away and make their environment resemble their regimental home. Unfortunately, Bessbrook was home to a great many regiments on regular rotation and each one rearranged the partitions to suit themselves. The result, as far as more permanent residents were concerned, was something akin to a permanently changing middle eastern souk.

One feature that did not change, however, was the sleeping accommodation. Situated on the upper floors, this too comprised a great many small rooms created by partitioning but once established, they were not altered. Access to these sleeping quarters was by a metal spiral stair, part of the original mill construction. This stair, when struck by the military boot produced a very distinct sound which, because of the lack of sound insulating properties of the partitioning material, invaded your very dreams and was etched on your soul. The temporary stairway at Riyadh Airport which I was now ascending, separated by 3000 miles from Bessbrook, made the same sound. It was uncanny.

At the top of the stairs a door opened out into, what I expect is now, the airport lounge. Then, it was just a large enclosed space, devoid of the desks, offices and the baggage carousels that you normally associate with such a place. The girders were still bare and the floor un-carpeted but the space was anything but empty. It was thronged with people, most of whom were engaged in that occupation which seems to take up half a soldiers life, waiting. Most were sat, slouched or hunched up in chairs which were obviously originally intended to serve the expected passengers once the building had been completed but now had been hurriedly pressed into service, as the remains of wrapping paper and plastic sheeting attested. Many of those occupying the seats were asleep or dozing, some were reading and there was the inevitable card game. I joined a short queue to a desk on which there was a cardboard sign which read, 'RECEPTION'. The airman, who was dressed in a standard blue RAF uniform, was checking the new arrivals against his list and directing them accordingly.

"Do you know where your going, sir?" he enquired as he put a pink felt tip splodge against my name on his list.

"JEMMY." I replied, confidently.

He looked at me blankly. "Never heard of that one, sir. Where is it?"

"It's not a where, its an operation. Op JEMMY." I was now feeling less confident. He still looked blank. I explained as much as I thought he ought to know, which was not far short of all I knew. "And I was told to say, JEMMY, when I arrived and you would know the next step," I finished, now feeling anything but confident.

"Don't mean nothing to me, sir," he said, "we have two C-130 Round Robins leaving tomorrow, sorry I mean this morning," he said, pointing to two large sheets of white paper, which turned out to be the backs of maps of some completely irrelevant part of the world and were now doing service as destination boards. "I'll try and find which one you want."

The C-130, (pronounced 'charlie one thirty') or Hercules or Herc for short, is the most successful military transport 'plane built in the West. It has been in production since 1955 and almost 1750 have been built for operations with 55 different countries. The RAF has about 50 C-130K models, 30 of which have recently been 'stretched' by the addition of a 15ft fuselage extension. These are officially known as C Mk 3 Hercules', but all the aircraft, long or short, are affectionately known by the nickname 'Fat Albert'. A Round Robin, by the way, is the name given to any form of military transport which travels a more or less circular route, dropping off and picking up passengers or freight as required.

"What time do they leave?" I asked.

"0600." was the reply. "Zulu," he added, seeing the look on my face. "that's - er - 0900 local, I think."

Zulu time, as I have explained, is used universally by civilian airline operators, the military and anyone else who is in regular communication with people in different parts of the world. It is supposed to make life simple by having a common time reference, but it often leads to a great deal of confusion especially when you are trying to translate it to the ordinary man in the street, or airport lounge.

"Is there anywhere to sleep?" I asked, looking at the rows of full chairs. He pointed to a pile of mattresses stacked by the wall

.

"Grab one of those and find a space on the floor, sir." he replied and turned to deal with his next customer.

I picked up a mattress and took it to the far end of the building where someone had thoughtfully removed the fluorescent tubes from the light fittings in order to create some semblance of night. Here were about 50 other 'bodies', in various stages of sleep and wakefulness. I found a space and occupied it. Then I remembered my tri-wall box. I ought to try and find it before it disappeared off to somewhere obscure. I made my way back down the 'Bessbrook' stair to the pan and asked one of the Kiwi movers where the kit from the TriStar had ended up, explaining that I was on one of tomorrow's Round Robins but, as yet unsure of which one. He pointed to a large pile of kit.

"It should be there," he said, "when you find it put it over there," and pointed to a roped off enclosure underneath the Bessbrook stair. " We can sort it out onto the right aircraft in the morning."

I thanked him and went off to look. Surprisingly I found it without too much trouble and, with the aid of a small fork lift truck, moved it to the prescribed enclosure.

As I re-entered the reception area, the airman behind the desk caught sight of me.

"I've been doing some inquiring, sir," he called out, "you are to go to Minhad and ask about JEMMY there. Get on Round Robin Bravo. It leaves at 0915- local."

These instructions seemed rather odd. Minhad was nearly 500 miles further east of Riyadh in the United Arab Emirates (UAE), just outside Dubai. It was also a long way from Kuwait; 500 miles in a straight line across the waters of the Gulf and another 150 miles if you went round the coast. The normal radius of action for a Chinook, as quoted in Jane's World Aircraft Recognition Hand Book, is 115 miles, so Minhad seemed an odd place from which to launch Special Forces' missions. But it was now 0230 hours local time and far too late to argue. I had little option anyway. I relocated my mattress, fell upon it and, still clutching my SA-80, dropped off to sleep almost immediately.

3 - THE HUNT FOR OSCAR - 12 Jan '91

At about 0630 on the morning of the 12th of January, a gradual stirring of the itinerants of the King Kahlid Airport lounge broke through my subconscious and returned me slowly to the land of the living. I had not slept particularly well and, after the initial period of perhaps an hour's relatively deep sleep, had drifted along just the other side of unconsciousness. As a rule I do not sleep deeply at the best of times. Some people can sleep through earthquakes, alarm clocks, the lot. But I am roused if the clock stops ticking. I have, therefore, learnt to doze, and that seems to be sufficient.

People, clutching wash bags and towels, were disappearing towards an internal stair well at the far end of the room and it seemed prudent to do the same. Downstairs was even more of a builders tip than upstairs, with girders, pipes and wires festooning the area and doing their best to live up to the image of concrete jungle. Shafts of light from the rising sun, shining through a doorway and illuminating the dust in the air only heightened the illusion. Momentarily, my jungle camouflage kit seemed quite apropos.

I followed the crocodile of men to what was a hastily constructed ablutions block. This area was obviously destined to be the toilet facilities in the finished airport but, like the lounge upstairs, it had been rushed into service in indecent haste and all the refinements, such as tiles and ceilings to the cubicles, were missing. Nevertheless, the facilities were functional, the water was hot and the plug for the electric razor produced a choice of 110 or 240 volts. What more can you ask?

Personal laundry complete, I returned to the lounge and, drawn by the smell of coffee, discovered another temporary/permanent feature doing its best to look and act like a cafeteria. There was no cooked food and it was self help, but there were cereals, bread and jam and urns of tea and coffee. Armed with a plentiful supply of these comestibles, I wandered back to where I had left my kit to find an airman waiting for me.

" 'You going to JEMMY, sir?" he enquired.

"That's the GEMMER-al idea," I said, but it fell on stony ground.

"Well, I'm to tell you, you want the other Round Robin. Alpha not Bravo. It leaves at '9.'"

"Are you sure?" I asked, "I thought I was supposed to go to Minhad, and that doesn't appear on the schedule for Alpha."

"Dunno, sir." He shrugged his shoulders. "That's what I was told to tell you."

"Alright. Thank you." I said. No future in shooting the messenger, but I would just go and check up. The day shift, at the reception desk, had a few more stripes than the night shift. I selected a flight sergeant who seemed to be in charge.

"JEMMY." I said. "I understand I now have to go on Round Robin Alpha."

" 'You Flight Lieutenant Small?" He asked.

"Yes." I replied. How many others, destined for this secret location, was he expecting?

"That's right," he said, "specific instructions. Round Robin Alpha and ask at Batin."

"You're sure?" I said with emphasis.

"Positive, sir." He replied. "Those were the instructions. If you would like to get your bits and pieces together about 0815, I'll make sure they're loaded on to the right aircraft."

I thanked him and went of to eat my breakfast. This made more sense. Batin was only 100 miles from the Kuwait border. Round Robin Alpha was scheduled to fly from Riyadh to Bahrain, 220 miles to the Northeast, and then on to Batin, a further 300 miles to the Northwest. At a cruising speed of 340 knots and allowing half an hour for the stop at Bahrain, I should be in Batin approximately two hours after take off.

Unlike the departure from RAF Brize Norton, there were few formalities and no boarding cards. Just before 0830, along with about 50 other assorted passengers, I made my way across the pan to where Round Robin Alpha was waiting.

There are three ways of getting onto a C-130. The first is through a small door, approximately 10ft aft of the nose on the port side of the fuselage. It is used mainly by the crew for, just inside the door, there is a stairway that leads to the cockpit and galley. Immediately to the right of this stair is an opening through a bulkhead which leads into the cabin/hold area.

As an aside, do you know which is port and which is starboard and what the appropriate coloured light is? Well, an easy way to remember is that all the longest words go together. 'Green' is longer than 'Red', 'Starboard', longer than 'Port' and 'Right', longer than 'Left'. Easy, isn't it? But I digress.

A second door is to be found, again on the port side, but this time near the back of the aircraft, just forward of the hinge of the loading ramp. This door leads directly into the rear of the cabin section.

The lower rear section of a C-130 fuselage slopes gently up from almost ground level to the underside of the tail. It is split in two and, by means of hydraulic rams, the top half can be lifted up into the roof and the bottom half lowered to form a ramp, up which anything, from small crates, through Land Rovers and 4 ton trucks to semi-dismantled Puma helicopters, can be loaded into the hold. This, then, is the third, and most usual route for entering the C-130 cabin. But today, so much freight had been stacked in the aft section of the hold and lashed to the ramp itself that access to the seats in the cabin via the two rear entrances was a non starter. I could not even see my tri-wall box, but as it was no longer in the cargo area under the Bessbrook stair, I trusted to luck that it had been loaded and, more to the point, was easily accessible. It took some time for us all to manoeuvre our rucksacks and rifles through the forward door, round the sharp right hand turn and into the cabin, but eventually we were all in.

For the C-130 to achieve universal renown as an extremely versatile transport aircraft, certain compromises had to be made by Lockheed, the manufactures; most of them at the expense of comfort of any passengers. The cabin is basically empty. The roof and walls are obviously structurally sound but no attempt has been made to hide any of the numerous pipes, control cables and wiring looms. Only where they might be damaged by passengers or freight or where they themselves might cause damage, is there any hint of shrouding or protection. There is a minimal amount of sound proofing, but this only extends from floor level to just above head height.

The floor is bare metal plate with numerous holes, slots and surface mounted shackles which are the key to the aircraft's versatility. To these many fixing points can be fitted a variety of features. Vertical posts, affixed to both floor and struts in the roof, can be used to carry either banks of seats or tiers of stretchers. The floor can be fitted with pallets of rollers on which very heavy freight may be easily manoeuvred before lashing down or which can facilitate the ease of exit of freight during para-drops. At the most basic, boxes and equipment can be simply stacked on the bare floor and restrained with strops (nylon webbing straps with hooks at either end and a tightening device in the middle) or chains, or placed under cargo nets and securely fixed by hooks or snap-links to the shackles.

All this freight handling is an art in its own right and is the domain of the aircraft loadmaster, usually a senior non-commissioned officer (SNCO), sergeant, flight sergeant or master air loadmaster (warrant officer). In these liberated days of equality there are more than a few female air loadmasters; unkindly but universally known as loadmattresses.

Our C-130, like the TriStar which had brought us out, was roled for both freight and passengers. As I have already said, the freight had been stacked in the rear part of the cabin, the front half being given over to seats. There are two things which make flying in a C-130 memorable. The first is the seats.

The seats, again, are a compromise. They are strong enough to support a fully kitted paratrooper but, of necessity, are light in weight. As a result they are not comfortable. They comprise lengths of nylon 'canvas', fitted around an 'L' shaped frame, have no springing or 'give' whatsoever and, for some unknown reason, are bright red. Banks of these seats are fitted along the axis of the aircraft, one on either wall, facing inward, and two, back to back along the centre of the cabin. This means that you fly sideways and, in the event of a crash, despite the safety lap straps, stand no chance of survival at all as there is little to stop you, and all the other internees, ending up at the forward bulkhead in one untidy heap like chickens in a deep litter house. The reason for this configuration is the ease of loading and dispatching paratroops and, from that point of view, is sensible. Can you imagine trying to get nearly 100 paras out of conventional cinema seats in time to drop them all on the same DZ (drop zone). You would be lucky if they all made it into the same country.

But back to the seats. Initially they are not too uncomfortable, rather like an upright deck chair, but after about 30 minutes the lack of 'give' starts to have an effect on the anatomy and the 'numb bum' syndrome ensues. Added to which, the seat is just high enough off the deck to enable the metal frame, which forms its front edge, to press into the back of your knee and restrict the blood supply to your legs. The resulting 'pins and needles' is, at the least, uncomfortable and, should you completely lose all sense of reality and fall asleep for a period of time, excruciating.

We stumbled about in the semi-darkness of the cabin, Hercules are equipped with an inadequate number of small windows, and, as I have previously suggested, sat in the first seat we came to, without undue fuss or confusion. There are no overhead lockers for cabin baggage so we dumped our bags on the floor or stowed them out of the way, under the seats, as best we could. The loadmaster appeared and, suspending himself from a section of framework which formed part of the internal structure of the aircraft and which would not have been out of place as wall bars in any gym, proceeded to brief us on how to fasten the lap straps and where to find the life jacket. What were we going to do with a life jacket in the middle of a desert at least a thousand miles in any direction from the nearest water deep enough to drown in? At least he did not go into details of how to inflate it or where to find the whistle.

The whistle has always amused me. The standard safety brief in a civilian airliner, given as you taxi out from the passenger terminal, invariably includes the immortal words, "and the whistle is for attracting attention." I have this vision of survivors, bobbing up and down in the Atlantic swell, blowing their whistles, trying to attract the attention of other aircraft, passing 36,000ft (11,000m for those who were born after the official demise of the Imperial age), above them and not succeeding. The safety brief complete, the engines started and the second thing which makes C-130 travel memorable then became apparent. The noise.

An RAF Hercules aircraft is powered by four Allison T56 turboprop engines, each developing 4,500 shaft horse power. Folklore has it, that because of the power developed by these engines and the lightness of the airframe, it is possible to 'prop hang' in a C-130. That is, to stand the aircraft on its tail and just hang about in mid-air. Officially it is denied but as the manoeuvre is also strictly forbidden ..... who knows? Whatever the truth of the matter one thing that is indisputable is that the undoubted power of these engines develop a considerable amount of noise. During my time spent on the GD Aerosystems Course at the Department of Air Warfare, RAF College, Cranwell, one of the more jingoistic slogans doing the rounds was. 'Jet noise. The sound of freedom'. It was even consigned to a wall in lurid spray paint. However, before it could be removed, some intellectual wag scrawled out the word 'Freedom' and inserted the phrase 'Thermal Inefficiency'. Such is the price of education.

Noise tends to be a personal thing and, although certain aspects of it can be measured, remains to a large extent subjective. When attempts are made to quantify it, it is often expressed in decibels (dB). A decibel is the amount of energy needed for the average person to appreciate that there has been a change in sound level. In real terms each of these steps is equivalent to an increase in power of approximately 25%. The Open University science data book gives the following as typical sound levels:

38

0dB - Threshold of hearing
30dB - A watch ticking at 1m
50dB - A quiet conversation
70dB - A loud conversation
90dB - A busy typing room
110dB - A pneumatic road drill
130db - The threshold of pain

Inside the cabin of a Hercules you can't talk to the person sitting next to you, you have to shout. At a guess, the noise level is around 95dB. A level which, if sustained, leads to hearing loss; 'industrial' deafness. Many aircrew, myself included, suffer from this to one degree or other. In my case, I suffer what is colloquially known as 'cocktail party' deafness. In a quiet room, such as that in which the annual hearing tests are conducted, I can hear very low levels of sound. My problems start in high noise environments such as parties or discos. I find it increasingly difficult to distinguish between one sound and another and voices just blur into the general noise of the background. In the aircraft it becomes harder and harder to hear what is being said on the radio or intercom and turning up the volume only makes the problem worse. That is one reason why an important part of any loadmasters job is to hand out ear plugs to the passengers. These are small, cylindrical pieces of yellow foam rubber, approximately 1cm long, which can be rolled and compressed into a sausage shape and placed in the ear where they expand and gently wedge. They do not exclude all the sound but they do reduce the distortion caused by excessive volume. They are also ideal for rock concerts and the like. You would think their application obvious but I have seen some of the lower forms of cannon fodder (common soldiery) try to eat them, and succeed!

Astonishingly close to the scheduled time, our 'Round Robin' took off and started its delivery run. The day was clear and fine with only the occasional puffy white cumulus cloud drifting past. Once airborne, I got out my book and started to read. I was fortunate. The gods had smiled on me. My seat was against the port aircraft wall and close to a window. The sun was shining through the window and made reading easy. Not like those poor so and sos on the other side, trying to read in the gloom. It took several minutes for me to realise that the gods were obviously having a bit of a joke.

Bahrain lies about 225 miles to the north east of Riyadh. At this time of day the sun is in the south eastern part of the sky. It should, therefore be shining through the starboard windows of the aircraft not over my right shoulder. I got up, and picking my way through the assorted bodies, found the loadmaster at the rear of the cabin checking the security of the cargo.

"Where are we going?" I shouted to him.

"What?" He said, and took of his ear defenders.

"Where are we going?" I repeated, " I thought we were off to Bahrain and Batin?"

"We are, sir," he shouted back, "via Tabuk."

"But that's at the other end of the Arabian peninsular." I protested.

"Yes, sir, but we had an urgent task come up to take some spares to the Tornados out there. That's what's in all these crates." and he gestured over his shoulder with his thumb at the wooden boxes piled up on the ramp.

"But we are still going to Bahrain and Batin?" I asked.

"Oh yes." He replied.

"What's the ETA?"

He thought for a moment and then started to calculate out loud. "That's 600 miles to Tabuk and about 800 back to Bahrain, call it 4 hours. Half an hour to unload and turn round; should be at Bahrain approximately 1345 local. Then another hour by the time we get to Batin. Say 1500, if we're lucky." he concluded.

Good grief! Six and a half hours locked up in this box of noise. I left him checking his strops and shackles and went back to my seat. I passed the news of our detour to the other passengers in my immediate vicinity but they did not seem either surprised or to care, and unconcernedly resumed their own particular form of in-flight entertainment.

The loadmaster returned from the rear of the aircraft and proceeded to distribute the ubiquitous butty boxes which he produced like rabbits out of a hat. There is a ritual that goes with the dispensation of butty boxes. Each recipient immediately writes his name on the box lid and then proceeds to check the contents, even though he knows exactly what to expect. It is culled from the following menu:

Two bread rolls or rounds of sandwiches - white.

Filling for above - spam/cheese/corned beef with appropriate salad accompaniment - lettuce/tomato/cucumber.

A slice of rich fruit cake.

Two Jacobs Cream Cracker biscuits with an ounce of cheddar cheese.

A packet of crisps.

A chocolate bar.

A box of fruit squash - usually orange.

A pot of flavoured yoghurt.

One stick of chewing gum.

A green apple.

A plastic spoon and knife and a paper serviette.

Doubtless it is a balanced diet and took a great deal of time and research to formulate but after 20 years in the service one longs for something different. There was just a chance that, because we were in 'foreign' parts there might be local variations to the theme, but the only concession was the Arabic writing on the Mars Bar wrapper. Variations and combinations are played on the flavours of the crisps and yoghurt and the type of chocolate bar. Very occasionally the cheese is replaced by a small tin of nameless pâté, but that is it. Nevertheless, it does offer a few moments of entertainment whilst cheese and cucumber is exchanged for spam and tomato or prawn cocktail crisps for salt 'n' vinegar. The chocolate bar is consumed immediately and the green apple consigned to the rubbish bag.

The excitement of the butty box having receded, the next highlight was a visit to the loo. This is yet one more compromise to the god of versatility. It comprises a chemical toilet, situated on the port side of the aircraft about three feet up the rear ramp. In order to effect a modicum of privacy, a 'shower curtain' frame has been fitted above it and from this is suspended a heavy duty green cotton curtain. The curtain does a good job in providing a visual screen but the problem is that it only just fits round the loo. There is little room for manoeuvre and it is almost impossible to 'drop ones trousers'. It is easiest to perform this preliminary operation in full view, sit down and then pull the curtain around you. Of course it lacks a certain dignity but it ensures that you do not run the risk of ending up looking like a mummy. Seasoned Hercules travellers pay no attention and anyone visiting the loo automatically becomes invisible for the duration of the visit but its an unnerving experience for the newcomer. It is, perhaps, for this reason more than any other that female crew and passengers were, until recently forbidden from travelling on the RAF's C-130s. But needs must, and in these days of equality the girls spend hours fighting inside the cotton curtain. The boys regard it as an additional form of in-flight entertainment.

However, today, there was little chance of seeing anything. The cabin was almost bulked out with freight and there was only just enough room to squeeze past at either outside edge. I negotiated this obstacle course but discovered that there was a queue. Boredom must either shrink the bladder or stimulate the production of urine, however, the queue provided the opportunity to stand in the space by the rear door and look out of its window.

The desert stretched as far as the horizon, and beyond. We were flying over the great Nafud (pronounced nefoot) desert which occupies about two thirds of the Arabian peninsula and covers somewhere in the region of half a million square miles of arid wilderness. The popular concept of a desert is that it is a flat featureless expanse of sand, but that is true of only a small percentage of the desert areas in the world. This one had distinct features, visible even from 25,000ft (7,620m). Some areas were definitely sandy, but they were not without features for they were covered with broad crescent dunes. In other places the surface appeared to be barren rock, pockmarked with valleys and ruggedly contoured outcrops. It is also a common misconception that deserts are, more or less, at sea level. Perhaps this stems from a subconscious association with the beach at the seaside, but, on average the surface of the Nafud is 2000ft (610m) above sea level and in some places tops 5000ft (1525m).

However, a common concept which is justified, is that deserts are empty. We flew for hundreds of miles and saw almost no sign of human habitation. Occasionally, however, a very odd, and, at the time, inexplicable feature drifted slowly through my field of view. There, on the ground, some 4¾ miles (7½ km) below us, would appear a cluster of perfectly round bright green circles. Not all exactly the same size, they were, on average, perhaps 100yds (91½ m) in diameter. Neither did they appear to be associated with any of the odd settlements which had managed to graft themselves onto the merciless landscape but seemed, instead, to occur at random, almost like colonies of mould forming on the surface of well past sell by date cream.

The queue, by this time, had moved on and I could no longer see out of the window. I relieved my boredom and went back to my seat. Some people think you need to slip into temporary suspended animation to be a successful Hercules passenger, but this is not so. It is imperative to keep moving to stave off the 'numb bum' and, often, to keep warm.

At 20,000ft (6100m) the outside air temperature is around -40°C (which, by the way, also happens to be -40°F). The aircraft is pressurised and by its very nature protects you from the chilling effect of the air as you rush through it, but the predominantly metal structure and skin tends to act more like a refrigerator than an oven. In the survival manuals you are always exhorted not to shelter in crashed aircraft but to build refuges outside using parachutes etc. A double skin of silk or nylon may not be physically very strong but, as I can attest from the experience of several survival courses, the layer of air trapped between the two material walls provides sufficient insulation to keep you snug in the snow or cool in the glare of the sun. A single skin of aluminium alloy does the opposite.

Heating for the cabin is provided by hot air, bled off from one of the compressor stages of the engines. However, the control is crude and it tends to be either off or on. The result is that you are either scorched or frozen to death. It is triggered, not as you would think by some sophisticated thermostat, but by a far more primeval mechanism. To offset the effects of the impending ice age, the passengers in the cabin get up and start to wander about. This obviously upsets the trim of the aircraft and the pilot despatches the loadmaster to see if the load is still secure. As he emerges from the benign environment of the cockpit the loadmaster is struck by the awesome scale of the mass migrations taking place amongst the herds and turns on the heat until the water holes have again dried to a sun baked concrete. This, in turn, stops the migration and the now perspiring herds return to their wallows. Equilibrium is restored and the captain is happy again.

It may, therefore, be injudicious to suspend animation but the noise and the extremes of temperature, together with the subdued light, require the passenger to suspend conscious thought if he is to arrive at his destination with any degree of sanity.

Thus it was that the two hours transit to Tabuk seemed to take only a short life time. The pitch of the engines changed, and the aircraft began to descend. As we approached the airfield I caught a glimpse of more of the strange green circles, much closer now, and the mystery became clear. They were nothing more sinister than fields of crops. They were circular because, in the centre of each was a well or bore hole, water from which was pumped in to a horizontal sprinkler pipe, suspended at intervals from wheeled supports. The whole affair was slowly rotated and, within the circular field so described, vegetation grew. The origin, perhaps, of crop circles.

Although there is little surface water in Saudi Arabia, there is a great deal just below it. The oasis and well have been the lifeline of the nomadic tribesmen since the dawn of time but the size and capacity of the underground reservoirs were not appreciated until the search for oil produced significantly more water than petroleum. Even now it is not seriously exploited, just the odd circular vineyard or camel pasture.

Tabuk airfield was huge. Originally built to provide a first line of defence against any incursion from Israel, it was now ideally situated as a launch pad to attack Baghdad through the back door. Every available space was filled with Coalition aircraft and there was a constant roar of jet engines as Arab, American and UK aircrew readied themselves for the inevitable conflict. As we taxied to our pan the loadmaster began to lower the ramp at the back of the Hercules, like a great drawbridge of some Norman castle, and even more noise and sunlight came flooding in. As soon as we came to a halt a small army of movers descended upon the aircraft and, with the aid of an Eager Beaver articulated fork lift truck, began to unload the crates from the hold. We were told that we could get out and stretch our legs, although in reality it wasn't the legs that needed stretching, but not to wander too far as we would be off again in twenty minutes time.

A small group of us wandered across to the edge of the pan and watched the activity. The sky was blue but, even though the sun was almost overhead, it was not particularly warm and the wind had a keen edge to it. A pair of Tornados taxied past and induced the Pavlovian reaction of a wave from us. Why is it that we wave at trains and boats and planes? Often we are too far away or the occupants too busy for them to see us. In our heart of hearts we know this is so but we still wave. Possibly in some abstract way it forms a connection and for a brief moment we are part of another imagined world. This time, however, the wave was returned by both pilots and navigators. Perhaps they too felt the need for contact with an 'other' world; the real world they were leaving before entering the unreal world of a combat mission albeit for the moment, simulated. A few moments later there was a thunderous roar, columns of smoke turned to pillars of flame as reheat was engaged and the Tornados accelerated, slowly at first but then with ever increasing momentum until, free of the bonds of earth they leapt skyward and literally disappeared into the blue. The noise was felt rather than heard and it reminded me of a song.

44

Songs feature significantly in service life and, in the airforce, particularly with the aircrew. In general they tell a story of a deed or act that has struck a chord. Rather, I suppose, in the style of the minstrel's lay of old. They serve to identify individual squadrons or sections, throw down challenges to all comers and act as territory markers in a crowded bar. They are habitually derogatory, frequently bawdy if not downright obscene, often set to a perfectly harmless well known tune and usually calculated to shock the unwary. They also function as a form of oral graffiti where a senior officer or establishment can be 'slagged off' without too much fear of retribution.

I have always thought that every station, squadron, regimental HQ or whatever should have a graffiti board for the 'men' to use; a no holds barred suggestion box that would tell the boss which way the wind was really blowing. But I suppose most bosses would rather not know. Anyway, back to this song. As background, you should be aware that, in 1978, at the Royal Review to celebrate the 60th anniversary of the formation of the Royal Air Force, the then Minister for Defence, one Fred Mulley, appeared in a photograph in the daily newspapers. Sat next to Her Majesty the Queen he appeared to be asleep.

The following song was composed to celebrate the fact and should be sung to the hymn tune, 'The Church's One Foundation':

> We are Fred Mulley's Air Force,
> We are the boys in blue.
> There are not many of us
> And fewer aircraft too.
> But when we get together
> The noise would wake the dead.
> But it takes more than the Air Force
> To wake up sleepy Fred!

The song tradition in the Support Helicopter Force, possibly triggered by exposure to the 'Fleet Air Arm Song Book', coalesced with the bringing together of the RAF and RN detachments (Junglies) in Northern Ireland in the mid '70s, with such notable renditions as 'The Battle Hymn of Camlough Mountain' and 'Do you Ken South Armagh?' Previously a tradition handed down by word of mouth, the songs were collected together and published in book form about 1980. Amendment lists (ALs) 1 and 2 were issued subsequent to the Falklands and Gulf Wars.

My reverie was broken by a call to get back on the Herc. It now seemed empty by comparison and we were able to get on by way of the ramp. My tri-wall box had emerged from the pile of cargo and was now visible underneath a restraining net. I knew it would be there, but even so I was pleased to see it again.

The journey to Bahrain was much as predicted and two and a half hours of noise, boredom and another butty box later we touched down again. The one difference on this leg of the journey was that suddenly, after 800 miles of sand, the beach ended and we came to the sea, Bahrain being an island.

Our halt at Bahrain was so brief that the pilot did not even bother to shut down the engines. We just taxied to a halt; the ramp was let down; several people got off, several more got on and we were on our way once more. The leg to Batin was relatively short, a mere 300 miles; we had hardly climbed to cruising height before it was time to start the descent again. This time the stop was longer as there was freight to unload, my tri-wall for a start, and it turned out to be fortunate as I was soon to discover.

As soon as the engines were cut I got out of the Herc and made my way to the Ops set up at the side of the pan. This comprised a couple of Portacabins set amongst a mountain of containers and other piles of freight. The warrant officer, who seemed to be in charge, met my enquiry with all the negative vibes of a rabbi in a pork butcher's.

"JEMMY? Never heard of them sir."

I briefly explained what I was seeking.

"The only helicopters round here are down at Al Jubail," he said.

"Where the hell's that?" I asked.

"Just up the coast from Bahrain."

"But I've just come from there." He looked at me as though he had a thousand other things of greater importance than a lost officer to attend to, so I quickly said, "Have you a 'phone that I can contact Force Headquarters with?"

He furnished the said instrument and a couple of telephone numbers and went off to deal with far more important things. The first 'phone number struck gold.

"Squadron Leader Ellis here. Can I help?"

I couldn't believe it. Here in the middle of nowhere was a voice I knew. Sam and I had been neighbours at RAF Odiham several lifetimes ago.

"Sam." I exclaimed, " It's Roger Small here. I need some help." I explained as briefly as I could my dilemma and as soon as I mentioned JEMMY he gave the distinct impression that he knew what I was talking about. "Thank God for that," I said, "you are the first person to recognise that word since I left Strike Command."

"Where are you now?" he enquired.

I explained the details of my journeys of the past six hours. "And as far as I know our next stop is back at Riyadh." I finished.

"Well," he said, "you should have been on the other Round Robin and got off at Minhad."

"But that was the original plan." I said, "At the time it did not seem to make too much sense, Minhad being so far away from the action and all, that when I was told to go to Batin this morning I did not question it."

"Nevertheless," he continued, "Minhad is where you should have gone but it's too late to start that journey now. Go back to Riyadh and get on the Minhad 'Robin tomorrow. I'll get on to the guys at Oscar and tell them to meet you."

"What's Oscar?" I enquired, hardly expecting a sensible answer.

"That's the code name for the base where the Special Forces are located. I can't say any more, especially over the 'phone, but do as I have instructed and you should meet up with them tomorrow."

I thanked him for his help and put down the 'phone. I ran back to the Herc just in time to see my tri-wall being unloaded. "Put it back." I cried "There has been a change of plan." The loadmaster just shrugged his shoulders and waved the forklift truck back again.

"'Happens all the time." he said. "Where are you off to now?" I explained. "Can't do much about that now," he said, "We'll take you back to Riyadh and you'll have to sort it out from there."

"That ties in with my information." I said. "When are we off?"

"Just as soon as those crates are loaded." He replied, pointing to half a dozen wooden boxes by the side of the pan.

He was as good as his word and fifty minutes later I was back where I had started, at the reception desk in the half built terminal at King Kahlid.

"Back again already, sir?" It was the airman I had first encountered last night, or was it this morning?

"Yes," I answered. "I should have been with the other coach party." He laughed. Two Royal Navy Midshipmen standing by the desk joined in the conversation.

"You think you've got troubles," one of them said, "we graduated from Dartmouth two weeks ago and have been trying to track down our ship ever since."

"Every time we get to its last known location, we find it has just sailed," added the other.

"Why don't you signal them and ask for their next port of call?" I queried.

"We've tried that," replied the first one, "but because of the security state they cannot or will not give us that information. All they do is send messages of their current location. However, because they don't know where we are and because we're always on the move trying to find them, by the time their message catches up with us and we have acted upon it, they've moved again. It's just one vicious circle. The latest information is that she is at Jabal Ali, just this side of Dubai, but God knows how old that is."

I wished them good luck and left them to it but I often wonder if they were ever successful in their quest or did they spend the rest of the Gulf War trapped in a time warp just one step behind reality. My immediate problem was what to do now.

"Another night on the mattress in the corner I suppose?" I said to the airman behind the reception desk.

"Oh no, sir," he replied, "There's accommodation for you down town. There's a minibus leaving in about twenty minutes."

It was about ten miles from the airport to the city of Riyadh. The road for the most part was a six lane highway rather like a British motorway but with one essential difference. There was almost no traffic on it. This ribbon of concrete and tarmac stretched off into the distance but, as far as the eye could see, was almost devoid of other vehicles. The road itself was the product of modern technology and civil engineering but at its edge all that stopped and, apart from the odd drainage ditch, there was nothing but desert.

There are strict speed limits in Saudi Arabia and to re-enforce them each vehicle is fitted with a device which produces a sound rather like doorbell chimes as the limit is approached. The closer to the limit the more frequent the chime until, at the limit itself the peel is continuous. The thing is, it is not an unpleasant sound and in no way deters you from breaking the speed limit, in fact it is rather soothing and every driver seems to go out of his way to purposely generate this melodious accompaniment to his driving. The authorities, however, are obviously not unaware of the situation and, just in case the driver should chill out too far, they provide a nasty surprise for him every so often.

At irregular intervals sections of road are paved with what can only be described as bricks set cornerwise. These have two effects. Firstly they produce a loud noise through the suspension of the vehicle, rather like driving over a cattle grid. Secondly, the set of the bricks physically throws the vehicle first to the left and then to the right, producing a distinct swaying motion. The combination of movement and noise wakes even the most somnolent driver in an environment where the heat and landscape unite to become soporifically deadly. Perhaps the UK could adopt the system to keep the sleeping holiday makers and lorry drivers on their toes.

We had not been very long on our journey to Riyadh when there appeared on the horizon, on the road ahead, a vision which at first defied interpretation. It was obviously a vehicle, a small truck or pickup of some description, but the load it was carrying was not familiar. From a distance it looked like two palm trees without leaves but as we got closer the truth turned out to be far more bizarre. The vehicle was indeed a Ford pickup and in the open back were two camels. They were tied into the vehicle in a sitting position but their necks were unrestrained and, from their movement, appeared to be taking a great interest in the surroundings as they passed. Consequently, as we overtook them, both beasts bent their necks towards our minibus and peered at us through the windows. It really was a most odd sight.

Talking of camels. Apparently it is a generally accepted law in the whole of the Arabian peninsular that, if a motorist hits a camel it is the motorist's fault. However, if he is in collision with more than one animal it is the fault of the camel herder. That is why you often see vehicles being driven erratically off the road and over the desert; the drivers desperately looking for another camel to hit so that they will not be held responsible for the original accident.

The remainder of the journey to Riyadh was uneventful. On the outskirts of the town we drew up outside a guarded gate set in a wall that seemed to encompass an entire block of buildings. The security guard was obviously expecting us as we were allowed straight in. The inside of this compound comprised several blocks of flats and was one of several such communities dotted around the city. They have been set up to house British personnel, working in Riyadh, and provide some measure of relief from the less than liberal regime outside. The dress code is relaxed and women, as well as men can parade themselves in shorts and tee shirts, or less if they feel so inclined, without the fear of being severely censured. Likewise, alcohol can be consumed openly, if it can first be acquired.

There is a general banning of alcohol in Saudi Arabia which stems from two sources. Firstly, the Koran is fairly forthright in its condemnation of drunkenness, however, it does not exclude alcohol completely. Any believer, fortunate enough to be called to Allah's bosom, is promised that paradise will flow with wine and be peopled with young buxom maidens. The idea of these two items being freely available on earth is an anathema to the more fundamental Moslems so it seems slightly odd that they should be available in paradise. Perhaps one cannot be tempted in paradise?

The second, and far more practical reason for an all out ban on booze in Saudi is for the simple reason that, some time ago, a royal prince was implicated in a case of death through drunken driving. His Highness King Fahd, the Ruler of the state, therefore decreed that there would be no more alcohol and, as he has sufficient power to make that kind of proclamation stick, it sticks. In some of the other Arab states alcohol is available in bars and hotels, although the punishments for abuse still tend to be severe. However, realising the need to encourage Westerners to Saudi Arabia and also realising that Westerners drink, a certain amount of common sense has prevailed and, whilst decadent western ways and blasphemous religions are actively discouraged in public, in private they are tolerated on the understanding that they are strictly segregated from the general public or anyone else who might be offended. In general it tends to work. It is a privilege that is too precious to jeopardise.

Our compound was functional rather than luxurious but it did provide an adequate meal, a couple of beers, a clean bed and a good night's sleep. Tomorrow was another day.

Tomorrow dawned much too soon and far too early. 'Round Robin' Bravo was due to depart at 0815 which meant breakfast just after 0600. Breakfast was a 'do it yourself' affair but the well stocked larder yielded all the makings of a bacon omelette, toast and tea. At the time this seemed a perfectly natural breakfast menu but I was soon to learn that bacon was not the easiest of commodities to get hold of in a strict Muslim country. Breakfast over, the minibus, complete with door chimes, ferried us back to King Kahlid International Airport.

Nothing had changed and at 0800, amid the ordered chaos, I found myself ensconced once more in the bowels of a C-130. This time we headed South Southeast. The aircraft was almost empty, its task today to pick up supplies brought in through Dubai, and my tri-wall box sat prominently in the middle of the ramp. After about 30 minutes the loadmaster came and found me.

"'Like to come upstairs for a cup of tea?" he shouted.

I nodded and followed him to the stairway at the front of the cabin. Perhaps stairway is a bit of a grand description for the steep ladder which confronts you; it gives the impression of going up into the loft of a house. Four steps later, I emerged into a reasonably well ordered galley, replete with bunk cum sofa. The loadmaster motioned me to continue on through a doorway into the cockpit.

"Make yourself at home," he said, "I'll bring the tea through in a minute."

This was luxury indeed. I made my way forward into the relatively spacious cockpit of the aircraft. At the front, obviously, were the captain and co-pilot. Behind them and on either side, facing their respective walls of dials and instrument, were the navigator and flight engineer. The Hercules is a product of 'old' technology and is labour intensive. In a modern civil airliner seldom do you find anyone other than the pilot and co-pilot on the flight deck, but then they are flying well established routes to strictly calculated schedules and the computer does the rest. Military flights, however, often end up at obscure places, having flown devious routes where the services of navigators and engineers are still required to manage the aircraft whilst the pilots wrestle with the physical problems of getting the aircraft to do things the designers never even dreamt of, let alone built it to achieve.

I was recently privileged to spend several hours in the cockpit of a Boeing

747 en-route from Bombay to Hong Kong where, as far I was concerned, the flight management computer did all the work. Even so, the pilot complained that, although this modern, silicon chip version of 'George' the automatic pilot took them from one waypoint to the next, automatically turned the aircraft onto the next programmed heading and even adjusted the engine throttles when there was a change in height, it did not 'match' the engines and he had to spend at least 30 seconds after each climb or descent making fine adjustments to the throttles so that all four engines were acting completely in unison. Some people don't know they're born. In a Puma helicopter if you can get the engines to within 2% of each other you count yourself lucky.

The 'nav' looked up and grinned. He was busy working out our position and calculating the heading for the next leg. Traditionally, the RAF navigator, who is usually the only person in the aeroplane with a map and any idea of where they are all going, is sat down the back, furthest from the windows. His work station is invariably placed so that it faces any direction other than the one in which the aircraft is heading and is equipped with a collection of technological crystal balls which tell him where the aircraft has been but only offer vague predictions as to where it might be at any given time in the future. If he is lucky he has a table big enough on which to spread out his map and make his predictions. If not, this black art is practised using nothing more than a knee pad, a stop watch, a wax pencil and several acres of map so folded that it would win a PhD in origami. You think I jest?

"Can you show me where we are and where we're going?" I asked.

He pointed to a sharp pencil line which headed Southeast, East and then Northeast, vaguely paralleling the Gulf coast of the Arabian Peninsula. It ended in a circle, in the top right hand part of the Peninsula, which surrounded the airfield of Minhad, just a few miles south of Dubai. This was the first time I had managed to get a good look at a map of the area and at last the geography of the area began to fall into place.

Minhad was in The United Arab Emirates (UAE) and while it was a long way from Kuwait and Iraq it was ideally placed as a supply staging area with several good ports along the Gulf coast and a major international airport at Dubai. The question in my mind, however, was what the Special Forces were doing so far away from the action. I was still not convinced that I was headed for the right destination but doubtless I would soon find out.

As I finished studying the map, the loadmaster appeared with a tray of cups of tea and coffee and proceded to hand them round. The engineer erected the 'jump' seat between the two pilots and motioned me to sit in it. Most larger aircraft have jump seats. They are temporary affairs, usually a tubular frame with a seat and collapsible back support which can be quickly erected for visitors to the flight deck and equally quickly stowed out of the way again.

I sat there and watched the world go past. There was not much opportunity to engage the pilots in conversation as they were busy on the radio most of the time. Although the Western forces had been cordially invited to help form the Coalition, with certain of the Arab nations to help repatriate Kuwait and act as a deterrent to any further aggression from Iraq, there was still an underlying mistrust of the Infidel and what he might do. Consequently, air traffic control procedures were 'rigorously' applied and the chat on the air waves almost constant.

The scenery was, for the most part, similar to that I had watched all day yesterday, but slowly the eastern horizon began to take on a distinctly rugged appearance and gradually the range of mountains that makes up the former Trucial State of Muscat came into view. We came within about 30 miles of the mountains, some of which rise to almost 10,000ft (3050m), before starting our descent to Minhad airfield. I was invited to remain in the jump seat for the landing and gratefully accepted. The landing was uneventful and, after we had taxied to a standstill, I said my goodbyes to the crew and returned to the cabin. The ramp was down and my tri-wall box had already been unshipped. I collected my rucksack and rifle and departed by the same route.

At the far end of the pan was the ubiquitous portacabin office and I made my way in that direction. The place seemed deserted for, apart from the marshaller who was already directing the Hercules in which I had arrived back towards the runway for take off, I could see no one. Even the portacabin failed to yield any human forms of life.

There was a crescendo of noise from the Hercules as it lumbered its way back into the sky and then all went quiet. The tiny figure of the marshaller was slowly making his way towards me. He was clad in khaki shirt, shorts, long socks and black RAF DMS (directly moulded soles) shoes. He plainly had not heard about the impending war. Where was his camouflage kit and gun? I started out to meet him.

"Where is everyone?" I asked, as soon as we were within shouting distance.

"'Gone for a NAAFI break, sir." he replied.

"What all of them?" I tried not to sound too incredulous.

"Oh there's only four of us," he said "And we only come up when there's something special coming in."

"Where do you usually hang out then?" I asked, wondering if I really qualified as 'something special'.

"Down at Dubai."

"We're all a bit relaxed, aren't we?" I said, "Where's your weapon and gas mask etc?"

"'Security state's relaxed here, sir. It's only Black Alpha[1] and we're not allowed to carry weapons when travelling between bases. Would you like a cup of tea?"

"No thanks." I said as he started to open the door to the portacabin. "By the way, do you happen to know what I am supposed to do next?"

He halted. "Ah! yes." he replied, "I was supposed to tell you. There's a Herc coming in to pick you up in about 20 minutes."

"But I've just got off one."

"Yes, but this one's to take you to Oscar."

"I don't suppose you happen to know where Oscar is?" I asked.

He waved his hand vaguely in a Westerly direction, the direction I had just come from, and disappeared into the office. Ah well, I thought, doubtless it will all become clear in the end, and I sat on a box outside the portacabin and waited. The sun climbed towards mid-day and it began to get warm. There was neither sight nor sound of any living thing.

Half an hour later the airman re-emerged. "Your 'plane's due in in five minutes, sir." he said and, clamping a pair of bright yellow ear defenders over

[1.] Officially there are three security states: Black, Amber and Red. Black is normal and entails a minimum security check at the gate by unarmed guards, more or less unlimited access to the base and freedom to park antwhere within reason. Amber is a heightened secuity level with security checks carried out by armed guards and access and parking restricted. Red is the highest security state. Black 'Alpha' is a compromise; not quite Black, but nowhere near Amber?

his ears, made his way off towards the pan clutching his marshaller's batons in his hands. Perhaps he worked by telepathy or second sight because I had not heard a telephone bell or radio call and I still do not know how he came by that information but, five minutes later, almost to the second, there was a sudden roar of engines and a pink Hercules, the same colour as the TriStar that had brought us from the UK, suddenly appeared over the top of the sand dunes. This time the colour seemed nowhere near as garish as it had back against the drab grey background of an English winter. I had never considered the desert to be anything other than yellow but my present surroundings had a definite salmon hue about them and the camouflage of this aircraft blended very well.

The Herc plonked itself down on the runway, engaged reverse thrust and came to an almost immediate stop. We usually only associate reverse thrust with jets but another feature which endears the C-130 to its users is the ability to reverse the pitch of the propellers, thereby producing push instead of pull. Not a thing to be done in the air but an extremely useful attribute once you are on the ground and trying to stop in a very short stretch of cleared bush or jungle strip. It is, likewise, invaluable if you find yourself at a location where the ground handling staff are negligible or without the niceties of tractor tugs and you need to back out of a tight parking slot.

The Herc had come to a stop so quickly that it was able to take the very first taxiway and creep up behind the marshaller. He tried to direct it to a parking slot with vigorous waving of his arms, but all his attempts were ignored and the aircraft executed what can only be described as a handbrake turn at the entrance to a pan and sat there poised to depart as soon as possible. The ramp was already down as it entered the pan and now that it had turned away from me I could see that it was empty. I mean empty. There was nothing inside it. The floor was completely bare and there were no seats to be seen. Standing on the ramp was a figure that I assumed to be the loadmaster but, instead of wearing the usual flying suit, he was dressed in desert camouflage trousers and jacket. There was nothing too unusual about this but what did make him stand out was his head gear. Round his head he wore a shemag, the archetypal Arab head-dress, on top of which was perched a pair of head-phones attached to a long intercom lead.

The shemag is an ideal garment for use in the desert. Developed over the last 8000 years, it is a simple piece of cloth that keeps off the sun, keeps out the wind and, more importantly keeps out the sand. It is, however, the base for the derogatory term 'rag head', used by those who know no better, to describe Arabs in general.

The loadmaster beckoned me to get on board and, with the help of the marshaller I loaded myself and my tri-wall box. Immediately we were off and, in very short order, airborne. The loadmaster offered me another pair of head-phones, which I put on.

"We're going back low level. OK?" he said.

I nodded. What option did I have anyway?

As a helicopter navigator, I am used to flying at low level. The philosophy is, the lower you are the less of a target you make. The Support Helicopter force therefore spends much of its time, both day and night, at very low levels nevertheless, the general public around Hampshire, Wiltshire and Surrey tend not to understand our continued need to practice this particular form of survival and constantly complain that we frighten the horses. From the number of 'avoids' that we have to plot on our maps, there must be more horses in Hampshire, Wiltshire and Surrey than people, and all of them Arab studs or polo ponies. I must admit that on one particular occasion we crested a hill somewhere just south of Salisbury Plain in our helicopter only to be faced with the local hunt in full cry coming in the opposite direction. From the confusion we left in our wake, I can only assume that, for once, Mr Reynard got away. But we don't do it on purpose, honest.

Low Level Herc

In the UK, fixed wing aircraft are not allowed to fly lower than 250ft (75m). I therefore assumed that the pilot of this aircraft was going to fly it across the desert at 250ft (75m). No such luck. At a conservative estimate, I believe most of the next 15 minutes flying was conducted at about 25ft (7 ½ m) Ok, these guys were part of the Special Forces support team, but I did hope the pilot would remember to climb a little before he turned. A Hercules has a wing span of 132ft (40m)! Not only that, but I was standing in the back of this aeroplane. No seat belts (no seats), no restraints of any kind. I took some comfort from the fact that the loadmaster was similarly placed. He obviously had implicit faith in the pilot, or was completely mad. The only thing to do was to enjoy the ride.

I was just beginning to get used to this style of flying when we climbed slightly, the starboard wing dipped and we entered a tight 180^0 turn to the right. A moment later we were level again and on the ground! There had been no warning. None of the usual lowering of flaps etc., although someone must have put the under carriage down, no fuss, we just landed. Again there was a roar and shudder as reverse thrust was engaged and I found myself hanging on to avoid ending up in a heap against the forward bulkhead. We taxied down a long concrete pan with two Hercules on one side and four Chinook helicopters on the other and parked at the far end of the line of Hercs. All the Chinooks were painted camouflaged pink but we appeared to occupy the only pink Hercules. The engines were winding down and the loadmaster was already stowing the cargo net he had used to secure my tri-wall box. I made my way to the back of the aircraft.

"Welcome to Oscar." said the loadmaster.

So this was it at last. This was the place that had haunted my dreams for the last four days. I jumped off the ramp to have a look. At the end of the pan, on the far side of a sand strewn, tarmac roadway, was the, now expected, collection of portacabins. These housed the workshops of the line engineers and all the others whose day to day job was servicing the aircraft, supplying the fuel, marshalling the freight, etc. To the right, there was a large hangar and behind it, what appeared to be two tall square towers. To the left, about a quarter of a mile away, there was a ten foot barbed wire fence and desert. A Landrover moved out from the side of the pan and drove towards me.

"Flight Lieutenant Small?" asked the driver, whom I vaguely recognised. I nodded. "Good to see you, sir. We were expecting you yesterday."

I was about to explain but then thought better of it. "What now?" I enquired.

"I'm to take you to Ops." he replied. So we loaded my tri-wall into the back of the 'rover and set off.

"Who's here?" I asked. The driver's answer rather took me by surprise.

"Three squadrons of SAS, one of SBS and the Herc and Chinook Special Forces support flights."

All of a sudden I felt safe. Since the first moment that I had learnt of my possible involvement in the impending Gulf War I had been apprehensive, to say the least. Now, however, with this select gathering of the world's elite as my personal body guards, how could I possibly come to harm. Noone in their right mind, even Saddam himself, was going to attack this place. At least that was what I hoped.

We rounded the hangar and the two towers I had seen from the pan came fully into view. They were attached to another large hangar and the whole structure looked like a huge grain silo. In between the two hangers was a single story, 'L' shaped, office complex. Each leg of the 'L' comprised 3 offices and in the corner was a kitchen and toilet block. In addition, two portacabins were positioned so that the whole formed an open square facing the 'grain silo'. The complex was surrounded by a wire fence with a gateway leading to a car park between the offices and the 'grain silo'. There was, however, neither gate nor guard at the entrance. On the opposite side of the road to the gateway lay a huge pile of breeze blocks which, in my ignorance, I supposed would eventually be used to construct some form of guard house. This could not have been further from the truth as I was to find out a little later.

Running in front of the offices was a paved area about five feet wide. The centre of the square, however, was rough, unmade ground, neatly enclosed by kerb stones. Facing the 'grain silo' were three hollow metal flag poles, without flags, but with halyards that constantly struck the poles in the wind to produce unexpectedly loud metallic ringing sounds. The whole camp had a new look about it and, like the King Kahlid International Airport, was obviously still under construction.

The Landrover stopped in the car park and, as I got out, I was greeted by two pilots whom I had known for some years. One of them, Flt Lt Liam MacFee (known to the world as MacHoot) said, "Come and meet the Wing Commander." and led me to an office. The office was about 15ft square and in the centre were four desks, side by side and back to back. Inside the office bedlam appeared to be reigning. A group of about a dozen people, mostly clad in flying suits, were gathered round the desks and poring over maps and documents. The walls were hung with maps of Iraq and Kuwait and one was covered with a sheet of white paper on which was printed, in large red capital letters, the word 'SECRET'.

As we entered, one of the figures at the desk nearest the door got up and held out his hand in greeting. "Nice to see you Roger," said Wing Commander Irwin, boss of No 7 Squadron RAF, "we were expecting you yesterday." I started to explain my exploits but, almost as though he had not heard me, he carried on. "I've got a couple of jobs I would like you to take over. At the moment two of the pilots are doing them but we're getting ready for a possible move and I want to release them. That's why I sent for you."

Not only was he not listening to me he also seemed oblivious to the fact that I had literally just stepped off the aircraft. I assumed he must have a lot on his mind and said, "Yes."

He lead me over to the 'SECRET' map and, lifting up the covering sheet, stuck it to the wall with a piece of masking tape. The map was of Kuwait and Iraq and covered in little symbols depicting missile and anti aircraft batteries. "We get regular INT (intelligence) reports on the positions and strengths of these things," he said, "and your job is to keep this map up to date. We're particularly interested in the low level SAMs (surface to air missiles) and the Triple A's."

Triple A or AAA is short for anti aircraft artillery. The most well known and widely deployed is the Russian ZSU 23/4. Pronounced, 'zed ess you twenty three four', it is a formidable weapon with an awesome reputation. It comprises a bank of four, twenty three millimetre guns, together with a fire control radar, mounted on the turret of a medium sized tracked, armoured vehicle. It has a maximum range of about 5000 metres (3 ½ miles) and a rate of fire of 4000 rounds per minute. However, despite these impressive credentials, its reputation is somewhat exaggerated.

Whilst the ZSU 23/4 can fire 4000 rounds per minute (1000 per barrel), the magazine only holds 3200 rounds (48 second's worth) and, if the vehicle is closed down for action, there is no way of getting any more ammunition to the guns. The gun barrels are water cooled but the cooling supply can only cope with 800 rounds per minute, any more and significant wear to the barrels occurs. Finally, despite being mounted on tracks, it is almost impossible to fire the weapon when it is on the move. It is, therefore, not the roving hunter killer with limitless fire power that haunts most helicopter crew's nightmares.

Nevertheless, it can still throw up a devastating wall of lead when defending a particular target, hence the Wing Commander's interest.

"The other job I want you to take over," said the Wing Commander, hardly pausing for breath, "is runnning the imprest. Del Boy's been in charge of it up to now so it should be alright. Any questions?"

Actually I had a whole list of questions like, where do I stow my kit? Do I have any accommodation? What time is lunch? And who the hell is Del Boy? But they all seemed irrelevant in light of the 'possible move', so I just shook my head.

"Good." he said, and turned back to his desk.

An imprest, according to the Oxford English dictionary, is 'money advanced to a person for use in State business'. As far as the RAF is concerned, it is the financial mechanism which allows the day to day running of a detached unit. It is meant to cover such contingencies as food and accommodation, the odd taxi fare and handling charges at civilian airfields. Normally an imprest has only to support a few people for a few days and seldom exceeds £20,000. Any moneys spent out of the imprest have to be accounted for scrupulously because it is 'public' money, and to enable you to do this the money is accompanied by reams of paper work. Trying to fiddle an imprest is one of the most common causes of courts martial. You would think, therefore, that every detachment would have, on its strength, an accounts officer. No such luck. It is a job that is traditionally given to the most junior officer in the crew because it is said to be character building and good experience but, if the truth is told, junior Bloggs gets it because it's a real pain. Aircrew come under the all encompassing heading of GD(Air) The GD stands for General Duties and it means that you are called upon to be a jack of all trades, but with a flying bias. Flying is obviously the primary duty but aircrew are often called upon to perform a legion of other tasks as secondary duties. You may think that 'flying pay' is the bonus aircrew receive for enjoying themselves whilst airborne but in reality it is a token gesture for all the other work they perform in their spare time.

It was obviously the end of the audience and, although I nodded greetings to several other people in the office whom I recognised, no one else seemed inclined to engage me in conversation. They were all very busy, planning. I went back outside and found MacHoot waiting for me. "What ever's going on?" I asked him.

"Well as you probably know," he replied in his soft Scots accent, "the ultimatum given to Saddam Hussein expires on Tuesday the 15th and word has come down that if he does not see reason then the Coalition Forces are going to strike. They've had enough of his games. If that happens we expect to be among the first in so we are busy planning all the possible scenarios."

"That would account for all the activity then."

"Yes as you can see we are having to plan combinations for all the forces that are located here."

"Just one thing," I said, "What about accommodation? I've literally just stepped off the Herc."

"Ah. That could be a problem. All the rooms up at the block are spoken for. I'm sure there's no room up there."

"Where's that?" I asked.

MacHoot pointed in the direction of the portacabins. "Behind there is the domestic block." he said, "Accommodation, admin and the mess."

"That's the first hint of food since I arrived." I said. "What times do you eat?"

"Oh the usual times." was the reply, "Breakfast 0630 - 0800, Lunch 1230 - 1330 and Dinner starts about 1830."

"That sounds awfully civilised." I said, "What's the food like?"

"Not bad. Lots of curry. In fact, it's coming up to lunch time now. I'll take you across and we'll try and find you a bed at the same time."

We made our way between the portacabins and the hangar and were confronted with a wire fence, beyond which was a good quarter mile of desert scrub. On the far side of this open area was another collection of single storey buildings and a single minaret.

"What is this place?" I asked MacHoot.

"Well," he began, "It was being built for the UAE parachute battalion, hence the two towers on the hangar, they're for the initial training jumps. We're actually in the middle of a large military complex, rather like a big sandy Salisbury Plain. There are several separate military camps and this one was being built for parachute training. It had almost been completed when this lot blew up and it was deemed suitably remote and secure as a base for the Special Forces to operate from. The runway was completed but none of the lighting has yet been installed."

"I bet that makes landing at night interesting." I said.

"It's not too bad," he replied, "we do all our night flying on NVG (night vision goggles)."

I had had some experience of these NVGs. Basically they look like a small pair of binoculars but each of the eyepiece tubes is an image intensifier. Any light picked up is magnified within the tube and presented on a miniature TV screen just in front of the eye. They work at very low light levels, star light is sufficient for them to 'see' in, and are therefore ideal for Special Forces operations.

There are two main problems with them. The first is that they only have a limited field of view and you have to spend your time continuously moving your head from side to side to give a complete picture. When you consider that these goggles, together with the helmet, battery pack and counter balance weight, weigh in the order four pounds you can see why aircrew engaged in night flying take large collar sizes. Their neck muscles are well developed.

The second problem is the colour, or lack of it. I said that the picture presented to the pilot was on two miniature TV screens but what I failed to add was that it was monochrome. Normally that is not too bad. It was not so long ago that we all had black and white TVs but these are not black and white, they are black and green. However, having said that they work and work well, allowing flying at night to be safely carried out down to 150ft above the ground.

By this time we had got to the fence. It was a standard wire mesh security fence except for the fact that someone had cut a hole in it to provide access. "Well," MacHoot said, pre-empting my question, "Otherwise we would have a journey of about 2 miles all the way round the perimeter road every time we wanted to eat."

"Who made the hole?" I asked.

"Oh, one of the 'boys'." said MacHoot, nodding towards the hangar. "That's where they've taken up residence."

We crossed over the waste ground towards the admin complex. To our left was an area, surrounded by barbed wire, that appeared to contain piles of boxes.

"What's in there?" I asked.

"That, is the ammunition dump." was the reply. It's as far away as we can get it from the domestic and flight sites without being impractical." Imagining the sort of fireworks that the 'boys' were wont to play with, it looked awfully close to me.

We arrived at another hole in another fence. "That is the mess hall immediately ahead of us," said MacHoot, "Lunch should be on in about 20 minutes."

The minaret I had seen from the other side of the camp was just behind the mess and was attached to a small mosque. "Do we have our own muezzin to call us to prayer?" was my next question.

"No." said MacHoot. "There's a large loudspeaker which appears to be fed from a central point for all the surrounding camps. It caused quite a problem for the first few days as the first call is just before dawn, about 0500, but the same guy who cut the holes in the fence used his wire cutters on the loudspeaker feed and its been quiet ever since."

"Didn't the locals complain?"

"To begin with, but it all seems to have died down now."

By now we had reached another open square, single storey complex of buildings but, unlike the office block, there was a roofed verandah all the way around the inside of the square. MacHoot knocked on the door of the first room. It was opened by a medium height, well built man with sandy hair who I judged to be in his early 50's. He was wearing a major's rank tabs. "Hello John." said MacHoot. "One more joining the party. Do we have a bed for him? John's the Quartermaster." he added turning to me.

"Not a chance." was the reply. John had a gruff voice but there was a twinkle in the depth of his eyes. "We're solid up here. Best I can do is give you a camp bed. You'll have to find yourself a few square inches of floor space somewhere."

"Just thought I'd ask." said MacHoot. "It looks as if you'll have to doss down with Sqn Ldr Kirby, the SENGO (senior engineering officer)."

"Where's he living?" I asked.

"In the office next to where you met the Wing Commander. He uses it as an office during the day and spreads out his bed at night. There's plenty of room in there."

I wasn't so sure, but at least it would be somewhere to put my tri-wall.

We made our way back to the mess and went inside. There were two identical dining halls separated by a central kitchen.

"This is the officers'." said MacHoot and led the way into the hall on the right.

The menu was impressive. I had expected COMPO (composite rations) but instead there was a choice of chicken, steak and the inevitable curry. I hadn't brought my mess tins or KFS (knife fork and spoon) with me but I managed to scrounge sufficient for the purpose.

There was a notice board on the wall by the serving hatch and among the notices detailing meal times, today's menu, etc., someone had pinned up the following cartoon and it caught my fancy. It summed up the gulf (no pun intended) between East and West, Moslem and Christian.

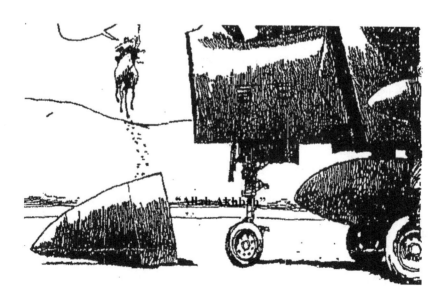

Lunch over, we passed through the two holes in the fences and returned to the office complex. I went and found SENGO and informed him I was going to live in his office. It was a nice big office next to the kitchen, as big as the Ops room next door but with only two desks in it. SENGO was a short, slight, squadron leader with an even shorter haircut. He did not seem particularly surprised and waved me to a far corner. "Dump your kit over there," he said, "You can put your bed up later." I was just about to open up my tri-wall when 'Del Boy' arrived. He turned out to be Flt Lt Jack Walsh, someone else whom I knew from RAF Odiham.

"'Understand you're taking over the imprest," he said, "I've got ten minutes, shall we do it now?" and he led off towards one of the portacabins that had been commandeered as a map store. "We should be relatively undisturbed in here."

The thought of taking over the imprest in 'ten minutes' immediately rang alarm bells. It could only mean one of two things. Either the imprest was not very large or complex, or the records were in a bit of a mess. Considering that the detachment comprised four aircraft and ninetyish personnel, most of whom had already been in the Gulf for upwards of two months and moved location twice, the chances of finding a simple and well kept imprest were remote. I was not disappointed. The central core of an imprest is the daily record sheet. This records, day by day, expenses incurred, by category; taxis, fuel, food, accommodation etc. Individual receipts are numbered for reference but kept in a separate folder or envelope. I was presented with a large, blue envelope folder which contained a whole sheaf of receipts, in no particular order and several sheets of A4 lined paper with some scribbled details.

Del Boy was in a hurry to hand over the imprest. Not because he thought that it wouldn't balance or anything like that but because he had a lot of 'planning' to do. If someone is planning something which may easily involve laying his life on the line then it is callous to quibble about something as mercenary as money. On the other hand it would be my reputation at the courts martial. We compromised.

"Let's just go over the major items," I said, "the day to day accounts I can sort out in my own time."

The list was short but impressive; one dozen portacabins together with air conditioning units, two RICOH colour photo copiers, six mobile 'phones and half a dozen assorted cars and 4X4s on permanent hire from Avis. There was obviously a little explaining to do.

"The need for portacabins I can understand, " I said, "but why have we bought them and not hired them?"

"What's wrong with that?" Del Boy asked.

"One of the cardinal rules of an imprest is that you can use it only to purchase consumables." I said. "It cannot be used to trade with. If you need something like a portacabin you are supposed to hire it. That way, at the end of the day all you have left are bills and receipts. All nice and tidy in accountant's eyes. When this is all over we shall have to get rid of the cabins somehow and unless we give them away they will generate money, and that is trade. The first sign of a fiddled imprest is one that makes a profit."

"Ah!" said Del Boy, "Then there is a bit of a problem."

"What do you mean," I queried, fearing the worst.

"We-ell. The last time I balanced the books we had a surplus of six hundred Dirhams (UAE currency @ approximately 10 DRMs to the £) that I couldn't account for."

"When did you last balance the books?"

"About ten days ago."

"It's supposed to be done at the end of each day."

"I know, but there just isn't time."

I had a certain sympathy. Whilst the gnomes at the treasury have steadily cut the men and equipment in the Armed Forces they have singularly failed to reduce the size of job by a similar amount. The result is that each individual is faced with more work, and not necessarily that which he was trained to do.

"Sixty pounds isn't a fortune," I continued, "but it's enough to smack of slack accounting and will provoke a witch hunt." Del Boy's face began to drop. " Never mind, I'll see if I can find it. That, after all, seems to be the job I was brought out here to do. Now, explain the photo copiers and the Avis vehicles."

The unusual aspects of the imprest revolved mainly around the fact that it was being used to support a covert operation, not quite secret nor yet clandestine, but obviously it was advantageous to all concerned not to advertise its presence. Additionally our host nation, whilst lending us all aid and assistance did not want the fact that we were operating from within its borders noised abroad. These limitations, therefore, made it somewhat difficult to plug into the usual military supply system. I had not been exposed to the detailed workings of Special Forces before and had never considered the logistics of such operations. In the end it proved to be very much a case of supply yourself and send in the bill, but don't forget that you still have to account for every nut, bolt, washer, bullet and hand grenade.

The explanations that Del Boy gave seemed plausible enough to me, I just hoped they would sound as convincing to the accountants back in the UK. The photocopiers had been purchased to reproduce maps from the core library. Many of the maps needed for planning the operations were, of necessity, very detailed and of obscure areas, and it seemed injudicious to advertise our interest in these targets by demanding maps of them through the usual channels.

"Fair enough," I said, "But why two?"

"In case we split up from the Hercules Det (detachment)." was the reply.

"Yes. I can see the logic." I replied, "Now explain the cars and mobile 'phones."

"The SF flight has no vehicles of its own," he began, "And up till now our operations have not lasted more than a couple of weeks, but this is different. We are 40 miles from the nearest town and .."

"Yes." I interrupted. "Point taken, but the 'phones?"

"Invaluable." he said. "Military COMMs (communications) are never good at the best of times. We are stuck out here on a limb, away from the main Force HQ and have two dubious telephone lines. Our operations can take us anywhere within the Arabian peninsula and beyond, and most of the places we end up in don't even know what a 'phone is. With these mobiles we can at least communicate with the rest of the world."

"You mean they're international?" I said.

"Oh yes." he replied. "You can stand out there and dial home if you wish."

"And security?"

"It's all monitored, of course, and there's no telling what the other side are doing. So you need to exercise a certain amount of caution."

At that moment the door opened and the Wing Commander came in.

"Everything going all right?" he asked. I nodded.

"Good," he said, "I'm sorry I was busy when you arrived but as you can understand it's all a bit hectic. There's a couple of things I need to make clear. Security here is very tight because we wish to keep our whereabouts as secret as possible. Of necessity therefore, access in and out of the camp is strictly limited. I want you to take over the task of issuing permits to anyone from our outfit who has to go down town. There are two reasons for this. Firstly, we need to know who has gone and why, and secondly, for their own safety we need to keep tabs on them and if necessary mount a rescue mission if anything happens to them."

"Is there much of a threat?" I asked.

"Because we are so far from the front line, the perceived threat is that of terrorist rather than full scale military attack. Therefore the orders are that, around camp, there is no need to have our NBC (nuclear, biological and chemical) suits and kit with us, just know were it is. However, we are to carry our weapons at all times. The only exception to this is if you go down town."

I gave him a quizzical look. "Surely if the greatest threat is from the terrorist, the one place we do need a gun is down town?"

"That may be so." he replied, "But the political climate totally forbids it. The other task I want you to take on," he continued, "Is that of censor. You are to read all out going mail and prevent any compromise of our location. I see you as our lynch pin and point of contact both while we are here and if and when we disappear up country. Likewise, when this has all finished it will be your job to close the place down when we have gone home. You know, last one out, switch off the light and shut the door."

Well at least I now had a better idea of what the job entailed.

When the Wing Commander had gone I said to Del Boy, "One last question, for the moment. Where do we get our supply of money from? You can't have brought out all you require in the first place."

"No." he said. "We've set up a bank account in the local branch of the British Bank of the Middle East and every so often Auntie Betty sends us a postal order." He fished about in the wad of papers and found a sheet of hotel note paper on which were written two numbers. "The first one is the account number at the bank, the second is the telephone number of a sergeant at HQ Strike Command Accounts back in the UK who actually feeds the money to us."

"Do we get regular payments?"

"No. I just 'phone up when I want some more. It takes about three days to come through. By the way," he added, "I think it's just about time for a top up and I suggest you go down to the bank tomorrow and introduce yourself to the manager. Nice guy. Mr Hunter."

For those who may be wondering, 'Auntie Betty' is a term of endearment used by servicemen when referring to Her Majesty the Queen, especially where the payment of money is concerned.

We left the portacabin and stepped out into the 'square'. It was mid afternoon, there was not a cloud in the sky, a light breeze was blowing from the south and it was warm. For the first time since I had arrived I now had time to have a good look at the people I had come to work with. The men of the SAS and SBS. Where were all these 7ft tall clones of Arnold Swartzanegger; heroes of the British armed forces who appear out of nowhere in a flash and a bang and leave almost as quickly having sorted out the world's ills?

Most, I knew, were housed in the 'grain silo' but those who were visible looked rather ordinary. I am only 5ft 8ins (172cm) tall and the majority looked, if anything, shorter than me. True they looked fit, some were walking about in just shorts and a T shirt, but they were not bursting out of their clothes every time they flexed a muscle. Also, there was no sign of any rank insignia anywhere. The whole air of the place was one of ordinariness, and that, of course, is one of their special attributes. The ability to blend into the background. There is a story, it may be apocryphal, of an SAS group that spent over a week as an observation team in the front garden of a house in Belfast and remained undetected. Now perhaps the owner of the house was no great gardener, but even so.

Outside one of the offices was a guy, stripped to the waist, lying on the ground, peering down the barrel of a rifle which was propped up on some books on the seat of a chair. I couldn't help myself. I had to go and ask.

"What are you doing?" I queried, hardly daring to hope for an answer.

He looked up and smiled, "sighting my gun." Seeing my incredulous look he continued, "If I adjust the sights to the target I can see down the barrel, hopefully that is where the bullet will hit." He said no more and after a few moments I left him in the sunshine making fine adjustments to the sights with a jeweller's screwdriver.

A few days later my curiosity again impelled me to ask one of the 'boys' what he was doing. I had seen this particular SAS man several times. He was short, slightly round shouldered and had a face that was a caricature of an Irish leprechaun. However, what had grabbed my attention was the fact that he always had a canvas bag, rather like a rough shooter's game bag, slung round his shoulder. Eventually I screwed up my courage and asked what it contained. A broad smile crossed his face and he proceeded to undo the flap. I honestly expected him to produce a brace of partridge but instead his large sunburned hand emerged cradling two hand guns. One was similar to the Browning 9mm pistol which, up until recently, had been the RAF officers' personal weapon, but this one was obviously of larger calibre.

"It's a '45' (0.45 inch/11.43mm)", he said, "'Packs more of a punch."

The other weapon was a medium sized revolver which I did not recognise and which he declined to enlarge upon. He popped them back into his game bag and went his way.

Those two examples typify the average SAS man as I found him. On the outside, ordinary; someone to whom you probably would not give a second glance. Inside, an eccentric professional whose constant practice at his unusual skills makes him appear superhuman to Joe Bloggs in the street.

I went on to explore the 'domestic' arrangements within the compound. In the corner of the two lines of offices was a kitchen and a loo. The kitchen was fairly standard in that it comprised a sink, draining board, and a bank of empty cupboards. The loo was not standard, at least to the Western way of thinking. It consisted of a small square room the floor of which can best be describes as a shallow, porcelain funnel. The hole in the centre was about 8 inches in diameter which, from the smell, appeared to lead directly into the sewer. On either side of the hole, moulded in the porcelain, were two slightly raised platforms, marginally bigger than the human foot. One was expected to perform whilst balancing on these two platforms, or get wet or dirty or both. There was no provision for a loo roll, just a tap for washing the left hand. That is why Arabs never eat with their left hands. In the film, 'Lawrence of Arabia', there is a scene, early in the film, where Lawrence takes some food offered by his Arab guide with his left hand. Had that happened for real the story would have ended there. Flushing the loo was achieved by employing the hose pipe protruding from one wall and the yard broom which stood in the far corner. For a Westerner, encumbered with trousers and a bog roll, going to the loo required a certain degree of dexterity which, nevertheless, was quickly learnt. The place stank!

I returned to my 'room' and started to unpack my tri-wall. I was particularly relieved to find that I had, after all, remembered to pack two bog rolls, they were going to be more valuable than fine gold. It was then I discovered the 'surprise' that Janet had said she had packed; three sugar mice. As far back as I can remember our family has always had sugar mice and chocolate coins on the Christmas tree each year and here were mine, left over from the festivities. I ate one immediately because I thought I deserved it but determined to save the others for strategic moments in the coming conflict; the end of the war and the order to return home.

Since the advent of EEC regulations, sugar mice have undergone a radical change. In the bad old days, every mouse had a string tail. This, however, is no longer allowed as string is regarded as 'foreign' matter and, as such, not to be included in food stuff. You can have a wooden stick in a lollipop, but you can't have a string tail in a sugar mouse. And they pay people a fortune to think up and administer rules like that!

I had just about organised myself when SENGO announced that it was time to make our way to the mess for dinner. "If you get there early," he said, "it gives you time for a leisurely meal and still get back in time for the Colonel's 'O' Group at 1900."

An 'O' Group, or Orders Group, is a periodic, usually daily, meeting held by the senior officer of a military formation. It is attended by the 'heads of sheds' (leaders of the various sections within the formation) and is rather like a board meeting where past events are discussed and outline orders for the forthcoming period are promulgated. The main difference between an 'O' Group and a board meeting is that members at 'O' Groups seldom, if ever, get the opportunity to vote on a proposition.

Dinner was, if anything, of a higher standard than lunch. The crowning glory was, however, the magnificent stilton cheese which stood at the end of the servery. Stilton as bought from your average supermarket cold shelf is usually sour or bitter tasting and lacks any bite whatsoever. A good stilton should be sweet, and I mean sweet, and burn the roof of your mouth. This was a good stilton.

In an ideal situation the stilton should be accompanied by a water biscuit and a pickled walnut. This was not an ideal situation but the Jacob's Cream Crackers made an acceptable substitute. There was a distinct lack of pickled walnuts but, by the side of the cheese, stood a large glass jar which contained, of all things, pickled jalapeno chilli peppers. If you have never eaten a jalapeno (pronounced halerpeeno), beware! They are regarded as one of the hottest. The combination of cheese and pepper, though unlikely, was a gourmet's delight. Fortunately, most of the other diners opted for the trifle and cheese cake. They did not know what they were missing and I was not about to tell them. There was a civilised side to war after all.

"Where ever did you find them?" I asked the chef.

"'Delicatessen in Spinney's, down town." he replied.

"What is Spinney's?"

"Oh, the local supermarket."

Obviously not the average Basingstoke supermarket. This would have to be investigated further.

The 'O' Group was well attended and about twenty people packed themselves into the aircrew Ops room. It was presided over by an SAS colonel, Sid Moore, a small compact man who walked with a distinct limp. The main item on the agenda was an update by the INT O (intelligence officer) on the general situation. There was no change. Saddam Hussein was still prevaricating, the deadline of the 15th of January was getting closer and the Coalition Forces were preparing for the inevitable.

The only other point of note, as far as I was concerned, was the MET (meteorological - weather) report that Riyadh was wrapped in cold, wet fog! Something else I had not expected of the desert. As it turned out, a great many others had also not considered the fact that winter in the desert can be very cold with bitter winds and snow. Two people paid for this miscalculation with their lives, but that will come later.

As the 'O' Group ended, several great, grey, plastic 'hessian' sacks of mail arrived. This was promptly sorted and handed out. I suddenly realised I was lonely. The last few days had been so hectic that I had not had time to reflect on my personal situation but, as letters were eagerly opened and avidly read, the fact that I did not have one made me feel very isolated from all that represented safety and security. I tried to console myself with the thought that, even if Janet had written a letter the moment I left RAF Brize Norton, it could not possibly have reached me. But there was little consolation in the thought.

I wandered round to SENGO's office to find that he had pushed his desk into one corner and was already assembling his camp bed. I did the same and in so doing discovered yet another use for the tri-wall box; it makes an excellent substitute for a bedside locker and, in fact, served me in this capacity throughout the duration. We made ourselves one last cup of coffee and went to bed.

5 - TRANSITION TO WAR 14/16 Jan '91

The 14th dawned bright but very hazy, due mainly to the strong wind which had developed during the night and lifted all the fine dust from the coarser material into the air. This was another aspect of the desert which differs from the average non-desert dweller's perception of what deserts are like. The grains in the half yard of sharp sand that you buy from the builders merchant are reasonably uniform in size because they have been sieved and graded and do not usually blow about because they are generally wet and stuck to each other. This does not apply to the desert. A desert, by definition, is an arid place. The sand, therefore, is usually dry and the grains free to move. Likewise, no one has been out there with a riddle and graded it to uniformity. I shall take time out here to describe just what is meant by sand.

When does dust become sand and sand become gravel? According to the Hamlyn Guide to Minerals, Rocks and Fossils (1976), grains of rock greater than 2mm (measured by the pitch of the sieve through they will pass) are classified as gravel, those between 2 and 1/16mm are sand. From 1/16mm to 1/256mm diameter you are in the silt category and anything less than 1/256mm is fine enough to form clay particles. As an aside, it is obvious that the Guide was written during the time of enforced change from imperial measurement to metric. Lip service to the metre has been paid but the imperial fraction still haunts the psyche. I expect by now the limiting sizes have been rationalised to 2mm, 0.625mm and 0.004mm respectively. Nevertheless, to the laymen such as you and I, gravel is still small pebbles, sand sand and dust anything which can be suspended by the merest breath of wind and is usually seen in the sun beams pouring in through the lounge window.

The action of the wind, constantly rubbing the sand particles together, causes them to wear and become rounded. The wearing results in dust and the 'roundness' allows the particles to be transported more easily by the wind. The end result is that the material of the desert gets everywhere. This raises several problems. Not only does it cause personal discomfort by getting in your hair, clothes and eyes; stinging your face every time the wind blows; adding a gritty texture to your food and giving even the softest soap all the abrasive qualities of wire wool but it also causes serious problems to mechanical moving parts. Of particular concern to ourselves was the sand blasting effect caused by the dust being sucked at high speed into jet engines. This was not so much of a problem to the fast jet and fixed wing fraternity, who spend much of their time above the general dust layer, but for the helicopters and tanks it was a nightmare. Not only are the latter close to the ground and therefore in the thick of it but their very presence stirs up even more dust thus exacerbating an already difficult situation.

Initially the problem was so bad that an unfiltered helicopter engine lasted, on average, only ten hours before the turbine blades were worn to such a degree that they needed replacing. Even in the benign environment of Europe the dust of simulated battle fields had proved to be a problem but filters were fitted and engine life extended to over one thousand hours. These filters, however, proved less effective against this fine desert dust and only managed to increase the life expectancy of an engine to about one hundred hours. There were echoes of British Rail's "the wrong type of snow" but in the end, the right type of filter was found for the wrong type of sand and reasonable engine usage was achieved but, the dust remained a constant problem. (In passing, it is worthy of note that these 'sand' filters have been found to be very effective against snow ingestion but that was not our immediate problem!) There was, however, one benefit. The dust in the air produced the most magnificent red sunsets and in the late evening reduced the sun's glare to such an extent that it was possible to regularly observe sunspots without any recourse to dark glasses.

I spent my first day at Oscar getting to know the place, the people and the routine, and routine always starts with breakfast. Breakfast comprised cereals, a full fry, toast, in fact all the works. There was certainly no intention of sending you off to work, whatever that might be, on an empty stomach. On the contrary, if the three meals I had already experienced since my arrival at Oscar were anything to go by there was a serious risk of putting on weight.

Back in my 'room', SENGO was trying to make it look like an office once more. So I tidied my kit up, stood my camp bed on end in the corner and helped shuffle the desks back into the centre. I then set off to try to do my bit for the war effort.

In Air Ops there was less bedlam than on the previous day. I discovered that the block of four desks was arranged such that one side was the Herc empire and the other belonged to the Chinooks and that there was a certain rivalry between them. This was not helped by the fact that both flights had originally been commanded by squadron leaders of approximately equal seniority. The question of who was in charge had been settled to some extent by the arrival of the Chinook wing commander but, even though he had tried to act impartially, the Herc boys were not convinced and, as an outsider, I thought I detected a certain atmosphere.

I asked the Chinook duty officer where I might find the latest INT reports so that I could update the 'Secret' display. He directed me to one Corporal Richards - Gaunt who was the ADMIN (administration) clerk and responsible for controlling the day to day trivia that the detachment received. Cpl R-G or just 'Argy', as he was universally known, had set up shop in the same portacabin that housed the map store and had made one corner an empire of pens, paper clips and files. He was a shortish man with a slightly sad expression to his face which belied his cheerful interior. One of his possessions was a steel box, approximately 2ft (61cm) long, 18ins (45cm) wide and 9ins (23cm) deep. On the lid of this box was a 'Manifoil' lock. This is the sort of lock beloved of 'movie' burglars who spend either hours or seconds, depending on the plot, twisting the dial first one way and then the other whilst listening intently to their results through a stethoscope.

This steel box was the detachment safe and housed all the secret and confidential documents. For extra security it was chained to Argy's desk by one of its handles. Ostensibly not the most secure arrangement in the world but, on the other hand, it was, in effect, guarded by four squadrons of the most revered soldiers in the world. The crown jewels could not have been safer.

At my request, Argy opened the safe and produced several pages of computer printout which detailed the last known locations of the enemy's SAM and AAA sites. I signed for them and took them across to Ops. The map was covered in little red guns and missiles. If this was Saddam's anti helicopter ORBAT (Order of Battle) then we were in for a rough time. I started to plot the new positions but soon realised there was something wrong. I went back to Argy.

"Is there another part to this signal?" I asked him.

"No." he said, "Why?"

"Well this list only adds newly occupied locations not previously reported. It does not list previous locations which have been vacated." He looked at me blankly. "There is no cancellation list." I continued. "In other words, we're just filling the map with symbols, not moving them about. The map in Ops is covered in SAM and Triple A sites. But whether they're actually active or even currently occupied is anyone's guess."

"I see what you mean." he said. The dawn of realisation lightening his face. "No one's thought of that before. I'll see what I can find out."

I left him to it and attempted my next goal, getting to know some of the people. Two people who turned out to be very important were John and Swede.

John, who I had met the previous day in my quest for a bed space, turned out to be the SAS Quartermaster; a soldier who had served his time with the regiment and had stayed on as a member of the staff cadre. Now, nearing the end of his service career and too old for active service or the rigours that training others demanded, he had been commissioned and given the job of supplying the 'boys' with their particular and peculiar wants and needs. Although his initial reaction to any enquiry was, "No!" his vast experience of life enabled him to service even the most outlandish requests, and usually in a surprisingly short space of time.

Of similar abilities but of completely different background was Swede. Swede was a short, plump airman, who, whilst not actually insubordinate, resented directly exerted authority and worked best from vague hints and suggestions. When he addressed an officer as, "Sir", you got the distinct impression that this was a phonetic alternative of the word "Cur". On the other hand, any officer whom he had decided was "all right", he lauded with the salutation of "sire". Swede could also produce the most unlikely items at the drop of a hat although it did not do to enquire too closely into their provenance.

I managed to cultivate the friendship of these two 'suppliers' and, as a result, spent the duration of the war in relative comfort. My first request to both parties was for a set of desert camouflage jacket and trousers. You will remember that the Brits had been sent off to the Gulf looking like well watered shrubbery in their jungle cam outfits, however, one of the things that struck me as soon as I arrived at Oscar was the fact that everyone here blended into the sandscape. My request provoked a mixed response. John said "No" and Swede was evasive but said he would see what he could do.

Back in the office it was time for the first coffee of the day. Coffee forms an integral part of SH life and is drunk constantly. We have never had 'tea breaks' as such because SH life is not ordered. You work when there is a job to do and drink coffee in convenient gaps. Usually it is 'NAAFI' (Navy, Army and Air Force Institute) coffee and fairly dreadful. I don't know where they get it from but I doubt that it starts its life as a coffee bean. It tastes rather like the result of mixing finely scraped burnt toast into hot water but it is often free and does seem to have a caffeine content and both of these features are important.

The time was approaching 0900 hrs (mid-day UK time) and one of the navigators, Flt Lt Mark Smith (Smithy) produced a small portable radio from which issued the tune 'Lilibularo' which was to haunt the rest of my time in the Gulf and still does to this day. Lilibularo is the signature tune of the BBC World Service and on the hour, every hour, there is a news bulletin. Many other countries provide similar world wide radio services, Voice of America and

Radio Moscow to name but two, but they are often heavily biased parochially or with propaganda. The BBC however, has an internationally envied reputation for telling a credible version of the truth. So much so that its transmissions are often jammed in parts of the world where the ruling regimes do not wish their subjects to be aware of what is happening inside their own country or around the world.

Until the advent of geostationary satellites, the only practical method of global communication was by short wave (high frequency (HF)) radio. You may recall that at the end of chapter 1, I mentioned that radio waves can only travel in straight lines. They may be transmitted in fan or cone like patterns to cover as great an area as possible but, in general, they cannot be bent over the horizon. The higher the aerial the greater the distance that can be covered, the same way that you can see further from the top of a tall building than you can from street level. That is why radio and TV transmission aerials are usually on top of very tall masts on the highest hill in the area. However, one of the properties of high frequency radio waves is that they can be reflected or bounced off the Van Allen Belts, areas of ionised particles which surround the earth at a height of some 50 miles (80km). This has the effect of providing a very tall aerial capable of effectively covering almost one third of the earth's surface. By a careful juggling of frequencies and the re-transmission of received signals it is possible to cover the whole world.

HF radio communications are, however, not quite as simple as I have just described. The areas of ionised particles are not stationary and their height above the earth's surface varies with time of day, particularly at dawn and dusk. Their reflective properties are also dictated by the vagaries of solar radiation, particularly that associated with sun spots. Anyone who has listened to HF transmissions will be familiar to the fading and whistling which characterises the 'unevenness' of this reflective medium.

As might be imagined, the signal at the receiver is pitifully weak after it has been transmitted these vast distances and, until recently, has resulted in the need for powerful transmitters and equally powerful amplifiers in the receivers. Not so long ago British expatriates who wished to keep in touch with the Old Country were forced to own wirelesses the size of tea chests containing racks of valves which required a small power station to drive them and yards of wire aerial to pick up the signal in the first place. I knew that modern technology in the form of the transistor and micro-chip had gone a long way in reducing size and power requirements but I was more than impressed at the size of the radio from which Lilibularo was now emerging.

"What ever is that?" I asked incredulously.

"The latest Sony gadget," replied Smithy, handing it across.

The radio measured 4ins (10cm) by 3ins (7.6cm) by ¾ of an inch (1.9cm) thick and was heavy for its size. It had an 18ins (45cm) telescopic aerial sticking out of one end and the top face contained a series of buttons, an LCD display, a loudspeaker grille and the ubiquitous brand name 'SONY' writ large in silver characters along the upper edge. However, the most impressive feature was the small writing around the LCD display which announced:-

FM 87.5 - 108 MHz AM 150 - 285/531 - 26100 KHz

"Does this little box pick up all these frequencies. Long, medium and short-wave and FM as well?" I asked.

"Yes." he replied, "Everything except the military, police, airline and emergency bands."

I was amazed. "OK." I said, "What's the catch?"

"It is expensive," he ventured "but worth every penny."

"How much is expensive?"

"About £150." was the reply.

Even so I was smitten. I had to try and find one for myself. This was my link with reality. My Walkman was fine but its limited radio band was designed for life in the city not for an isolated existence in the middle of the Arabian desert. Nevertheless, however fine this marvel of modern electronic technology was, it did not bring particularly good news. Saddam Hussein was reported to show no signs of acceding to UN resolution 678 and war seemed inevitable. A small crowd had gathered, drawn by the strains of Lilibularo, but little comment was made and, with the end of the news headlines, each individual returned to his various tasks with his private thoughts.

I went to find John to see if there had been any progress on the desert cam. There had not, however there was a large tri-wall box in the middle of his store room.

"And what do you suppose is in there?" he asked.

"I have no idea," I replied, "Knowing you lot it could be anything."

"Well," he continued, It's full of track suits and ladies knickers."

I was beginning to believe almost anything of the SAS but this needed some explanation. "What are you up to now?"

"Nothing." he said with a grin. "You remember the hostages Saddam was holding as a human shield?"

"Yes."

"Well, when the British Airways flight came in to pick them up after their release it brought with it a supply of spare clothes in case they were needed. These were left over."

And he was right. Inside the box were about 40 track suits in the dark blue and red BA colours with the BA logo and goodness knows how many pairs of ladies white cotton briefs.

"But how did they get here?" I asked.

"That's a long story," he replied "Let's just say that there has been a certain amount of scavenging and leave it at that."

"What are you going to do with them?

"I'm sure the lads will find a use for the track suits. The knickers will probably make their way to the local British Consul's charity box and his wife will see they go to a good cause. I think the colonel has already had a word."

It was not the sort of statement that you expect from these roughy toughies but despite their rugged public persona they actually spend quite a lot of time doing good. Since their earliest campaigns in Malaya, when they discovered that the local population were far more likely to be friendly when offered medical and 'engineering' aid, the SAS have developed a policy of hearts and minds. In contrast to the often brutal oppression meted out by special forces of other regimes, this unusual combat tactic has often yielded much needed local support in the form of shelter, information or even just being ignored at a critical moment. It doesn't make the headlines because it is not headline material but then they are not a very public organisation anyway.

"There's one thing that we are not finding so easy to get rid of though," John continued.

"What's that?" I asked.

"Those breeze blocks outside the entrance to the compound." he replied.

"They're yours? I thought they had been left over when this complex was built."

"No, they're ours and they are also connected with the hostages." I was intrigued and he went on. "When the hostages were first captured we were given the task of engineering their release. This entailed a lot of detailed planning, including careful study of the buildings in which they were held. To this end, we were on the point of building replicas of their prisons in order to practise assaults on them before the real thing. But just as the blocks were delivered, Saddam ups and releases the hostages without so much as a 'bye your leave'. Left us a bit embarrassed he did."

"What are you going to do with them now?"

"We-ll." he smiled, "If we're here long enough we might just build a swimming pool."

The war ended sooner than most of us expected and when I left, almost three months later, the breeze blocks were still in an untidy heap just outside the gate.

When I returned to Ops I was informed that, as it looked as though armed conflict was inevitable, part of the afternoon would be spent being 'jabbed up' by the Doc in case Saddam 'threw' anything nasty at us. This was something that had been in the back of all our minds. Saddam Hussein was reported to have large stocks of all kinds of chemical and biological weapons at his disposal and, if the reports of mass deaths in his war with Iran were to be believed, then there was every chance that he would not hesitate to use them against the Coalition Forces. Therefore, after lunch we duly assembled at the medical centre. I have no particular fear of needles but the one the Doc was waving at us did seem to be backed by an awfully large syringe.

"What's in it then, Doc?" we asked, eyeing him dubiously.

"Oh just a little cocktail." he replied, all too nonchalantly for my liking.

"Yes, but what's it supposed to save us from?" we persisted.

"Anthrax, plague and whooping cough."

"Is that all? Are you sure you've covered all the possibilities?"

"No," the Doc replied, "but this will do for a starter. By the way," he added, "the day before you go forward you should also start taking your NAPS tablets."

The NAPS (Nerve Agent Pre-treatment Set) tablets are designed to reduce the deadly effects of certain chemical and biological compounds used in warfare. They come in bubble packs of 21 and look for all the world like contraceptive pills. In fact they probably have the same effect as they are said to contain eighty five percent bromide. If all this pre-treatment was necessary it did make you just wonder how effective our NBC suits and respirators (gas mask) really were.

The NBC suit, known colloquially as the 'goon suit', offers physical protection against gas and liquid chemical attack and very limited protection to alpha and beta radiation. The suit comprises a smock with hood and trousers, which are made of layers of material impregnated with carbon and fullers earth, both of which are capable of absorbing and holding large quantities of harmful liquids or vapours. Rubber gloves, overboots and gas mask complete the outfit which offers protection that is reputedly the best in the world.

The goon suit was devised at Porton Down Chemical Defence Establishment on Salisbury Plain. Contrary to its reputation, Porton Down was not established to produce nerve gases and the like. Quite the reverse, its main aim is to develop counters to the effects of biological and chemical agents that others may, from time to time, see fit to deploy against the British serviceman. Long may its work continue. If, however, despite all these precautions you still get a whiff of nerve gas, there is one last line of defence. The Combo pen.

The Combo pen is an auto-injection syringe containing, among other things, 6 mgs of atropine. Atropine is a poison derived from deadly nightshade (Atropa Bella-Donna) but, as any homeopath will tell you, many substances, which are in themselves poisons, if administered in measured doses will act as antidotes to other poisons. Atropine is apparently the antidote to nerve gas. The problem is that if you mistakenly diagnose yourself as suffering from the effects of nerve gas when all you have is a hangover and inject yourself with atropine you may do yourself serious damage. Just 100 mgs of atropine can prove fatal to a healthy adult male. If, on the other hand, you have inhaled nerve gas but do not inject you may well die within nine seconds. The training manual states that there are three stages of symptoms which indicate that you have suffered a nerve gas attack:

Early Symptoms

Pin pointing of pupils and dimness of vision.
Running nose, increased salivation.
Tightness of chest, difficulty in breathing.

Later Symptoms

Headache, increasing salivation, drooling at mouth.
Dizziness and general weakness.
Excessive sweating.

Danger Symptoms

Nausea and vomiting.
Involuntary urination and defecation.
Muscles twitching and jerking.
Stoppage of breathing.

The manual ends by saying 'write down these symptoms and learn them.' Bearing in mind that nerve gas can kill in nine seconds, you've got to be pretty sharp to recognise the problem and react with the antidote. However, even correct diagnosis leaves you with several problems.

The Combo pen is sealed in a vacuum-pack plastic sachet. Although there is a 'V' notch in the wrapper to aid tearing we all know how difficult it is to undo such packaging. Inside, the 'pen' has a plastic cap to protect the syringe needle and auto-inject mechanism. This cap must be removed and the pen pushed hard against the leg in the vicinity of the outer thigh muscle mid way between the knee and the hip. This action releases a spring loaded needle which penetrates your clothes and thigh muscle and automatically injects the contents.

Consider, also, that you are trying to carry out this procedure with your hands enclosed in rubber gloves, your gas mask is filling with saliva and vomit, your trousers are beginning to resemble a baby's nappy and your whole body is twitching and refusing to breathe and you can see that your reaction to a nerve gas attack needs to be pretty slick.

Contrary to what the popular press would have you believe, sticking a needle in yourself is not a natural act for the majority of people and, besides, very few have even seen an auto-inject device. The more inquisitive, therefore, wanted to know just how hard you had to push the Combo pen against your leg in order to make it work, how long was the needle, and other basic questions like that. However, taking into account the warning of atropine poisoning it was concluded that a non-human guinea pig was needed for the trial. After much discussion, an orange was selected as a suitable victim, mainly because the fruit and veg rights people were thought to be less militant than their animal counterparts. Several people had a go and the orange was duly injected about six times in all. With their questions answered the inquisitive dispersed about their various tasks and no more was thought about it until some poor innocent, who had not been party to the original discussion, was seen staggering around, pupils dilated clutching a half eaten orange! The initial reaction was to give him a whiff of nerve gas to see if that was an antidote to atropine poisoning but fortunately the Doc arrived on the scene and managed to dissuade us. He administered a rather more tried and tested form of treatment which, I am glad to say proved successful, but the victim was not a well bear for several days. All in all, nerve gas appears to be something to be avoided.

There were, however, unwelcome side effects from this legitimate medication, although, at the time, the connections were not obvious for people had other things on their minds and the phrase, 'Gulf War Syndrome', had not yet been coined. Most suffered two or three days heavy cold symptoms but this was put down to 'a change of environment' for those who had just arrived and 'the effects of the air conditioning' for those who had been in theatre for some time. For those who did not fit either category it was just a cold that was 'doing the rounds'. In my own case it was like having a head full of glue and necessitated much washing of hankies when the supply of tissues ran out. What tissues?

Subsequent to the end of the conflict, Gulf War Syndrome has taken on a more sinister aspect. Sufferers claim all manner of ills to be the results of the various drugs taken whilst in the desert and are trying to get suitable compensation. The MoD is naturally sceptical. I will cite two cases. A very good friend of mine, Flt Lt Rob Brown, spent six months at the front with the army in the thick of it and ended up in the oil fire polluted atmosphere of Kuwait. To my knowledge he was given nothing, by way of preventive medicine, which differed from that taken by myself. However, I did not get to Kuwait and I led a relatively stress free existence. Since my friend's return from the Gulf, he has suffered from several unidentified muscle complaints, pneumonia and a kidney cyst which resulted in surgical removal of same. On the other hand, the only major complaint that has troubled me is that I seem to be getting older.

I do not deny that drugs, even those given for the best possible reason, can and do have harmful effects but I wonder if that is the whole story. Trauma, deprivation and bad diet can all harm the body in their own way and it may be a combination of these circumstances together with the drugs that has lead to this 'syndrome' which appears to have manifested itself in myriad forms.

There were, however, other afflictions which were common among the troops. Many people suffered either from constipation or 'a certain looseness of the bowels' or both, but not at the same time. These effects are universally attributed to COMPO (composite rations). It is widely believed by many that COMPO is specifically designed to 'glue you up'. On the other hand, others swear that there is nothing like an excess of COMPO bacon burgers and beans to keep you more than regular. Looked at dispassionately COMPO is not bad. It is designed so that it can eaten cold or heated, is palatable (in fact the bacon burgers are decidedly tasty) and a 24 hour pack is designed to be well balanced and nutritious. Typical contents are:

Breakfast:

Biscuits, service brown,	3 oz	1 packet
Porridge mix	2 ½ oz	1 sachet
Bacon burger	5 oz	1 can

Snack:

Biscuits, service brown	3 oz	1 packet
Beef spread	2 oz	1 can (easy open/ring pull)
Milk chocolate bar	4 oz	1 pack (Cadbury's)
Boiled sweets	2 oz	1 tube
Chocolate caramels	4 oz	1 tube (Rolos)
Dextrose tablets	1 ½ oz	1 tube

Main Meal:

Instant soup	½ pint	2 sachets
Steak and kidney pudding	5 oz	1 can
Baked beans in tomato sauce	5 oz	1 can
Fruit salad	5 oz	1 can
Biscuits, fruit filled	3 ¼ oz	1 pouch

Sundries:

Chocolate drink mix	3 oz	1 sachet

Coffee, instant	1/6 oz	2 sachets
Tea	½ pint	6 tea bags
Beef stock drink	½ pint	1 sachet (OXO)
Non-dairy whitener	1/10 oz	16 sachets
Sugar	1 oz	6 sachets
Orange drink powder	1 oz	1 sachet
Chewing gum	?	1 packet (Wrigley's)
Matches	-	1 booklet
Matches, waterproof	5	1 sachet
Water purification tablets	6	1 foil strip
Toilet paper	10 sheets	1 pack
Can opener	1	loose

Compared with the American MREs (meals ready to eat) COMPO is a gourmet's delight. The steak and kidney pudding, in particular, is to be recommended although its popular name, 'babies heads' tends to put off those of weaker dispositions. Its superiority was proved time and again by the vast number of American camp cots (aluminium framed, nylon webbed camp beds) that were exchanged for 24 hour COMPO ration packs.

Back in the Ops room the apparent chaos was beginning to make more sense and it was becoming obvious that the aircrew were winding themselves up for the big day. There was a great deal of speculation as to what the precise role of the Special Forces was going to be but at this stage that was all there was, speculation. There did not appear to be any specific objective and all the training was of a 'general' nature. Indeed, as it subsequently transpired, Norman Schwarzkopf was initially very sceptical about the Special Forces being involved at all. His judgement was, no doubt, coloured by the less than wholly successful results achieved by the American SFs in former actions in places such as Iran and Grenada. It was not without strenuous lobbying by General Sir Peter De La Billiere, himself a veteran SAS commander, that a role was found for them. Even so the 'job' had no specific target but was merely to create a diversion in the western desert whilst the preliminary air war was engaged and to try and convince Saddam that it would be from that direction that the main ground thrust would come. However, as someone remarked, that was how it all started with David Sterling in the North African desert back in the Second World War. Back to basics was the general feeling.

With the next day came my first chance to go 'down town'. The engineers needed to buy one or two items that even Swede could not supply and it was therefore an ideal opportunity to make contact with the bank and establish my credentials in order to draw money for the imprest. I went and changed into mufti and waited for my chauffeur. Mufti, by the way, is an Arabic word which means 'plain clothes worn by one who is entitled to wear a uniform.' A few moments later, my 'chauffeur' turned up in a rather neat little red Mazda 242. Sgt Reid (Rabbie), was an individual of medium height but well built. To give you an idea of how well built you must realise that Rabbie played 'lock' for the London Scottish rugby club. An ideal 'minder' if I was going to wander about carrying large sums of money.

"What are you going down town for?" I enquired.

"Ten gallons of black paint and some sewing machine needles." replied Rabbie. This sounded improbable enough to be true but I was intrigued.

"And what, pray, are you going to do with those items?"

"Well," he said, "You have seen the pink Chinooks?" I nodded. "That camouflage works well enough in the daytime but at night, when most of our operations are conducted, they look like pink Chinooks. We are going to try and tone them down a bit."

"But if you paint them black they will stand out during the day." I remarked, stating the obvious.

"True," he replied "so we're going to try stripes, rather like a zebra."

"And the needles?" I asked, now willing to believe anything.

"For the safety equipment workers." He answered with a smile. "Repairing harnesses, flying suits and the like."

I got into the car and off we went. We stopped at the guardroom at the entrance to the camp to register our departure. There was strict control over both entry and exit, mainly in an attempt to maintain the anonymity of occupants of the camp. The guard room was staffed by 'our people' whilst the actual gate/barrier was manned by local soldiers. Nevertheless the whole security set up was inconspicuous. As we drove up to the barrier Rabbie wound down the car window and spoke to the guard.

"Salaam Alaikum." he said. The guard replied something that I did not catch and lifted the barrier.

"What was that, the password?" I asked, as we drove up to the main road.

Chinooks - Pink and 'Zebra' Colour Schemes

"No." replied Rabbie, "It's the standard Arabic greeting and reply."

"Say it again slowly." I requested.

"Salaam Alaikum," (pronounced Sal-arm aly-coomb) he said. "and the reply is Alaikum Salaam."

"What does it mean?"

"Literally translated it means 'the peace of God be upon you' and the reply is 'and the peace of God be upon you also. Whilst we are learning the lingo the next most useful word is 'shukran'. (pronounced shoo-crarn) It means thank you. With those two phrases and a lot of hand waving you can get away with most things."

By this time we had turned right onto the main road. I mentioned earlier that Oscar was just one camp in a large military complex. This road was the main feeder road within the complex and stretched out before us in a straight line as far as the eye could see. At odd intervals other encampments were glimpsed on either side of the road but to all intents and purposes the place was empty.

"How far is it to the main gate?" I asked Rabbie.

"About ten miles." he replied. "Straight on for seven miles until you come to a roundabout, then left and another three to the gate."

"Where do we go from there?" I asked. "I know it might sound like a silly question but where exactly are we? And don't say 'it's a secret'."

Rabbie looked at me a bit one sided. "You really don't know where you are?"

"No." I replied. "I know we're in the UAE and from the time it took to fly from Minhad we can't be too far from Dubai but as to our exact location ... no idea."

"Well at least the security works." he said. "We're about an hour's drive from Abu Dhabi, our nearest town. That's where we are off to now."

The road to the main gate was as Rabbie had described it, dead straight for seven miles then sharp left at the roundabout. Not only was the road straight but it was flat as well and this induced the obvious temptation to speed. In an attempt to negate this the authorities had built sleeping policemen at intervals along the road. These were considerably larger than those usually encountered in the UK and resembled hump back bridges with kerbstones and would have delighted anyone building fortifications as a tank trap. They should have commanded respect as the only way to emerge on the other side with your vehicle's suspension intact was to negotiate them at less than walking speed. However, as there were only two of these constructions along the whole of the seven mile stretch they patently failed in their intended function. It was common practice to burn along the road for several miles as fast as your car could go and only reduce speed for the fifty or so feet that these humps occupied. Nevertheless, from the piles of wrecked vehicles surrounding each of them it seemed that many drivers had either not seen them (unlikely) or simply tried to ignore them (probable). They may not have reduced speed but they were efficient at reducing the number of cars on the road.

At last we reached the main gate and, after another ritual of 'Salaam Alaikum' and document inspection, we turned right on to the main highway. This road was a modern two lane dual carriage way and, unlike the camp road, was neither straight or flat but followed a series of graceful curves round the undulations of the countryside. The surroundings were, as I had seen from the air, sand, dunes and the odd outcrop of rock and, at first sight, rather featureless. However, later on, after I had made this journey several times, I began to recognise individual hill shapes and rock formations. It occurred to me that, contrary to our western conception that Arabs found their way across the desert by means of the sun and the stars because there was nothing else, they probably navigated much of the time by 'common knowledge' of the area rather as we find our way around towns by recognising the pubs, shops, churches and other familiar landmarks. We travelled along this road for about ten miles and saw very little other traffic.

"How long have you been out here?" I asked Rabbie.

"Since the end of October."

"Have you been up at Oscar all the time?"

"No. We moved in there just after Christmas. Until then we were based at Bateen, a military airbase on the outskirts of Abu Dhabi. It's full of Spams (Americans) but serves as our airhead. You can get the heavy transport in and out of there. The Galaxies, Starlifters and the like. At Oscar a Hercules is about the limit."

"Did you stay on base?"

"No. We all lived down town in the Gulf Hotel. Very plush. It was a bit of a culture shock to move out. Still you have to make the best of what you've got."

That, I thought, sums up the British. Phlegmatic to the end.

"Sergeant!"

"Yes Sah"

"Cancel all leave 'till morale improves"

"Yes Sah"

Then another thought struck me. "If you stayed all that time in the Gulf, where are the bills? I've seen nothing in the imprest accounts."

"Don't know." was the reply. "I thought it was paid on the AMEX (American Express credit card)."

"Whose AMEX?"

"The one that came with the imprest."

"Oh Lord." I thought. "I wonder where that is and who's buying what with it now?"

The road ended in a large roundabout. There was quite a lot of traffic on it but most was travelling at right angles to our line of advance.

"The main coast road." Rabbie explained. "We're going straight across into the town. It's another 20 miles or so."

I was not prepared for the surprise that greeted us on the other side of the roundabout. The road widened out into a six lane highway with a broad central reservation. But the shock was the vegetation. The desert had suddenly ended, at least as far as the immediate proximity of the road was concerned. Both the central reservation and the verges for about 50 yards on either side were covered in herbage. Palm trees, bushes and grass, many of the bushes covered in spays of bright red flowers which subsequently turned out to be some type of bougainvillaea.

"It's all very beautiful but what's the point?" I asked.

"A visible indication of wealth and power." came the reply. "Anyone who can 'tame' the desert on this scale must have considerable wealth and as far as the Arabs are concerned if you've got it you've got to flaunt it so that everyone else is aware of the fact. Besides which if you've got as much money as Sheikh Zayed you have to spend it on something."

The flora remained unbroken for the next 10 miles but through it could still be seen the omnipresent desert, the sand slowly giving way to salt marsh, as we neared the coast. In the middle of all this 'waste' land was Abu Dhabi International Airport but this did not surprise me. I was beginning to become used to this country of vast nothingness interspersed with islands of twentieth century technology and innovation. Eventually we came to the Al Maqta bridge, one of only two which connects the island which is Abu Dhabi city, to the mainland and crossed into yet another completely different world. This time it was a world familiar to western eyes, streets full of shops, offices and houses; commerce and everyday life going on all around.

The street down which we were travelling was dual carriageway, three lanes either side of the central reservation. In the UAE, as in most other parts of the world, the traffic is driven on the right-hand side of the road. However, one of the things that immediately struck me was that, unlike the strict British rule of only overtaking other cars on the 'outside', here, if you wished to pass another vehicle, you simply aimed for any convenient gap. The system seemed to work quite well and one of the benefits was that you were actively encouraged to execute 'U' turns at road junctions and gaps in the central reservation, as long as you were in the 'outside' lane. The remainder of the traffic got on about its business and avoided you, well, most of the time at any rate.

Eventually, having negotiated a large and complex roundabout / underpass, we turned off into a side road and parked in what appeared to be the entrance to a building site. It was now just past one o'clock and the sun was high and warm. The street was thronged with people. The crowd was made up mainly of men, dressed almost exclusively in the Arab 'thobe', best described as a long cotton night-shirt affair with pockets. All wore headgear of some description, from the ubiquitous 'shemag', through variations of turbans and complex woolly creations, more usually identified with Afghans, to simple fezzes and cotton/lace skull caps. I must admit that I was rather surprised to see the latter as they gave an oddly 'Jewish' air to the assembled throng.

Whilst the interpretation and implementation of the Koran in the UAE is less rigorous than in other parts of the Arab world, there were significantly few women to be seen. Those that were out and about either observed the tradition of 'purdah' by wearing the all enveloping 'burka', a tent designed to completely camouflage the female shape and thus curb the passions of the men, or western style dress. The latter, however, usually comprised either trousers or long skirt and long sleeved blouses which, to some extent, paid lip service to the maintenance of the lady's "modesty". Even the western women appeared, in general to observe this custom. One aspect of Arab street life which immediately strikes the newly arrived western visitor as distinctly odd is the large number of men walking around holding each other's hands.

"Surely they can't all be queer?" I asked Rabbie.

"No." He replied, "It is just their custom. You will find they all do it no matter what their rank or status."

We turned the corner into the main road and walked up to the door of the bank. It was closed! We asked the guard, standing outside, "Why?"

He looked at us as though we were mad and then, in a tone which left us in no doubt that we were stupid infidels, replied, "Because it always closes at one o'clock."

"When will it reopen?" we asked.

Again, with an air of incredulity, he replied, "Tomorrow at 0730. As it always does."

We decided that we were not going to gain any points in this contest so, having thanked him politely, we crossed the street and tried to act as if we had really known all the time that banks only open in the mornings.

"Well that was a wasted trip." I said to Rabbie.

"Not altogether," he replied, "We still need the paint and needles and besides which it's always worth a rummage round the souk."

The souk lived up to most of my expectations. It was not exactly a labyrinth of dark alleys, but was about five acres of closely packed shops, lock ups and 'other places' from which people conducted their various businesses. It was a hive of activity. A throng of people buying, selling, trading, eating, exchanging money, in fact anything you care to think of and many things that you might not. The basis of all this commerce, however, was haggling. The British understand the practice but tend not to indulge in it as they have been brought up in the belief that they will be asked a fair price and be expected to pay it. That is why the British workers are poor and remain so to the everlasting incredulity and profit of the fat cat bosses. The Americans simply don't understand the process and get ripped off unmercifully.

"What's the form then?" I asked Rabbie.

"Oh, in general, halve the asking price and then offer half that again." He replied, "You will probably end up somewhere in the middle. However, remember," he added, "once you have shown an interest, an Arab is very loathe to let you go without closing the deal. Sometimes they will even sell at a loss just to save face, but don't count on it happening every time. They work on the concept that a good deal is one where both sides believe they have a bargain."

Rabbie obviously knew his way around as he made his way straight to a warehouse with a small frontage which belied the depth of the cavern behind it. It was stacked from floor to ceiling with paint.

"I reckon 10 gallons ought to do it," he said, "Matt black for preference."

This we acquired in short order and, together with 6 four inch brushes went off to look for sewing machine needles.

"I didn't notice a great deal of bargaining for the paint." I commented.

"No," he replied, "But then it wasn't a bad price in the first place and Auntie Betty's footing the bill anyway."

"As I'm keeping the books now, you'd better give me the receipt." I said.

He handed it over. It was a typical small trader's receipt but untypically, for me at any rate, covered in Arabic scrawl. "I wonder if there are any Arab linguists in Command Accounts," he mused, "If not you should be able to hide all sorts of sins under a few well chosen bills."

"Don't tempt me." I said, "I'm going to have enough problems sorting out Del Boy's attempts at trading without creating pitfalls of my own."

As we were searching for a source of Singer Sewing Machine needles we passed a hardware stall. No, it was not an IBM outlet but an emporium stacked, high with all manner of pots, pans, crockery, and anything else of domestic use that you can imagine. "Just a minute," I said to Rabbie, "I am going to treat myself to a decent plate and mug."

The standard eating/cooking equipment of the British military comprises two rectangular aluminium mess tins which have hinged handles, nest one inside the other to form a 'box and lid' and fit neatly into one of the pouches which form part of your '58 pattern webbing. Your cup is the top cover of the water bottle. It too has hinged handles but is made of a hard black thermo-plastic material, probably PVC, and holds approximately one pint of whatever liquid you happen to be eating/drinking . Whilst all these items are very practical in camping and survival situations, the result of years of experience, they are less than aesthetically pleasing and the mess tins produce a nerve jarring screech when you scrape them with a knife or fork. Also, being rectangular, they are not the easiest of things to wash up. As it looked as though I was going to spend this war in relatively civilised surroundings I decided that conventional plates and a mug were the order of the day.

The mug was easy. A conventionally shaped, pillar box red, specimen caught my eye. It would be difficult to lose and had a stamp of individuality about it. The plates needed more thought. Military meals usually comprise two courses; cereal and fry up, main meal and pudding, therefore, if I wished to continue to receive my full rations, two plates were required. Military food also tends toward the liquid; stews, curries, gravy, custard, they all need to be contained, so the plates have, of necessity, to have fairly deep sides. I ended up with what can best be described as a dog bowl, for porridge and the like, and a larger shallow bowl with a lip for bacon and beans. They were white with a tasteful black and orange network pattern around the rim and, along with the mug were made of 'melamine'. Melamine is a brand name for a particularly hard wearing thermo-set plastic used extensively for the production of inexpensive crockery. It has the added advantage of being almost indestructible and happily survives the rigours of the dishwasher. My mug, in particular, has been in constant service since its purchase and after five years of use and abuse shows little sign of wear.

Another item that caught my eye was clothes pegs. Not very interesting I hear you say but when you are faced with doing your own dhobi (washing) previously uninteresting everyday domestic items take on a whole new meaning. Clothes washing facilities were available at Oscar, in fact there was a modern laundrette. However, it was run by two of the locals who, in true dhobi wallah tradition, did not always get things right. It was true that if you put in three pairs of pants and five pairs of socks to be washed that is what you got back but they were not necessarily yours and the socks seldom matched, and they charged you for the privilege. You would be surprised just how many combinations of khaki socks there are.

My purchases complete I looked round for Rabbie. He too had made a find, the very sewing machine needles that we had been seeking. We left the souk feeling that the visit to Abu Dhabi had not been a complete waste of time and returned to Oscar via an ice cream parlour. As we sat eating the ice cream it suddenly occurred to me that today was the 15th of January. The date by which, according to United Nations Resolution 678, Saddam Hussein was to quit Kuwait or face the consequences. I could not help but feel that the whole situation had a rather surreal air about it. I mean, not five days ago I was an ordinary helicopter navigator back in the UK not expecting to be involved in a conflict that was remote from my job. Now I stood at the brink of serious war, attached to the premier fighting force in the world, dressed in civvy clothes, shopping for paint and eating ice cream. It was decidedly odd.

The atmosphere back at Oscar, however, was noticeably more tense. The deadline had passed without Saddam showing the slightest intention of relinquishing his prize. I believe he thought his bluff would still work and that, despite the Coalition military build up, the combined armies would never actually go to war. Certainly he found it hard to credit that such staunch supporters of the Islamic faith as the Saudis would even contemplate allowing infidel forces to operate from their territory. Nevertheless, even if this unthinkable event took place, he still had one ace up his sleeve and that was to attack Israel, forcing them to retaliate and so split the Arab/Christian coalition down the middle. In the end the opposite happened and, ironically, future historians may see Saddam Hussein as the person who actually united Arab, Christian and Jew!

However, the gods devise strange ways of executing their plans and, as events turned out, pre-positioning the SAS forces in the western desert to act as decoy units inadvertently placed them in exactly the right place to operate against the SCUD missile launchers, shipped out to the western borders by Saddam when he realised that his Israeli ace had to be played.

As the deadline had passed, Oscar was now a hive of activity with soldiers and aircrew making final preparations to deploy as soon as, or even before, hostilities were formally declared. As a mere functionary, I was not sure how much of this deployment forward and behind enemy lines was going to affect me, and no one seemed to be able to give me an answer. "Just make sure you get that money tomorrow," was my only positive direction. So for me the events the next day followed a very similar pattern to the previous one except that we did not buy paint or needles but returned to Oscar with a rather neat little dark blue vanity case with combination lock containing 100,000 Dihram (£13,500).

Derek Hunter, Assistant Manager of the British Bank of the Middle East was more than helpful. Over the ubiquitous cup of coffee, he seamlessly transferred, to me, the legal control of the account which Sqn Ldr Steve Fields, the flight commander of the Chinook SF unit, had set up when the detachment had first arrived back in October. This done, we reviewed the account and I discovered that there was enough in it to meet our immediate needs but that was it. No contingency fund. Del Boy was right, it was time for a top up. I withdrew most of the balance, which I estimated would cover our outstanding bills and anticipated running costs for the next couple of days, and put the wad of notes into an A4 brown envelope which I secreted in my cheap plastic document case. It was not the most secure of arrangements but it was all that I had with me. If anyone had briefed me that I would be running an offshoot of Securicor I might have brought a small safe with me. But they had not, so, in usual military fashion, I had to make do. Rabbie was equally concerned.

"You really could do with a cash box or something." he opined. Let's go across to the souk and see if we can find one."

Now, tradition has it that you can find anything in a souk, but could we find a cash box? Could we - hell. The only thing that came close was the aforementioned vanity case, complete with mirror and combination lock. The mirror I can understand but why should you need to lock up your lipstick and eye shadow? Anyway, it fitted the bill. Not that it was overly secure. With a hefty blow from a hammer you could easily have smashed the box open or prised off the lid with a half decent screwdriver. Nevertheless it was the best that circumstances would allow and it provided psychological security both to me and my honest companions. The money was locked up, therefore by definition it must be safe. During the following weeks, that little blue vanity case became my trade mark. Whenever I turned up with it, the assembled company knew that money in some form or other was going to be dished out, payment of a bill for petrol or outstanding water allowance, it mattered not. The sight of me carrying that box meant that money was forthcoming. But the matter of a further supply of money was becoming critical. It was time to contact base and see if I could raise more funds.

When we returned to Oscar I called into Ops and announced that I wanted to 'phone home'.

"Not much chance at the moment," replied the watch keeper, "all the lines are very busy. Rumour has it that something's about to happen."

"All the more need that I get through then," I said, "You can't go off to war without an adequate supply of the readies. I think rape and pillage on the first day might be looked on a little unkindly. I need to speak to the accounts people."

"Try this then." he said, handing me a mobile 'phone. "Have you got the international dialling code?" I nodded. "The place for the best reception is out there in the middle of the square."

Feeling rather obvious and not having a great deal of faith, I went out into the bright sunshine and switched on the 'phone. It squeaked and beeped and indicated that reception was 'fair'. I then dialled a seventeen figure number and waited. Not more than five seconds elapsed when ringing tones started to emanate from the ear piece. Almost immediately there was the sound of the receiver at the other end being picked up and a voice said.

"Good morning. Can I help?".

To say that I was surprised is an understatement. The reception was as clear as a bell and there was none of that annoying time delay which often accompanies long distance telephone calls.

"Sergeant Jackson?" I ventured.

"Yes." came the reply, "Who's calling?"

"Flight Lieutenant Small, Op JEMMY." I replied, bracing myself for a long explanation.

"Ah yes," he said, "I've been expecting a call from you. What do you want?"

"You've been expecting my call?" I said incredulously.

"Oh yes," he replied, "Sqn Ldr Sanders has briefed me on what you are doing. How much money do you want?"

This was too good to be true. I just hoped that Don Sanders had briefed the good sergeant with more details than he had me. I had pondered the question of how much money I would need all the way home from the bank and had come up with a figure based on pure guess work which I would find hard to substantiate if pressed to do so. I had also reasoned that a regular injection of cash would make life less precarious than the 'cash on demand' regime that had existed up till now. Now that the moment had arrived I was terrified of asking for too much. As I hinted earlier, dealing with 'public' money is fraught with dangers.

I grasped the moment with both hands. "Twenty-five thousand pounds immediate top up and then twenty-five thousand each month beginning on the first of Feb." I said, all of a rush. That was more than I had actually guessed at but I would rather have fat than lean. The current business practice of tight budgets and hand to mouth living is all very well if you are in the city where an unforeseen short fall can be easily remedied, but out here in the desert, miles from home? No I'll build in a little leeway just in case. It can always be put back if you can't find something to spend it on. There was a long pause at the other end. "Oh God!" I thought. "I've blown it." Then came the reply.

"Is that all you need?"

It was my turn to pause. Eventually I said, "Ye-es," and then in as jocular manner as I could muster, "Why? How much should I have asked for?"

"Well," said Sergeant Jackson, "Let's put it like this, I have two imprests at the moment which are swallowing one million a week. Each! They are Tornado detachments and are having to pay for their own fuel." he added, "Even so.... No matter," he continued, "Your's is easy. The money should be with you tomorrow afternoon. Anything else you need, just give me a bell." And the 'phone went dead.

I stood looking stupidly at the 'phone. That was too easy. There had to be a hitch. But there wasn't. Sergeant Jackson was as good as his word. That payment and all my subsequent requests were met with equal efficiency.

The tension continued to mount and the centre of attention became the Comms (communications) room where any message to move would first be received. The Comms room was housed in the end room of our leg of the office block. The room had been divided in two. The outer section housed a clerk who acted as a filter between the outside world and the secret world of the Comms and crypto machines that lay in the inner sanctum. It also provided a home for less sensitive communications equipment such as the humble telephone, the time honoured signal pad and SBVM (signals by visual means).

SBVM was the military's forerunner of the internet and superseded the TELEX. It was, and still is, a godsend to those who have been shuffled off to remote parts of the world with little better than a cleft stick and lame runner as their sole means of remaining in contact with the outside world. It comprised a keyboard, a computer, a screen and, somewhere out in the wide blue yonder, a satellite. Once you had managed to crack the code to get into the system you could type up a message and send it, via the satellite, anywhere in the world, providing of course that your addressee was also similarly equipped. The beauty of the device was that it was secure, it did not rely on land lines to connect one terminal with another and messages of up to and including SECRET could be passed on it. SECRET is the fourth level of security, the others being: UNCLASSIFIED, RESTRICTED, CONFIDENTIAL. Once you get beyond SECRET you are dealing with items, the breaching of which would seriously damage national security (and your career!).

Another endearing feature of SBVM was that it did not matter if the person you were trying to contact was not at home. His machine stored the message and alerted him to the fact when he next logged on. If, on the other hand, he happened to be at the keyboard when you made contact you could hold a form of 'conversation' limited only by the speed of the slowest typist. In this aspect it was far superior to the traditional 'signal' which, unless of FLASH priority (the highest priority which even gets the prime minister out of bed) could take several days to be sent and answered. It sounds like 'old hat' now with e-mail and the like but I first came upon it in 1983 in Beirut and it proved to be a giant step foreward. It meant that you could contact your rear base with relative security and communicate in more or less real time on any subject, logistics, tactics or even an on going game of battleships.

The back room contained even more sophisticated machinery which had to be filled with complex codes of the day, soup, aspirins and a whole host of other things before you could make any use of them. Sometimes they worked and sometimes did not. It was the SAS commanders' link between their lords and masters and the men in the field. You needed the security clearance of God to get near any of it but sometimes, from this inner sanctum, you could hear, from what I assumed to be some form of long range HF radio, continuous low whooping noises rather like a flight of geese honking as they fly inland at dusk after a day feeding in the salt marshes.

As the night of the 16th of January fell, while Oscar waited and the rest of the world held its breath yours truly climbed into his sleeping bag, pulled the hood down over his head and went to sleep.

6 - THE MOVE FORWARD 17/19 Jan '91

At about 0300 on the 17th I was dragged back to the edge of consciousness by what sounded like a flock of geese fighting and someone shouting at them in a loud but unintelligible voice. I can remember thinking, "It's that bloody radio in COMCEN (communications centre). The operator must have gone outside for a fag and turned it up so that he can hear if anything important comes in." But, being in the forces teaches you to ignore things that do not directly affect you and, as no one came and tipped me out of bed and the noise seemed to abate, I turned over and went back to sleep. It was not until 0630, when my alarm clock went off, and I staggered into an upright position, that I discovered that all the previous night's noise was in fact signals traffic heralding the beginning of the conflict. I had, in effect, slept through the start of the war.

There was a distinct air of gloom about the place, a tangible despondency. All at Oscar had been so certain that they would have a role to play long before the outbreak of formal hostilities that the news of the first air strikes at 0001 GMT had come almost as an insult to their manhood. Nevertheless this was short lived.

At a general briefing later that morning the assembled company was informed that an FOB (forward operating base), from which sorties were to be launched, was to be established at a small airfield approximately 1000 miles Northwest of Oscar on a plateau 2000ft above sea level in the middle of the Nafud desert, close to the Syrian border and just 100 miles south of the Iraqi border. An ideal place from which to instigate sorties into the Iraqi western desert but not the easiest of places to supply. This FOB came to be known as 'Charlie'. Because of the distance between Charlie and Oscar, it was decided that the Chinooks, with their relatively limited radius of action (approximately 350 miles) would move up en masse leaving a small logistics element, including me, behind. The SAS would move troops back and forth as operations dictated and the Hercules detachment would remain at Oscar to act as the logistics link.

This decision brought forth a series of mixed reactions. The SAS remained as impassive as ever but there was a distinct increase in activity in their compound as the ubiquitous pink Land Rovers, fitted with all manner of brackets, rails and racks more usually associated with the underside of a fighter aircraft's wing, emerged from the hangars. The Hercules crews seemed ambivalent, as long range covert supply was part of their normal role anyway. The Chinook element broke into the factions that had always been there but until now had remained hidden just under the surface.

It was the first time that this Chinook SF unit had been called upon to operate in a war situation. It was true that the squadrons from which the unit was culled had been involved in operations in hostile environments. Their members are littered with campaign medals for Northern Ireland, Lebanon and The Falklands but whilst there was the ever present danger in these theatres none of them not even the Falklands had the aura of this coming conflict - all out war. A crisis inevitably shows people in a different, some say their true, light and the prospect of imminent action is as good a trigger as any for this phenomenon.

The Air Force is peculiar among the armed services in that, in general, it is the officers that go off and fight whilst the 'men' stay at the rear and patch up the crews and aircraft upon their return. The advent of the nuclear bomb brought an end to even SNCO aircrew, certainly a far as pilots and navigators were concerned, as it was considered that they could not be given the responsibility for such weapons. Why? I am not sure. If they could be trusted with bombers carrying 21000 lbs of high explosives or incendiaries or fighters with 30mm cannons and rockets why not a megaton nuclear device? Whatever the political whys and wherefores, the province of the pilot and nav became exclusively that of the officer. SNCO aircrew were, however, retained in multi-crew aircraft as radio operators, engineers, crewmen and the like. This situation has inevitably bred a feeling of us and them, mostly submersed, but always there.

The helicopter crewman is caught very much in the proverbial cleft stick. In the early form of the helicopter, such as the Whirlwind and Wessex, his place was firmly down the back. There was no other place for him as the designers had isolated the pilot on top of the engines and gear box and safe access to the cockpit could only be gained from outside with the aircraft shut down. The crewman, whilst lord of the cabin and all that went on 'downstairs', had no opportunity to become involved with flying the aircraft. However, as time went on, he was encouraged to carry a map and keep one eye on the navigation out of the side door. The advent of second generation of helicopter design changed all that.

Modern helicopters are designed with engines, gearboxes and rotors 'upstairs' which, in turn, facilitates easy walk through access from cabin to cockpit. A centre 'jump' seat between the two pilot's seats is often provided, and this the crewman is encouraged to occupy when he is not engaged in securing troops or freight in the cabin. Financial constraints dictate that, although there are two pilot's seats, in peace time, only one is normally occupied. The crewman's role, therefore, developed by default to that of part-time navigator and pilots' little helper and most became very proficient at the job. So much so that crewmen are often entrusted with much of the sortie planning and all the decision making that that entails. There is no more pay or status for these extra duties. A helicopter crewman enjoys exactly the same remuneration and promotion structure as a cabin attendant on a VC10 or TriStar. His only benefit is a self induced pride in a job well done and a subconscious thumbing of the nose at the authorities who had come to believe that NCO aircrew are second class citizens.

In war, however, the situation changes. Both front seats are occupied, either by two pilots or a pilot and navigator. The crewman is sent back to his 'proper' place as baggage handler and his considerable expertise and experience is ignored. He is, in his eyes, further humiliated because he is no longer invited to take part in the sortie planning and thereby deprived of the confidences that emanate from those occasions. His exclusion by the 'drivers airframe' is mostly unintentional but it has roots in the deep seated differences between officers and 'men'. However, the Chinook crewmen at Oscar had even more cause to feel slighted.

Traditionally, the British support helicopter has not been armed. There has always been provision for the mounting of a submachine gun in the doorway but this is more for effect than anything else. Nevertheless, the potentially dangerous nature of the SF sorties persuaded someone in authority to sanction the fitting of the 'Mini-gun' to the Chinook forward door position. The Mini-gun is a small gatling gun. It has 6 barrels and is capable of delivering up to 6000, 7.62mm high velocity rounds per minute. It is not particularly accurate and it cannot claim to be a long range weapon but it is very effective at keeping heads down if you happen to find yourself in a tight corner. With its introduction the crewmen saw their moment of glory and visions of 'mid uppers' and 'tail end charlies' hove into view. The dream was quickly shattered however, as the same authority who had sanctioned its introduction decreed that a weapon of this complexity and potency should be handled by 'rocks apes' (RAF Regiment personnel, so named after the rock apes of Gibraltar whose mental capacity and habits they are traditionally supposed to mirror). So the trade of 'Air Gunner' was temporarily re-established and 'rock' corporals were paid flying pay to enjoy themselves. This did nothing to ameliorate the already strained relationship between the front and back end crew members.

A further rift emerged, but this time between the aircrew as a whole and the ground crew. Again, this is a traditional hate. On the one side the aircrew demand the impossible and then return the toys, broken, without even so much as a please or thank you. On the other, the engineers will, without any warning, remove a perfectly serviceable ac (aircraft) from the flight line and spend weeks taking it to bits and re-assembling it under the pretext of a deep servicing programme. This action often seems to coincide with an overseas 'jolly' to which the GCs (ground crew) have not been invited. It is a classic case of lack of communication and has been actively pursued since Pontious was a pilot (Pilate?)! Even though the two parties tolerate each other, depend on each other and have even been known to drink beer together, at the end of the day there is little love lost between them.

Although many contingency plans had been made, because of the uncertainty of the exact role of the SF prior to the start of the war, precise details could not be formulated. However, now a definite-ish goal had been established and was to be achieved ASAP (as soon as possible) it was inevitable that orders regarding what stores and equipment to take were issued and then countermanded as the plot unravelled. Nevertheless, the fact that each of the four Chinooks were loaded and then re-loaded three times, and a Chinook can hold 12 tons of freight, did nothing to improve aircrew/groundcrew relationships.

The Wing Commander had already given me the job of censoring all letters home and, whilst the sole object of this censorship was to exclude any references to the location of the unit or its purpose, I could not help but gain an intimate knowledge of the individuals and their relationships with each other from the letters. Because of my unique position I assumed, by default, the role of father confessor in the midst of all this turbulence. I was accepted by the pilots and navs because I was a nav though not of their unit nor in post in a flying capacity. I was accepted by the crewmen because I had, in the past qualified in their trade and served a tour as such. And I was accepted by the groundcrew because, not being intimately involved with the preparations for departure to Charlie, I had time to listen to them and besides, I held the imprest which paid their allowances.

You should not take what I have just written as overt criticism of my fellow airmen. It is not that at all. It is just my observation of a particular reaction to a peculiar form of pressure and stress and a universal manifestation of human nature. There is, however, always a relief valve and in this case it was the proliferation of a poster that had been in the background for some time. It featured 'Baldric' of Black Adder (a TV programme) fame and showed him dressed in his WW1 private's uniform uttering the immortal lines:

"Don't worry sir. I have a cunning plan."

Copies of this picture suddenly appeared everywhere and our supply of photocopying paper and toner diminished accordingly. Its droll message fitted the situation admirably and gave a strong visual message to all concerned that, in spite of individual feelings, there was a job to be done.

Part of the preparation for this forward push, although in reality it was more of a jink to the left, was the issuing of a personal survival pack which comprised 20 gold sovereigns, a goolie chit and an escape map. You read about such things in WW2 escape stories but somehow I had not believed them to be real and yet here they were; to be used if one inadvertently found one's self in hostile territory. It only needed the compass in the heel of the flying boot to make it complete.

The gold coins were sealed in individual plastic envelopes and formed into a strip. Their value was approximately £1300 sterling and were to be used only in extreme circumstances. The penalty for their loss was severe, so much so that one of the pilots, Flt Lt Ivor Draper wrapped his up in black bodge tape and hid them at the bottom of his rucksack. He calculated the risk of losing them to be far greater than ever finding himself in a position to use them to any great effect.

The goolie chit harks back to colonial days when soldiers who, finding themselves prisoners of the rather more colourful tribesmen, were handed over to the women of the tribe who relieved them of their wedding tackle in long and painful ceremonies. In order to try and retain their manhood, and their lives, each man was issued with a card, printed in the several languages and dialects of the area, promising large sums in gold if the prisoner was returned intact. Although you might think the world is now more civilised you have only to look at Saddam Hussein's treatment of his own people to realise that any aid to the safe return of a prisoner is worth while. Therefore, the aim of the modern chit remains the same but is now operated through the Red Cross.

The escape map was another link with the past. In WW2 aircrew were given maps, printed on silk, of the area over which they were operating. They were printed on silk in order that they could be folded up small and concealed without damaging the information. In extreme cases they could even be used as a handkerchief. Nothing has changed! The maps issued to us were made of a piece of fairly heavy gauge white silk approximately 30x40 inches but which could, with very little effort be folded into a 'hanky' measuring 3x4 ins. Each one weighed 2 ¼ ozs and was printed on both sides with topographical information and the location of airfields. There were two to the set and the area covered included the whole of the Arabian Gulf, Northern Saudi Arabia, Iraq and part of Iran. They were, in effect, the standard Operational Air Navigation

Chart (scale 1:1,000,000) but printed on silk instead of paper. There was, however, just one thing wrong. They were not up to date. God only knows where they came from but they may well have been left over from the 1957/62 Arabian Peninsular Campaign for a note printed on the bottom said:

"Base information October 1959, revised March 1967. Air information current through April 1967."

I know that topography does not change very quickly but even in the desert roads are built and it would have been nice to have know the location of the latest Iraqi airfields.

On the other hand the American escape maps were a completely different kettle of fish. Someone had obviously given a great deal of thought to the problem and had come up with not just a map but an escape aid in its own right. They were up to date too. The copies I managed to get hold of were dated July and August 1990 respectively, just six months old. The background colour of the maps was a pale olive drab and the surrounding borders were a pastel disruptive camouflage pattern, not like the bright white of the British silk. The borders also contained a mine of information about the area covered by the map, local plants (both edible and poisonous), what climatic conditions to expect at different times of the year, first aid hints, escape and evasion tips (including how to find water in the desert) and celestial and terrestrial navigation for beginners. One whole folded section was printed with the 'Stars and Stripes' in case you wanted to identify yourself to a passing nomad. However, the most intriguing information was the section entitled 'other uses of this map', I quote:

"The material used for this chart is sturdy but not indestructible. Avoid sharp sticks and rubbing against rocks or sand. Wash the map if dirty. If the edge of the map is cut it will continue to tear easily. Although flame resistant, it will melt or burn if it gets hot enough. The evasion chart has many other uses beyond being a navigation aid. Some suggestions are:

1. Catch rain for drinking water.
2. Shade/shelter from wind/rain.
3. Cape or blanket.
4. Use as bag to haul water/food.
5. Line a hole to use as a wash basin.
6. Wrap clothing when swimming or fording streams.
7. Wrap vegetation and use as floatation device.
8. Use as extra layer of clothing.

9. Wrap sleeping gear in foul weather.
10.Splint a broken wrist.
11.Plug a sucking chest wound.

The mind boggles! I particularly like the last suggestion. If you can do all that with just an American map no wonder they beat the Russians to the moon. Needless to say, the British maps were kept as souvenirs, the American ones taken on the operational sorties.

The 18th of January was my 44th birthday. It was notable for several things. I was given a desk, it was one of the driest birthdays I had celebrated for some time and I discovered that I was suffering from 'trench foot'.

The imminent departure forward involved a lot of packing and included much of the Ops set up. Paper, pens, files, maps and one of the photocopiers were all crated up ready for the move. This produced a rather strange result. On the one hand, the occupiers of the desks in Ops were forced to relinquish their tenancies which meant I could now establish my own little empire but on the other hand, much of my empire, including the SECRET map that I had carefully stuck coloured pins in, was rolled up and taken away. There really was not a lot for me to do. I fetched and carried and packed maps in boxes but I felt rather detached from the proceedings. I was not closely involved with this move and it seemed that my best course of action was to keep out of the way. One job I could get on with, however, was to censor the latest batch of 'blueys' that were waiting to be posted home.

A bluey is the popular name for MoD Form No. 674 - the British Forces Mail Aerogramme. It is an A4, single sheet air mail letter form. It has two advantages. Firstly, it is of limited size. Therefore, you can write every day and fill it easily, especially if your handwriting is large. Secondly, it is free! This is a great boost to morale as it makes you feel that you are actually getting something out of the government for nothing. In fact it is estimated that for the duration of the Gulf War, the bluey cost the British government almost £2 million but, from a morale boosting point of view, it was considered to be worth every penny.

The postal system developed to serve the troops involved in the Gulf War was a combined military and GPO operation. It proved to be unusually efficient and mail seldom took longer than 4 or 5 days in either direction. This was greatly envied by the Americans who's letters were often 4 weeks out of date by the time they received them.

Another feature of the Gulf War postal service was the creation of BFPO 3000. This was a post office box number in the UK to which the general public could send mail to unspecified recipients in the Gulf. These letters (and parcels!) were then distributed around the various units. This probably did more for the self esteem of the troops than anything else. It is one thing for your General to stand up in front of you and tell you what excellent men you all are and that he knows that you will give your all. You don't have much choice in the matter. But when literally millions of unsolicited letters arrived addressed to 'An Airman' or ' A Soldier serving in the Gulf' giving support and wishing good luck you suddenly realised that patriotism was not dead. The letters were from all ranks and classes; from school children, old soldiers, lonely widows and just the ordinary man and woman in the street. Many were the result of newspaper campaigns, and none the worse for that, but a large percentage seemed to just fulfil the need for an outlet of people's feelings and not just about the war. It was a cross between a pen-pal's and lonely hearts' club. Even though we were a relatively small unit we still received, on average, two sacks of BFPO 3000 mail a day and that in addition to personal letters. The amount spent on postage by the British public must have more than offset the cost of the blueys.

My task in all this was three fold. In the first place, I wrote more than my own fair share letters, to my wife, family, friends and as many BFPO 3000 authors as I could find time for. With modern communication systems the art of letter writing has almost vanished. It is only when you are placed in a situation were the written word is almost the only option that you wish you were more articulate. Conversation contains a great many 'ums', 'ahs' and exceedingly bad grammar, and spelling does not enter into the equation, but putting your thoughts coherently onto the written page is another matter. As with all things practice makes perfect. Certainly, towards the end of the war, I had developed the art of holding quite an effective one sided conversation with a piece of writing paper, and not just because of too much sun.

Secondly, as I have said, part of my job was that of censor with a mandate to exclude any reference to our location or operational details. On average, I had about 200 letters a day to read. To read each one in detail would have been a full time task and a deeper breech of privacy than was necessary. Fortunately, in a very short while I managed to cultivate the knack of skimming the letters without reading the contents and only seeing names of places or equipment. In fact, the integrity of the men, who's letters I monitored, made my task almost pointless. Only very occasionally did someone make a slip and then it was invariably by accident. Nevertheless, I am sure that if anyone had wished to leak details they were mostly bright enough not to entrust them to the page of a bluey. Certainly, before leaving, I had arranged with my wife that if either of us wished to send a message which we felt we could not trust to the open page, then we would use a code based on a book, a copy of which we both possessed. Neither of us found occasion to use it.

My third part of this task was to act as postman; to sort and distribute the mail as it arrived. This proved to be a pleasant task for, as with the allowances, people were always glad to receive the letters and some of this pleasure rubbed off on the person dispensing it.

Unlike Saudi Arabia, alcohol is not forbidden in Abu Dhabi. The stricter adherents to the Koran obviously do not indulge but there are bars in the hotels and restaurants and it is only during the holy month of Ramadan that they are closed. Nevertheless, it had been strictly laid down that Oscar was to be a 'dry' camp, certainly until the conflict was at an end. This did not bother me particularly for, although I like a drink with the best of them I can go without. The only thing I really missed was my habitual G&T before dinner. I therefore prepared to celebrate my birthday with lemonade. However, after dinner, one of the Herc guys whispered that if I cared to pop round to their 'basha' (a Southeast Asian word for a rough hut or shelter) they might be able to find something a little stronger. I was touched to be taken into this confidence and very pleased that, despite the rivalry between the fixed and rotary wing factions, they were willing to befriend me. I therefore duly made my way to their block at the back of the mess.

The aircrew accommodation block was a single story building with a central corridor on either side of which were five rooms. Each room was approximately 7x10 ft and occupied by two people. Furniture was minimal, comprising a camp bed for each inhabitant and whatever boxes could be scrounged which served as chairs and cupboards. I do not remember there being any air conditioning. The privacy accorded by these 'cells' was given to the aircrew as it is decreed that they need relatively undisturbed surroundings because of the nature of their work. A stark contrast to the air conditioned luxury hotel rooms that many of the fighter boys managed to appropriate. A similar block next door housed the Chinook aircrew.

Groundcrew accommodation was even more spartan. Housed in separate buildings, it consisted of a series of large rooms into which up to 20 camp beds were fitted. Their 'furniture' was their rucksacks and their privacy was what ever they could conjure up in their own minds. It made my shared office seem quite palatial. Washing and toilet facilities for all were in a common ablution block.

The SAS, when they were at Oscar, were housed in one of the large hangars that made up the 'grain silo' complex. Their camp beds were dotted around the walls of this great barn but most, if not all, had built himself a personal 'fortress' or tent of boxes around his bed space and covered it with cam (camouflage) netting. When occupying one of these 'bashas' you got the distinct impression of being in a jungle clearing. Many of the guys added to this effect by cooking meals on camping gas stoves at the doorway of their 'tents'.

"What would you like to drink?" asked Alan Tribe, one of the Herc pilots.

"What have you got?" I asked.

"Scotch, mainly," was the reply, "Although I think there's some brandy left."

"A little scotch then, please," I said, Where did you get it from?"

"When we get food parcels from home we often find that things like washing up liquid bottles have been tampered with and contain whisky instead of Fairy Green Liquid." he said and winked.

The plastic bottle was duly produced and a generous measure squirted into a paper cup.

"Soda or American Dry?" he asked. "Sorry there's no ice."

"No thanks. I'll take it as it comes." I said.

"Happy birthday." he said, handing it over.

The taste was not quite what I had expected. I have drunk a fair selection of whiskies and some of the more peaty malts, like Laphroaig, are an acquired taste but this one had a definite soapy twang to it.

"That's one of the problems." said Alan, in answer to the obvious grimace on my face. "It doesn't matter how hard you try it is impossible to get rid of the taste. You think you've got the bottle smelling sweet but the scotch seems to fetch it out of the plastic. Still it's better than nothing. Try some American Dry, it hides it some what."

The dry ginger made it a little better but it was still like drinking rather fiery washing up water, nevertheless, it was a convivial end to my birthday. However, on the way back to my bed I decided that I was not that desperate for a drink and would wait until I could find something in a glass bottle before taking my next one. In fact, it did not turn out that way, but that is a story for later.

During the last couple of days there had been moments when both my big toes felt numb. An odd thing to say I know but one does notice these things. I had not given it a great deal of thought except to note that it seemed to occur whilst I was wearing the bush boots that had been issued to me at RAF Odiham. They appeared to fit and did not seem tight so I put the problem down to them being new and stiff. As I took them off this evening, however, I could not help but notice that something was very wrong. It had been a warm day and, not unnaturally my feet had perspired a little. So much so that you could actual wring moisture out of my socks. My feet, all pink and wrinkled, looked as if I had spent the day in the bath and both big toes were completely without feeling.

"You've got trench foot." ventured SENGO, "You know, like the soldiers of WW1 got from spending their time up to their necks in water."

And so it turned out. The boots had been carefully designed to a specification that seemed like a good idea but that no one had really thought through. The requirements were for a lightweight desert boot which had, at the same time, to be water/oil resistant with toe 'tectors suitable for engineering/ hangar work. The result was as requested. A lightweight suede top, with a steel toe cap, that had been welded to a rubber compound sole. The whole thing had been treated with a waterproofing agent that would not been out of place as a marine varnish. Unfortunately, not only did this boot keep water from getting in it also prevented any moisture escaping. The result? A mobile foot bath.

Fortunately I had brought my own bush boots with me. A pair of Clarke's best suede, crepe soled brothel creepers. They are not waterproof, in fact they are a disaster in wet weather, but they do allow your feet to breathe when they get warm. I wore them from then on and had no more problems.

The 19th of Jan, the day of departure for Charlie, was a day of great turmoil. An early start with another unpacking and re-packing of the aircraft did nothing to improve the general ambience. I sat at my desk pretending to juggle with imprest figures and generally kept out of the way as far as possible. Just after breakfast the Wing Commander came in to the office with a heavy looking rucksack and bulging brief case.

"Ah - Roger." he said, in a voice that usually heralded a long, complex and impossible task, "I've got something for you." and he handed over a key. "It's the key to my room." he added, "You might as well use it while I'm away. It will stop someone else stealing it."

I could not believe my luck. The senior officers quarters were where MacHoot had taken me the day I arrived. A room to myself, and with a veranda too. This was luxury indeed. However, there was no time to go and view my newly acquired property, that would have to wait until all the hullabaloo was over and the aircraft and troops had departed. By mid-morning all was ready. The four Chinooks, by now all resembling pink zebras, started one by one, each creating its own mini sand storm at the edge of the pan. Starting a Chinook is not a particularly quick procedure. First, the pilot starts up the APU (auxiliary power unit), a small jet engine, hardly bigger than 5kg bag of potatoes, located in the tail pylon immediately above the ramp. This drives an hydraulic pump and electrical generator which allows operation of the aircraft systems without having the main engines running and the blades turning. Having tested the flying controls and the auto-pilot functions and got all the nav equipment on line and set up, one of the main engines is started and set to run at ground idle. Ground idle is about 60% of the engine's max power and is sufficient to turn the rotors but not enough to get the aircraft airborne. Unlike a fixed wing aeroplane, where each propeller is powered by its own engine, in a helicopter the output from all the engines is fed into a common gearbox from which the main and tail rotors are driven. This ensures that the speed ratio between the rotors is kept constant. As the Chinook has two main rotors, the blades of which overlap by a good 20ft, you can see that this synchronisation is very important. Once the blades are turning and everything has stabilised, the pilot then advances the throttle to flight idle, about 75% max power. The second engine can then be started.

At this point, it is worth taking time out to describe briefly how a helicopter flies. The short answer is that no one really knows. It is like a bumble bee, inherently unstable and apparently without sufficient power to get it into the air. The theory of flight apparently works but the mathematics have never been completely and satisfactorily resolved. So next time you get into a helicopter remember it's only a theory that is keeping you airborne.

In a conventional aircraft, where the engines either push or pull the whole thing through the air, the wings are simply passive appendages which force the air downwards and ergo the aircraft up, thus providing lift. If you wish to climb, you point the nose of the aircraft up and in so doing increase the angle at which the wings cut through the air and thereby force more air downward.

However, this will decrease your speed unless you increase the power output from the engines by opening their throttles.

With a helicopter the opposite occurs. The wings (blades) are moved (rotated) at a constant speed through the air whilst the aircraft stands still. Like a fan, the rotor blades are made to deflect the air downwards and when the force of this air equals the weight of the aircraft it becomes 'weightless' and flies. The amount of lift is regulated by adjusting the pitch of the blades independent of the fuselage attitude. As the pitch of the blades is increased the rotor tries to slow down because it is having to do more work but this is countered by an automatic opening of the throttles and consequential proportional engine power increase. The helicopter is manoeuvred forward, backwards and sideways (or any combination of these) by tilting the whole rotor in the direction desired. You must, however, not forget that the rotor, in addition to acting as a giant fan, is also, by its very nature, gyroscope and therefore, any force to the rotor head must be applied at right angles to the desired direction of movement.

Despite a degree of automatic symbiosis between these various elements the pilot still has both his hands full, literally. Where a fixed wing pilot has only one 'joystick', a helicopter driver has two. One, the collective, for up and down. The other, the cyclic, for left, right, forward and back. With these he maintains a delicate and precarious balance for, left to itself, a helicopter will try to turn upside down and thrash itself, and those inside and outside within reach of its blades, to death. This said, flying in a helicopter is statistically far safer than travelling by car on a motorway. The mode of death is, however, more spectacular!

Eventually, all four Chinooks taxied slowly out to the runway and lined up in box formation for take off. Box formation is as the name suggests; a formation of four aircraft, two at the front and two at the back, with no apparent lead aircraft. Another feature that made Oscar different from other airfields was the total absence of air traffic control. There was radio communication with the Ops room but it was more of a chat frequency than anything else and there was certainly little control. If you intended to take off or land you simply made a blind call with your intentions and it was up to anyone else in the area to look out. This may sound rather haphazard but if the discipline of calling on the frequency is strictly maintained the system works very well. The proof is Bessbrook Mill in South Armagh, Northern Ireland. It is reputedly the busiest Helipad in the world for sheer number of movements and yet there is no air traffic control, just a single contact frequency. Since the beginning of 'The Troubles' in the late '60s there has been just one serious accident, a record that a great many fully controlled airfields would envy.

Once airborne, however, it was a different story. The movement of aircraft within the war zone was strictly controlled and monitored. Although there were land based radars, overall control was exercised by the mighty Boeing E-3A Sentry or AWACS (Airborne Warning and Control System); the flying radar station. These modified Boeing 707s, with their characteristic black and white striped mushroom radar scanners and answering to the call sign "Magic", patrolled the skies throughout the war. They performed two main functions. Firstly, they reported the movement of any hostile aircraft and directed interceptors towards them as required. Secondly, and as it turned out more importantly, they provided co-ordination between the hundreds of allied aircraft which filled the skies day and night. You may think that I exaggerate when I say hundreds of aircraft but the following may give you some idea of the scale of the allied air operation.

Each evening a list of the next day's scheduled air sorties was published and sent to all the relevant air operation cells. It was a computer printout with approximately fifty five lines of print to the page. Each line detailed one sortie, however, individual sorties were often composed of four, six, eight or more aircraft. On one particular evening we received our copy of the schedule which comprised 746 pages!

The Chinooks departed in formation and described a broad 270^0 arc to fly low over our heads in a farewell salute. As they clattered off over the sand dunes into the distance all those remaining wished them good luck.

By the time I got back to the office there had already been some changes. My counterpart on the Herc flight had started to re-arrange the office. Pete Craven was, like myself, a Flight Lieutenant navigator.

"Come on," he said as soon as he saw me, "Let's organise things to suit us while everyone else is away. This office has been a real bear garden and if we've got to work in it I want to be able to control it."

As I have mentioned before, there were four desks in the middle of the office aligned end on to the doorway. This allowed all and sundry to just wander in and disrupt what ever work was in progress. Two of the desks we turned through 90° and placed them side by side about two thirds of the way in from the door. For the remainder of the war we two camped out behind this defensive site and fought off all who sought to occupy the position for themselves. The other desks we placed one against each side wall. I know it sounds trivial, but even in an office you are more effective when you feel that you are operating from a secure location.

Our first task was to organise the Herc shuttle to supply the detachment newly departed to Charlie and for the next two days there was a constant flow of men and equipment forward. I am not a Herc man myself and have only the most scant knowledge of their capacities and limitations. I can, however, shuffle schedules and lists and answer the telephone and, as the days progressed, this became one of my major roles. The Ops desk had to be manned 24 hours a day so, between us, Pete and I worked out a shift pattern which allowed him to be on duty when technical decisions had to be made and left me the so called 'quiet' hours. In practice we both regularly worked in excess of 18 hours a day, overlapping from late morning to early evening.

Two other characters took up partial residence in our office. They were a sergeant and airman of the 'load handling' trade. Simply known to all and sundry as John the Mover and his mate Andy, it was their job to prepare the loads and passengers for air transport. In fact, we seldom saw them for, contrary to the widely held belief that movers are over staffed and dilatory, these two worked their balls off. At a large airhead there are usually more movers than you can shake a stick at, each one having his own small empire to defend. But, being our exclusive selves, we could not afford this luxury of numbers so John and Andy were responsible for gathering the freight together, breaking it down into manageable units, loading it onto palettes and then fork-lifting or manhandling the palettes on to the aircraft where the aircraft load master supervised its securing. All this activity was, of course, accompanied by a mountain of triplicate paperwork. You may think that once they had established a routine the whole thing would have gone smoothly, but consider for a moment who the customers were. The wants and needs of the Special Forces are not routine. The loads were, therefore, often made up of the most incongruous items and no two were ever the same.

After a very long day I decided it was time to inspect my new quarters. The departure of the Chinook personnel had not only provided me with a room of my own but had also inadvertently furnished me with my own transport for it had been decided that the little red Mazda 242 was not the sort of thing to cart off to a forward base. I therefore duly commandeered it and managed to hang on to it until the last week before our eventual return home, when I aspired to something much grander. But more of that later.

I backed the Mazda up to SENGO's old office and found that, although SENGO had only departed a few hours earlier and my kit was still stacked in one corner, the office had already acquired a new tenant. Colonel Sid Moore, the SAS CO, had conducted a similar operation to that carried out by Pete and myself in that he had moved the furniture round and now occupied an unassailable position facing the door.

"You won't be needing this office any more?" he queried as I entered. The inflections in his voice, however, gave the impression of a statement rather than a question.

"No," I said, "I'll just remove my things and be out of your hair." So saying I loaded my tri-wall, camp bed and ruck sack into the hatch back and set off in search of my new lodgings.

Wg Cdr Irwin, having been one of the senior officers at Oscar, had, naturally, acquired one of the better rooms in the accommodation block. In fact it was not a room but a suite. Situated in the left hand corner of the open square, as observed from the open side, it comprised three rooms. The first, which you entered from the verandah, was approximately 12ft square and the main bed/ sit room. It was carpeted with bright green nylon carpet and contained a single bed (with mattress and headboard) and an easy chair (an arm chair but without arms!). Both these items were comfortable pieces of furniture, not in the least way military, and would not have been out of place in a modern hotel room. There was, however, nothing else in the room. Having spent the last week in cramped and crowded accommodation the sudden luxury of space was a little daunting.

To the left of the main room, as you entered, was an internal door which led into an area which is difficult to categorise but can best be described as a kitchen. There were cupboards, shelves and work surfaces but no sink, stove or refrigerator. Obviously the occupant was not expected to prepare anything more exotic than a pre-packed sandwich, certainly nothing that required washing up, and, being intended for Moslems, there was no need for a 'fridge to keep the beer cold.

At the far end of this 'kitchen', through an open doorway on the right, was a bathroom. Again this is a best description as there was no bath. There was, however, a curtained off shower, a wash basin with mirror and shaving point and, joy of joys, a western style loo! Above, and to the left of the wash basin, was a large electric water heater which looked capable of supplying all the hot water one could need. I decided to christen the loo and upon completion attempted to flush it but without success. The cistern was empty. My trepidation increased when I turned on the taps of the wash basin which similarly yielded no water. However, my eyes lighted on a stopcock which, upon investigation, proved to be turned off. Turning the cock on resulted in the welcome sound of water flowing into the cistern and heater. Unfortunately that was not all that filled up, within moments the floor was awash. The two flexible couplings joining the main pipes to the various appliances both leaked like sieves and upon inspection, although new, proved to be damaged. The only way to use the en-suite facilities was to place a bucket or similar container under the offending plumbing, turn on the stopcock and then isolate the whole system again when one's ablutions were complete. Still, it was better than nothing and the sit down loo was worth its weight in gold.

I returned to the main room and inspected the bed. Firm but comfortable was the verdict. The only minor problem was the complete lack of bed linen. I dragged my bits and pieces into my new quarters, set up the tri-wall as a bedside table and unrolled my sleeping bag on top of the bed. Underneath the sleeping bag was my sand wedge. I don't know what possessed me, we do odd things in odd circumstances, perhaps it was all this green carpet but the urge to chip a few balls came over me. The ceiling was just high enough to accommodate my swing but I was not sure that the walls would survive a golf ball. Nevertheless, necessity is the mother of invention and some screwed up newspaper wrapped tightly with bodge tape made a very serviceable practice ball. After half a dozen swings the madness left me. Enough was enough. It was approaching midnight and tomorrow was another day. At least I now had the foundations of comfort and entertainment. I could build on them as time and circumstances allowed.

7 - THE AIR WAR 20 Jan / 23 Feb '91

The start of the air war brought the months of uncertainty to an end and with it came an unexpected period of stability. All through the build up phase no one had any real idea of what was going to happen or how they would be involved. In fact right up to the point of declaring war it was not even certain if the Special Forces would be used at all. The time was therefore spent in planning contingencies and 'what ifs?' and that inevitably resulted in schedules being changed at the last minute, hopes raised and then dashed and a general air of ambivalence. Not that there was inactivity. Every spare moment had been spent preparing and modifying the aircraft and honing the skills of the men. For the aircrew, this meant hours spent low level at night on NVGs and coming to terms with a new navigation aid GPS.

GPS (global positioning by satellite) has become THE navigation aid. Units are cheap, small, light and user friendly. Add to this the fact that they will tell you where you are, in three dimensions, to within 100m or better, anywhere in the world and you begin to wonder how we ever found our way before. However, at the beginning of 1991 the system and equipment was still relatively new and, not only did the crews have to learn how to use it, but they also had to learn to trust it. It could give a very false sense of security. Certainly you knew where you were to within 100m but when you were surrounded on all sides by 1000 miles of desert that information was not necessarily of much use. It is like the case of the two men in a balloon basket who, having spent some hours in cloud and out of sight of the ground, suddenly find a gap in the cloud and see a man sitting on a grassy bank reading a book. One of the balloonists shouts down to him,

"Where are we?"

The man on the ground looks up and replies, "In a balloon."

At that point the clouds reform and the balloonists again lose sight of the ground.

"Well," says the second balloonist "That was damn all use."

"No," says the first, "I now know exactly where we are. We are directly overhead   Boscombe Down.

"How come?" says the second.

"The information they promulgate there is absolutely precise," continues the first, "But of little use to anyone but themselves."

(For Boscombe Down read any government establishment)

In the event the GPS lived up to its reputation and proved to be a great boon.

Now that the war had started and a definite course of action had been embarked upon, routine set in. You should, however, not confuse routine with uniformity or run away with the idea that every minute of the day was a repetition of the same minute the day before. Far from it. For us in the SF the routine of an operational environment is a framework on which to hang the unexpected. For my part the routine consisted of manning the Ops desk. Very quickly Pete and I established the following working arrangement:

0300 Pete takes over the desk and starts to translate the tasking requests into a workable schedule together with flight plans and basic planning for theHerc crews. I go to bed.

0830 - 0930 I get up after 5 hrs sleep, grab a cup of coffee and return to Ops.

0930 - 1230 We both deal with the inevitable crises that launching aircraft generates.

1230 - 1330   We spell each other for lunch (usually just a sandwich).

1330 - 1800   Watch keeping duties (generally the quietest part of the day).

1800 - 1930   We spell each other for dinner (main meal of the day).

1930 - 2100 One of us attends the colonel's O Group. Sort and distribute any incoming mail. Pete to bed.

2100 - 0300 I receive daily movements schedule, signals and codes, update the imprest and write my diary.

This then was the pattern of our routine for the next month. However, as I have indicated many other things happened in the interstices.

One of my first tasks was to establish my credentials with the members of the Chinook flight that had remained at Oscar. When the main party moved to

Charlie only those thought to be essential to the maintenance of a forward operating base were taken. Not that that left many behind. There were about a dozen in all, engineers, storemen, clerks and cooks. They formed a first reserve echelon and, in effect, maintained the rear position. I was the only officer and therefore their CO. Now it may sound strange, but in the twenty years that I had served as an officer in the RAF I had never held a position of command. To members of Army and Navy this may seem an impossible situation but in the RAF it is not uncommon. It applies particularly to aircrew whose main function is to fly aeroplanes. If you are the captain of a multi-seat aircraft then you certainly have command of the other crew members, though it is seldom, if ever, the rigid command found on the parade square and if you are a single seat pilot there is no one to command but yourself. Obviously you do not live in isolation and have to give the odd order:

"Chief! Get the kite ready for 10 o'clock, there's a good chap, 'going to have a go at the Hun."

But he is not YOUR Chief, he is under the command of the engineering officer and what you have given is more of an authoritative request than an order. Many aircrew never hold a position of command and those that do may not have commanded men until they have reached the position of flight commander and the exalted rank of Squadron Leader. As a Flight Lieutenant specialist aircrew I therefore suddenly found myself in a position for which I was not well prepared.

During the working day my men inhabited one of the hangars which had been commandeered upon their arrival. I made my way down there and found them drinking tea in one of the offices. "Now," I thought, "What approach would the training staff at the Officer's Command School recommend for this situation. Have them parade for inspection, possibly. Interview them individually, probably." But looking at them looking at me none of this seemed appropriate so I simply went in, sat down and said, "Tea, milk, no sugar, please." The cup was there in a trice and the ice was broken. My salvation came in the form of C/T (Chief Technician) Matthews a doubty SNCO who became my number one and, being an NCO had had command of men since he had been a corporal. We therefore followed in the long standing military tradition; I gave the orders but only after due consultation with my sergeant and with his blessing.

"What do you think of the situation, sergeant?"

"Dreadful, but not without hope, sir."

"Very good, sergeant. Carry on."

I explained the situation as I saw it and the men seemed to understand. I concluded with the old standard, "And if you have any problems my door is open. Just come and see me." The difference was that I meant it. I made a point of visiting 'the men' every morning just in time for tea and tried to let them know what was going on. Most of the time they knew as much as I did; sometimes, I suspect, more. After a couple of days of this 'care bear' approach, two of the cooks who had been drafted to help the army in the general running of the kitchen, came to me and asked if they could have a bed.

"What do you mean?" I asked. "Where are you sleeping at the moment?"

"In the store room in a make shift bunk." was the reply.

"How long have you been doing this?"

"Since we got here, sir, about 4 weeks."

So for 4 weeks two of our men had been without adequate sleeping accommodation. Perhaps it was their fault for not speaking up but I feel that someone in authority should have made sure that all members of the party were properly set up. The mission obviously has priority but it will founder if the nuts and bolts are not looked after.

I returned to Ops and found one desert camouflage jacket and a pair of desert camouflage trousers on my desk. I have detailed them as two separate items because they did not actually match. Both jacket and trousers were undoubtedly desert cam patterned but they were of distinctly different shades of that well defined colour, sand.

"John brought them in," said Pete, "Said he hoped they'd do."

At last, by courtesy of the SAS, I no longer had to walk around looking like a badly watered privet hedge, I could merge into the background. I put them on. The jacket was a perfect fit, the trousers, on the other hand, were the correct waist size but the inside leg was about seven inches too long. "No problem," I thought, "Cut them to length." But that was easier said than done. The bottom of each trouser leg was fitted with a drawstring so that it could be tied tightly around the ankle, thus restricting the ingress of sand, the odd camel spider or scorpion. It took me most of the day, in between other tasks, to hem the bottoms and re-thread the chord. I am no seamstress and the stitching was irregular but, at last the job was done and the finished article served until I returned to the UK. There was, however, an unplanned bonus to all this needlework. With the trousers now more or less the correct length, I was left with two pieces of desert camouflaged material, seven inches wide and just over twelve inches long. This was not to be wasted. I was sure I could put it to good use.

I learnt at an early age that I was not destined for high office. I came from a humble, hardworking background but have, nevertheless, in the eyes of my parents, 'done well for myself'. Even so, I lacked the classical education, the connections, and, probably most importantly, the double barrelled name, all of which, whilst not guaranteeing, seem to ease the path to the more exalted ranks. One thing I do possess, however, is the ability to play the fool. I mean this in the classical sense of 'court jester'. The trick is to be unpredictable but not to lose your credibility; to be mildly eccentric or just outrageous enough to make people believe that you are still serious. It is a fine balance but if you can achieve it the benefits are enormous. It is also something that you must do consciously; you are playing the gallery for laughs and the effect of every act must be calculated beforehand. With this in mind I decided it was time to test the ingenuousness of my fellow inmates at Oscar.

The first piece of surplus trouser leg material I converted into a bow-tie. Now it is a tradition in the Officers' mess that bow-ties shall be tied properly. You may challenge anyone by walking up to them and giving their bow a tug. If the person so challenged is found sporting a 'ready made' he is fined a bottle of port. If, on the other hand the bow proves 'proper' and comes undone in the hand of the challenger then it is he who must provide the port. Unfortunately, the material that I had was not long enough to make a complete tie and I had to content myself with a fixed bow and a neck band, the latter being joined with a piece of Velcro which I obtained from the safety equipment section. I would just have to take the risk that no one would challenge its authenticity. Subsequently, I wore it on several occasions and it was never once questioned. Perhaps it was because I was the only one dressed correctly for dinner. Possibly, a more likely reason was that it was camouflaged and therefore remained unseen.

From the second piece of cloth I manufactured something equally bizarre. A medal. There had been much speculation as to the number of medals that might result from the Gulf War campaign. Some thought one, some two, some as many as five, UK, UN, Saudi, Kuwait and perhaps even one from the USA. However, being the eternal pessimist and knowing the reticence of the UK authorities to issue campaign medals, my money was on another clasp for the GSM (general service medal). I therefore decided to make my own from this piece of camouflage material at my disposal.

The medal itself I made from a UAE bronze 10 fils coin, the suspender from a spring clip that I found in the stationary store. I had great difficulty in making a hole in the coin by which to fix the suspender for, whilst I managed to acquire a drill bit of approximately the right size, I could not find a drill. They had all been taken forward to Charlie by the engineers. I was, therefore, reduced to 'twiddling' the bit backwards and forwards with my fingers until the hole was formed. It took me the best part of a day. This accomplished, I covered the coin with the camouflage material and sewed it up as neatly as I could at the back, rather like covering a button. I had, however, omitted to mark the position of the hole that I had so laboriously bored in the coin and it took me some time, probing with a needle, to re-locate it. and so fix the suspender. The 'ribbon' was a relatively simple affair even though I added a 'bar' for effect. The whole thing was attached to a safety pin and my camouflage medal was complete.

I pinned the medal to my battle blouse and waited to see what reaction it would provoke. It took three days before anyone noticed (camouflage does work after all). One evening at the end of an 'O' group, the Colonel looked at me and said, "What's that?"

"The CM, sir." I replied. "The Camouflage Medal, for remaining totally inconspicuous throughout."

He looked at me long and hard and then said, "Ye-es, very good. Get it off!"

So I did, but it had achieved its purpose. It had entertained me for several days and advanced my standing as an eccentric among a group of guys who are all basically eccentric.

In the event, the British Forces received three medals, UK, Saudi and Kuwait, with permission for only the UK one to be worn officially.

Not long after the departure of the Chinooks to Charlie we took delivery of some long awaited emergency services equipment in the shape of a fire engine and water bowser. Up to this point both Chinook and Hercules aircraft had been operating out of Oscar with no crash or fire cover beyond the odd hand held fire extinguisher. Even so that was all we got, just the equipment because the request had failed to ask for qualified crew to man it, and you only get what you ask for. We therefore took it upon ourselves to find out how it all worked. Now it seemed logical to us that if you could drive a car or truck then there would be no problem with a fire engine. Wrong. This fire engine, and I assume others must be the same, proved to be an unnecessarily complex piece of machinery. You needed a handbook just to start the thing and the multitude of gears were in all sorts of unexpected places. There appeared to be comprehensive instructive notices all over the inside of the cab but, as they were in Arabic, proved to be of no use whatsoever to us. Nevertheless, by a system of trial and error, we eventually found out how to start the beast and get it into first gear. We then all took turns driving this great red monster, together with its 500 gallons of water, which weighs almost 2 ½ tons, round the aircraft dispersal area. Trying to corner and stop with all this water sloshing about was an art in itself but we managed without coming to grief.

Fortunately we never had to contend with an aircraft accident. This proved to be most fortuitous for, much later, as we were preparing to pack up and leave for home at the end of the conflict, our lack of skill at fire fighting was exposed. A great bonfire was lit at the far end of the camp to dispose of all the accumulated rubbish and a 4 ton lorry was pressed into service as a refuse wagon. On one of its many trips this truck was inadvertently parked down wind of the conflagration and duly caught fire. The unfortunate driver came running into the Ops room bewailing his plight and a group of airmen, who were standing around at the time, saw this as their moment of glory. They leapt into the fire tender and made for the inferno, lights flashing and sirens wailing. Unfortunately, whilst we had all learnt how to drive the thing, no one had thought to find out how to turn on and operate the pumps. The would be fire crew returned 30 minutes later with an intact cargo of water and the report that the lorry was now a twisted heap of burnt metal.

At about this time items of humorous prose started to appear. God only knows where they come from for they are always anonymous but they are part of the ironic trench humour which is synonymous with the British at war. I will inject them at intervals but as a first offering this one seemed particularly apropos. As with much trench humour it has a 'religious' foundation. It is entitled:

THE PLAN

1. In the beginning there was the rumour of a plan, and both the plan and the rumour were without substance and void.

2. But the rumour was spread abroad and it came to the notice of the men and the men liked it not.

3. And the men said unto the Corporal, "This plan is a heap of shit and the whole thing stinks."

4. And the Corporal, being mindful of the welfare of the men, went unto the Sergeant and said, "This plan is a load of crap which smells to high heaven."

5. Then the Sergeant went unto the Duty Officer and, standing to attention, sayeth, "Sah! This 'ere plan, wot 'as been brought to my notice, his hay bucket hov hexcrement, the hoder hov which his wery hobnoxious. Sah!"

6. Then the Duty Officer, having pondered the plan, presented his draft report to the Adjutant, saying, "Verily this plan is a vessel of fertiliser which only the strongest can abide."

7. When the allotted time had come to pass, the Adjutant briefed the Staff Officer and reported unto him, saying, "This plan contains that which promotes growth and is very powerful to him that beholds it."

8. And in the fullness of time, the Staff Officer went unto his General and, laying the plan before him, sayeth, "This plan is powerful. Verily, it will ensure the development of all who have dealings with it and he who exhorts it, even unto the highest, shall be covered in sweet violets."

9. Then the General, being cognisant of the wider issues and mindful that the plan not only contained power but glory as well, hinted at it to the Minister.

10. And verily, the Minister saw that it was good and formed it into a policy and, in due season as it bore fruit, showered those about him with honours and decorations.

11. But when the men learnt of the policy they perceived the enormity of their folly and of the folly of those about them, and they smote their breasts and rent their clothes and cried with a very loud voice, "SHIT!"

Four days after the departure of the Chinooks to Charlie I received an urgent message from the detachment. They required money, £10,000 in Saudi Ryals and they wanted it tomorrow. So, I dropped everything and made my way post haste to the bank in Abu Dhabi. I had to extract the said sum in UAE Dirhams and then convert it; all extra commission for the bank but then that's how banks make their money. By the time I returned to Oscar, 3 hours later, there was another message waiting for me to the effect that the cash was required in US$ not Saudi Ryals. Now one of the rules of an imprest is that you keep the exchange of one currency into another to an absolute minimum, that way you cannot be suspected of speculation with public money. However, I had little choice. I turned the car around and re-traced my tracks back to Abu Dhabi and the bank. I arrived just as it was closing and explained my problem to the Deputy Manager. He sympathised with my predicament but said that the branch did not have that amount of US$ in stock and it would take at least a day to obtain it. However, he did have a solution although it took me somewhat by surprise and was certainly not one I would have arrived at on my own.

"Your best bet," he said, "Is to go down the souk and exchange your Ryals with the money changers. No." he added, seeing my look of disbelief, "I'm serious, and you'll get a better rate than I can offer you. They don't have our overheads. However, you might have to spread that amount around four or five dealers."

So, with a certain feeling of trepidation, that is what I did. In fact it took six separate transactions but not once was a eyebrow raised or any hint of surprise shown. With each dealer it was purely a business transaction. If they had dollars to sell they sold them to me. It says much for the integrity of the people of the souk for at no time did I feel that there was any threat to me or my burden. My biggest problem was that I got several different rates, all better than the bank's as predicted, but slightly different. The imprest accounting was going to be interesting.

It was late in the afternoon when I once again returned to Oscar. I was met with yet another message saying that perhaps some Saudi Ryals might be useful after all. This was too much. Was the situation at Charlie changing minute by minute or was it another case of someone making a plan and then altering it without considering the consequences? I managed to get a call through to them on a telephone line that sounded as if it had been trampled by a herd of camels and succeeded in making them understand the difficulties my end. I ended by saying that if they wanted the money on tomorrow's shuttle then it was US$ or nothing. The dollars suddenly became acceptable.

The Herc for Charlie was due to leave Oscar at 0600 hours the next morning. By 0530 I had presented myself, complete with gun, gas mask, sleeping bag and other necessities (not forgetting the $15,000) for at least one night's stop over, to John the Mover. "'Soon as these crates are loaded you can get on." he said. "There are twelve of you going up to Charlie but you are going via Riyadh to pick up some more boxes." The aircraft already seemed full to me. There were no seats and we had to wedge ourselves in amongst the crates and netted loads as best we could. "So much for passenger transport regulations." I thought, as I secured a berth on a relatively comfortable packing case and stowed my rifle on the floor underneath my rucksack.

'First Class' Travel

It took just over two hours to get to Riyadh and, after a brief stop to pick up the aforementioned freight, we were on our way to Charlie. I made a stern resolve never again to forget my book and spent the whole journey zombie like in the half light and noise. Once we had all shaken down, the trip was not particularly uncomfortable but there was little room and trying to get to the loo was rather like an expedition through the foot hills of a minor mountain range. Much to my surprise, the in-flight meal had not been forgotten although by now the supply of 'butty boxes' had failed and we were reduced to what the Navy call 'Bag Rats'; rations in a paper bag.

Two and a half hours out of Riyadh we made our approach to Charlie, landed and taxied past lines of Fairchild Republic A-10 Thunderbolt aircraft, affectionately know as the 'Wart Hog' because of its unlovely appearance. However, the saying "looks belie the man" certainly applies to the A-10. Designed specifically as a 'tank buster', it has a radius of action of 620 miles but is slow for a jet aircraft with a combat speed of only 390 kts (knots - nautical miles per hour) or 450 mph. However, this very lack of speed enables it to be highly manoeuvrable which makes it both difficult to avoid and difficult to hit. It is heavily armoured and can withstand small and medium artillery and missile attack with relative impunity. Its arsenal is formidable and is capable of carrying 12,000 lbs of bombs, rockets and guided missiles on its external underwing weapon pylons. Even so, it is probably best known for the seven-barrelled, 30mm gatling gun mounted in its nose. This gun is capable of firing 6000 rounds per minute and the shells are made of depleted uranium.

Depleted uranium, as its name implies, has minimal radioactivity but retains all of the density of a material of atomic weight 92. It is one of the most dense commonly available metals being almost twice as dense as lead and therefore has considerable kinetic energy. In other words, once you have got it moving it takes an awful lot of stopping. The awesome power packed by this gun will rip light and medium armour (including tanks) to shreds. I have witnessed a demonstration on Salisbury Plain where, in a single pass, a light tank was literally cut in half by the gun alone.

The A-10s at Charlie were working a continuous shuttle system throughout the hours of daylight. There was an endless stream of aircraft fuelling, arming and then departing to 'spoil someone's day'. The ironic thing is, that just before Saddam Hussein invaded Kuwait, the US military had decided to pension off these veritable war horses. The cold war had come to an end and with the spectre of phalanxes of Russian tanks disappearing into the blue the Americans could no longer see a role for the A-10. Rather in the same way that the British decided to dispose of its bomber force only to be faced with the invasion of the Falkland Islands shortly afterwards. It was rather more by luck than anything else that the RAF were able to resurrect the remaining few Vulcan bombers and make a 'show' of strength. In the Gulf War the A-10 re-found its raison d'être and proved to be a formidable asset.

In peace time Charlie is a small civil airfield though from a practical point of view there is little evidence of any community for it to serve for there is hardly a soul within a hundred of miles. Nevertheless, it is there and is one of the many strategic airfields scattered throughout the area. It is kept at a care and maintenance level against just such an eventuality as the Gulf War. Would that we had the foresight. The Chinook detachment had established its HQ and Ops in the Departure/Arrivals lounge and was utilising the baggage conveyer as a long 'desk'. The helicopters, needless to say, were on the far side of the airfield where a certain amount of hangarage and engineering facilities were available. The troops were living in a tented city at the northern end of the airfield and had already made themselves at home. Rows of separate 12x12 (12ft x 12ft ground area) tents formed the sleeping accommodation whilst an amalgamation of 12x12s formed the kitchen and mess area.

The 12x12 is the ultimate in frame tents and is the backbone of the British military in the field. The frames are built from stout, 3ft lengths of aluminium pole connected by short spider like union pieces. These spiders are so designed that any number of tents may be joined together to form large open spaces under canvas. The whole thing is then nailed to the ground with foot long 'skewers' and can be storm lashed with main guys if it is considered necessary.

128

The SAS had similarly established themselves but in a remote corner of the airfield away from prying eyes but could be identified by the strange collection of pink Landrovers, sand-buggies and motorbikes that littered their 'car park'.

It was the wind that immediately caught my attention as soon as I stepped off the Herc. It was blowing about 20kts and whipped up the fine red dust so that all the time you were exposed it was like standing in a sand blasting machine. It was cold too, about 15°C colder than at Oscar and at night the temperature regularly dipped below zero. The effect was a numbing chill against which the desert camouflage battle dress offered little protection. Indeed, back at Oscar, Swede's two most pressing tasks had been to obtain arctic sleeping bags and Parka anoraks for the detachment, much to the incredulity of the blanket stackers back at the main supply site.

Despite the urgent request for money I now found it a difficult task to find anyone willing to sign for it. Every last cent had to be accounted for as it was, in effect, a sub-imprest. Finally, SENGO was persuaded to take charge of it and promised faithfully to keep accurate records for me. I was happy, I had a signature. The first rule of any imprest is to get rid of as much money as you can in exchange for signatures. You are less likely to lose triplicate signatures than you are wads of cash.

By the time I had unloaded the money, the Herc, on which I had arrived, was long gone and was not due to return until the afternoon of the next day. Fortunately I had come prepared for this and all I had to do was to locate a bed space. This I duly did but then found I had nothing else to do. As soon as the detachment had arrived at Charlie it had been engaged in the night time insertions and extractions of SAS patrols. Therefore, during the day time there was little going on. Also, I was an outsider in as much as I was not intimately involved in the detailed planning or execution of any of the missions. Special Forces are notoriously reticent about discussing their operations, even to each other, working on the premise that what you don't know cannot be extracted from you.

You may see, then, that I was left much to myself and I spent the time observing and gleaning what information I could. I observed the relentless assault of the A-10s, the spiralling of eagles in the late afternoon thermals and the ritual slaughter of a goat by some local soldier/tribesmen. They left a fearful mess in the ablutions block much to the consternation of the western inhabitants, particularly the Americans for whom everything is sterilised and comes out of a vac pack. The Arabs, on the other hand, genuinely could not understand what the fuss was about. For them eating bacon burgers from a 24 hour ration pack was a far greater sin than leaving a few goat's entrails in a sink. What is a little disease born of a lack of hygiene compared with the wrath of God for failing to observe an age old custom?

As evening fell the night shift began to appear and it was clear that there was to be another operation that night. By the odd judicious question and a great deal of listening to other's conversations I managed to form a picture of what had been going on. The original concept for the Special Forces was their classic role of providing maximum disruption and deception in an area well away from the intended main thrust. These tactics were two fold in their intentions. They were designed to give the impression of a much larger force than was actually present and therefore to tie up a great many soldiers which Saddam Hussein could usefully use elsewhere and to cast doubt in his mind as to the actual line of assault on Kuwait. Indeed whilst all this action was going on in the western desert, the SBS were involved in similar deceptive missions in the waters off the eastern beaches and helping to create the impression of an impending sea borne invasion. However, within a few hours of the allied forces' initial air raids, Saddam Hussein played one of the few aces that he held and came within a hair's breadth of not only causing serious disruption to the allied plans but also possibly precipitating WW3.

On the evening of 17/18 January, Saddam ordered the launch of a series of SCUD missiles at Israel. For eight minutes, the time between the detection of the rocket launch to the time of impact, the world held its breath. It was known that Iraq possessed considerable stocks of chemical and biological agents that could easily be formed into munitions as had been adequately demonstrated in their conflict with Iran. It was also known that, under the guise of civil power production, they had been working frantically on a nuclear weapons programme. What was not known was the stage that these programmes had reached. Had viable missile warheads been developed and if so, could they be delivered? The SCUD rocket is an early Soviet design and, in reality, little better than the German V2s of WW2. But had Saddam been able to modernise and modify it sufficiently for his purposes?

Two rockets fell on Haifa, four on Tel Aviv. Fortunately, Israel did not disappear in a nuclear flash and mushroom cloud, neither did its inhabitants start dying in their thousands of plague. The warheads were conventional and not particularly potent. No one was killed and actual damage was slight but Saddam Hussein had brought Israel to the brink of war. It occurred to me that perhaps this act could establish his name in history as the man to unite Arabs, Christians and Jews but on reflection I think that his plan was far less altruistic. I believe he saw in this as an opportunity to advance global Muslim dominance with himself as leader.

130

By placing his own people and country on the sacrificial altar, Saddam hoped to drive a wedge between the Coalition Forces. He was certain that Israel would retaliate and in so doing place an unendurable strain on the Arab nations currently fighting along side the Americans and other western nations. Israel would have to cross Jordanian air space to get to Iraq which, he calculated, would bring the Jordanians into the conflict. There was also an outside chance that such a strike might persuade Iran to temporarily bury the hatchet and come in against the common enemy. If that had happened who knows what the reaction of the rest of the Muslim world would have been?

It almost happened. According to official sources, the Israelis actually launched a significant F-16 fighter bomber strike force but it was recalled before any serious political breach had been occasioned. Unofficially and strongly denied, they also went as far as rolling back their nuclear missile silo covers. Baghdad came within an inch of being vaporised. It was only intense diplomatic pressure that prevented a holocaust and a key part of that jigsaw was the SAS.

SAS Transport

In order to strike at Israel, Saddam Hussein had had to launch his SCUD rockets from sites in the south-western corner of Iraq thus demonstrating that his scientists and engineers had not been able to radically improve their range. The SAS, whether by divine intervention or otherwise, were also in that neck of the woods. It was therefore inevitable that their peculiar talents should be directed and concentrated on finding and destroying the SCUD missiles and launch sites. Again, unofficially, it is acknowledged that the Israelis only acceded to Western requests to stay their hand when they were assured that it was the SAS and the SAS alone who were to spearhead this task. Such is their reputation. The job of the Chinook SF detachment was to support the SAS in this vital task; to ferry SAS teams deep into Iraqi territory and re-supply them or withdraw them as required.

It had been a long day and I retired to my bed before the crews had finished briefing but I awoke at the sound of their departure and again, 3 hours later, upon their return.

The journey back to Oscar the next day was similar to the one up to Charlie, cramped and noisy. We arrived just in time for dinner and I spent the evening catching up on the happenings from Pete. Nothing untoward had happened and the routine of Oscar was settling down into ritual.

A spoof INTSUM (intelligence summary) had appeared on the grapevine and was duly posted on the notice boards. INTSUMs, as the name suggests, are brief, one or two line synopses of much larger intelligence reports. The humour of this spoof document was directed at current and traditional targets/victims. It read:

INTSUM No. 1

1. The Swiss Navy has finally gained control of Lake Geneva.

2. Italy reports that its war command bunker at the North Pole is nearing completion. The previously reported missing combat aircraft has been found at Rome International; there is no sign of the crew.

3. The Irish, having been invited to support the Coalition Forces in the Golf War, have banned all sport and mounted an attack on the main Dublin Volkswagen garage.

4. The price of sand has doubled but a spokesman for the Government said this did not go against the grain.

5. Forklanders, aware of the knife edge situation, have taken the opportunity to invade Argentina and liberate the Fray Bentos islands.

6. Russia denies that its troops are sweeping across Europe and claims that it is just the start of the holiday season.

7. In Gurf Wal, a hitherto little known Alaskan town, Chinese paratroops have landed and set up an air head. Commander Wing Wong denies confusion over the letters 'l' and 'r' in their orders to re-supply Coalition outposts. He is quoted as saying. "Soon pranes fry and tloops can expect lice and other supprys."

8. Supplies of 'Baghdad' and 'Kuwait' Hard Rock Cafe tee-shirts are now available.

The last item was, in fact, true but, although the shirts appeared widely throughout the Gulf, I suspect they had not actually been sanctioned by the Hard Rock Cafe company. They reminded me of one I had acquired in a previous conflict which proudly stated that "Real men drink in Beirut!"

The air war continued. Not that it was much of an air war as such. In the early stages there was a token resistance by the Iraqi air force but within 10 days, thanks to the low level airfield denial tactics of the RAF Tornados armed with JP233 mine dispensers and the American fighters, all the enemy's aircraft were either grounded, destroyed or dispersed. It was, and still is, unclear whether the aircraft that 'dispersed' to Iran did so of their own volition or were under orders to save them for another day. It may have been yet another ploy on Saddam's part to try and involve Iran in the conflict. If they had operated out of Iranian airfields, the Coalition Forces probably would have retaliated which, in turn may well have stung Iran into some form of action. In the end nothing happened and the Iraqi air threat ceased to exist. With total air superiority established the Coalition was free to concentrate on the second phase of the airwar: the subjugation of the enemy ground forces.

The plan was simple. The Coalition decided that it would use its air forces to achieve a 50% attrition of enemy ground forces before sending in its own armies to re-take and secure Kuwait. The official policy was the out and out destruction of military targets such as airfields, radar sites, artillery and tank positions and the cutting of logistic supply lines. Day and night targets were identified and attacked. To the outside world the whole war seemed to be conducted with all the precision of a surgeon wielding a scalpel as they were fed the spectacular film footage of LGBs (laser guided bombs) being directed through a particular window or vent. It was indeed spectacular but, in fact, a very minor part of the overall offensive. Contrary to popular belief, LGBs are nothing more than conventional iron bombs with the addition of movable fins to give some element of directional control and a laser detector unit fixed to the nose. The laser guidance system simply hones the precision of the delivery. It is still up to the skill of the pilot to put the bomb into the right 'ball park' in the first place. To make the system work, the target must be illuminated by a beam of laser light. The nature of a laser is such that the beam of light does not spread out very much and can, therefore, be pinpointed on small targets. The laser beam reflects from the target and bounces back into the air. It is coded in order that the detector on the bomb's nose does not react to any other lasers that may be flashing around the battle field at the same time. If a bomb is dropped into this cone of reflected light the detector will sense it and cause the fins on the tail of the bomb to move thus trying to keep the bomb in the centre of the cone and hence to the source of reflection, ie. the point which the laser target marker is illuminating.

The LGB has no forward propulsive power of its own. It has the initial forward momentum of the aircraft that has delivered it and is often 'tossed' to give it greater range but at the end of the day it is subject to the laws of gravity. It must be dropped in the correct place and with more or less the correct trajectory and, because of these requirements, it is almost impossible for the aircraft delivering the bomb to illuminate the target for itself. Therefore, in order to deliver an LGB you must have two elements, an aircraft to deliver the bomb and a means of illuminating the target with the laser until the bomb impacts.

Until the outbreak of hostilities the majority of training undertaken by the RAF using LGBs had been conducted using ancient Blackburn Buccaneers as the laser target designators whilst Tornados delivered the bombs. Despite the Buccaneer being 21 years old, this partnership had proved to be a deadly combination. However, when it was decided to send troops and aircraft out to the Gulf, the powers that be, ever mindful of saving the odd pound, decreed that the Tornados would do their own laser designation. As soon as hostilities commenced the error of this decision was uncovered and an urgent signal sent to the UK for Buccaneer support. They arrived five days later, painted pink and ready to go like Jack Russells in a barn full of rats. The strike rate went up immediately and the results vindicated the cost.

But back to the air war! The official policy of the air phase was to achieve a 50% reduction in the effectiveness of the Iraqi military might. The general public could be forgiven for believing that this was achieved purely by the destruction of armour and facilities with a minimum of unavoidable casualties because this was what the newsreel footage showed. What is generally not realised is that a major part of the attrition was the active demoralisation of the Iraqi troops themselves. This was achieved by systematic and intensive bombing raids on troop concentrations. A tactic widely used was to select a particular area (usually a 1km x 1km grid square on a map - to make navigation easy) and drop leaflets on it, informing those on the ground that at such and such a time the next day the same area would be subject to bombing raids. The troops on the ground were invited to surrender, retire, desert or face the consequences. It was no idle threat for, at the advertised time, the sky would fill with B-52 bombers and each one would unleash 60,000lbs (nearly 27 tons!) of HE on the surrounding countryside. The next day the leaflets would re-appear saying "We told you so. Now get out or it will happen again." And it did and it did and it did.

What the public and possible many of our own troops did not realise was that not only conventional HE was employed. Although it is difficult to authenticate there is evidence to show that fuel/air bombs were also used in this demoralisation campaign. Known colloquially as "Blues Brothers" these devices are simple in concept and devastating in result. They comprise either 15,000 or 30,000lbs of high octane fuel. It is dropped in a container to the desired height where the fuel is dispersed as a cloud of vapour or small droplets by a non-igniting explosion. When the dispersion has achieved the optimum fuel/air mixture it is ignited by a secondary small explosion. The process is somewhat similar to that of an internal combustion engine but if you consider that in a standard family car the amount of fuel used in one cylinder for one explosion is only approximately 0.0000125 (12½ millionths)lb, you may begin to realise the power of this weapon. The shock wave from the explosion is said to be as close as you can get to that of a nuclear bomb without going nuclear.

It is impossible to imagine the effect on those under such a barrage. You may, however, gain some idea from the Iraqi officer who, even though trapped between his own barbed wire and mine fields in front and Saddam's execution squads behind him, still managed to escape and surrender to the Coalition Forces. On interrogation it was discovered that he had not even come from one of the targeted areas. "That is true." he said, "But I have seen an area that was targeted!"

The 29th of January had been a day like any of the preceding few, warm, sunny and mundane. We had had some rain, in fact a cloud burst the previous day had turned the square in front of the offices into a pond several inches deep, but it was only temporary and soon everywhere was sun baked hard and dusty again. Some house martins had appeared and started to build nests in the eves of the buildings and several large dragonflies could be seen flitting among the buildings, gorging themselves on the myriad house flies that had been sent to plague us. I had always associated dragonflies with lakes, ponds and such like and thought it rather strange to find them in this arid setting. They could obviously derive sufficient water from their food supply and that was abundant indeed. We tried various sprays and even fly papers in an attempt to keep the house flies at bay but it seemed to make little difference. The only really effective deterrent was the good old fashioned fly swat, but that was labour intensive.

The time was approaching 2215 hrs and I was just considering sliding off for an early night when the SAS Ops officer, a Warrant Officer whom we knew as Charles King, rushed in and said that one of their patrols had taken a 'hit' north of Charlie and there had been an urgent request for a Herc to 'CASEVAC' (casualty evacuation) the wounded. The standby crew were hauled out of their beds, briefed and got airborne in very short order. The immediate panic over, I asked Charles if he had any more details but, true to SAS tradition, he had little to say. The CASEVAC Herc returned the next day with the report that the whole thing had been a panic reaction to a rumour. However, the truth was rather different.

What we had witnessed was the opening scenes of the 'Bravo Two Zero' saga which has been told in detail elsewhere. The details of this exploit unwrapped slowly even for those closest to the action. Initially, all we knew was that an 8 man patrol, on a SCUD hunting expedition had been rumbled, involved in a fire fight and failed to make it back to the pre-arranged emergency rendezvous point. Every sortie into enemy territory has an emergency back up plan built into it whereby, if things go wrong, those involved know of a location and times when friendly forces will attempt rendezvous and rescue.

The first concrete evidence did not come our way until eight days later when one of the patrol, "Chris", walked into the British embassy in Damascus. He had travelled nearly 190 miles, averaging 23½ miles a day, through territory that was both geographically hostile and swarming with enemy troops. His rations had comprised two packets of biscuits and very little water. He lived literally off body muscle, weighing 40lbs less at the end of the mission than when he began it. A full account is given in the book "The one that got away". It is a classic story of survival and the will to live and yet another testament to the training of the SAS. They are, however, not given to extolling their achievements publicly and Colonel Sid's only comment was typical of the low key play down that they adopt when among 'strangers'. "Hm," he mused, "I drove from here (the UAE) to Damascus before they built the road."

Subsequently, it transpired, that of that patrol two died (one as a result of gunshot wounds and one of hypothermia) three were taken prisoner and three evaded capture to eventually return 'home'. Of the three captured, it is worth noting that one of the soldiers was thought to be dead. He had been left by the patrol shortly after the initial exchange of fire with severe leg and thigh wounds and was believed to be bleeding to death. He was fortunate in that his captors took him to a nearby field hospital where there happened to be an Iraqi major, surgeon. A combination of his medical skills and military rank undoubtedly saved the soldier's life for, with the subsequent exchange of prisoners at the end of the war, he appeared, unlooked for.

In my role as quartermaster, one of the stranger requests that I received from the front line was for 60 pillows. It was argued that as the aircrew were regularly engaged on arduous missions then life in their tented city should be as comfortable as possible. At the time I could not fault the logic. I just hoped that the accountants back in the UK would be similarly swayed. Nevertheless, it provided me with an ideal excuse to go down town and attend to some shopping of my own.

As I have mentioned, the plumbing in my new quarters was less than perfect and I was in desperate need of two flexible couplings and an adjustable spanner and these the souk yielded without any problem. The main item on my personal shopping list, however, was some tea and coffee. Most of the time we drank coffee and I mean most of the time, but the three Ops officers, myself (Chinooks), Pete (Hercs) and Charles (SAS) had formed a 'tea club' and, when circumstances allowed, had taken to imbibing a cup of tea on the 'verandah' outside the office in the quiet period which seemed to occur most days between 3 o'clock and 4 o'clock in the afternoon. Now, NAAFI tea and coffee are all very well, particularly if you want to creosote a fence or de-scale a boiler, but as beverages they lack a certain finesse. My mission, which I readily accepted, was to find something a little better.

I had already been told that 'Spinney's ' supermarket contained a rather better than usual delicatessen and so made that my first port of call to see what they had to offer. The range offered was select if not vast and yielded a most acceptable Lipton's Earl Grey tea and Douwe Egberts full aroma coffee. We managed to procure a stainless steel teapot which, with the aid of a funnel and filter paper, doubled as a coffee pot and, from somewhere, Charles produced half a dozen bone china cups and saucers. At first it was viewed as rather eccentric but after a while became accepted as part of the scene and even Colonel Sid graced us with his presence on the odd occasion.

In the midst of all the official signals that came winging their way across my desk, one in particular caught my fancy. It was headed 'SUBJECT 7RS 3825-99-7686507 BRUSH RUNWAY SNOW CLEARANCE' and read as follows:

"SUBJECT ITEM SUPPLIED BY DSM IN D OF Q BOX PPQ 16. ATLAS 10 DATA BASE IN PROCESS OF AMENDMENT TO READ SAME, UNITS ARE TO REVIEW REQUIREMENTS AND RESUBMIT AS REQUIRED. SURPLUSES ARE TO BE RETURNED TO DSM ASAP."

I pondered this and drafted the following reply:

"THANKYOU FOR YOUR ENQUIRY REF BRUSH RUNWAY SNOW CLEARANCE SURPLUSES. WE HAVE DECIDED TO RETAIN OURS - JUST IN CASE. RGDS LAWRENCE."

I received no further communication. To be fair I should put this seeming farce into context. The UK was experiencing the heaviest snow falls for some years and signals are often sent out on standard address lists which cover all and sundry addressees. At least I appreciated the humour.

Another signal I received, however, was of much more practical interest to everyone. It contained written authority for a daily issue of a water allowance. The SF are, by their very nature, mobile and secretive. It is, therefore, unwise for them to pitch up at regular intervals at communal watering holes, neither is it practical for them to transport large quantities of water in bowsers. To overcome the problem, they had been forced into the practice of buying bottled water as and when they could. However, they had had to fund this out of their own pockets and it had been a bone of contention for some time. In their usual bureaucratic way, the gnomes of the treasury had seen fit to spend millions of pounds on arms, ammunition and the requisitioning of civil transport to augment the force they had just finished depleting in the name of cost saving, but jibbed at the paltry expense of providing the fighting man with the one most important thing necessary for existence in the desert, water. Nevertheless, even though the signal gave authority for an individual water allowance it was still redolent of the fear of all accountants that the money would be misappropriated. The exact wording of the signal was:

"AFTER CONSULTATION WITH J1/J4 STAFF HERE, YOU ARE
AUTHORISED TO PROVIDE FLUIDS FOR PERSONNEL AT A COST OF
UP TO 25 DIRHAMS PER MAN PER DAY. MONIES ARE NOT TO BE
PAID DIRECTLY TO THE INDIVIDUAL."

The last sentence highlighted the fact that whoever had given the authority
had missed completely the point of the exercise. In our case it was not the
authority to purchase water that we wanted but the authority to allow the
individual to do it for himself. If you cannot trust a member of the SF who can
you trust? I overcame the problem by paying the money to the men but
accounting for it en-bloc. There was one bright spot, however. The allowance
was back dated. This gave me an excuse to travel up to Charlie and spread the
largesse.

In the ten days since my last visit the Chinook detachment had done much
to make itself as comfortable as possible. It was still cold and windy but a lot
of time and effort had gone into improvising some semblance of normality.
The mess, although still a tented city, was comfortable and sported easy chairs,
a bar, a tv/video and a library. God knows where the things came from. For
my part I was very relieved not to be asked to fund them out of the imprest. The
cooks had set up a kitchen to rival the best of restaurants and produced the most
extraordinarily tasty and imaginative meals out of very ordinary ingredients.
The issue of the water ration money was received with great joy and made me
the most popular person in camp; for about half an hour. Thereafter, I was,
once again, left to my own devices until transport back to Oscar arrived the next
morning. I filled my time by gleaning what information I could to flesh out the
gaps contained in the official communications and news reports.

I got the impression that the general feeling at Charlie was less fraught than
it had been on my last visit. It was still tense, hyper-active and the interfactional
rivalry remained lurking just below the surface but the fear of the unknown had
to some extent dissipated as all the crews had, by now, been across the border,
some several times. There had, however, been one or two 'hairy' moments.
Two crews who had ferried an SBS raiding party to a point just under 40 miles
from Baghdad on the Basra road, 250 miles inside enemy territory at ultra low-
level, had had to land and shut down all but their APUs to wait for almost two
hours whilst an attack on a major communication cable network was carried
out. They sat there in the darkness watching the 'fireworks' going off around
Baghdad and expecting discovery at any moment. However they remained
undiscovered and the raid was successful. All returned safely but the crew's
fingernails were significantly shorter.

Another crew had an equally nail biting time, at the hands of their navigator, Flt Lt Mark Smith; not as you might suspect by getting them lost, but by assuming control of the aircraft when the pilot was taken violently ill and unable to fly. At the time they were well inside enemy territory and, although the mission had to be aborted, he successfully recovered the crew, passengers and aircraft to Charlie. That the journey was conducted below 50ft, at night, on night vision goggles is further tribute to the skill, dedication and flexibility of the personnel who make up the SF units.

The SAS, too, had taken on a different guise, in fact you might say that they were now indeed wolves in sheep's clothing. The unexpected severity of the highland desert winter, having already accounted for one of their number, and the need for more ethnic camouflage, had encouraged them to seek a local tailor who fitted them out with bespoke 'posteens' (heavy woollen great coats), which not only made them look like goatherds but smell like them into the bargain. When they completed the disguise with a 'shemags' (the ubiquitous Arab cotton head scarf) it was almost impossible to detect them among the locals, particularly as they had also taken to toting AK-47 Kalashnikov rifles.

Then there was this new crew that had arrived and included Pete Lacey and Roly Brown who were established 'characters' in the SH world. The sort of people that every squadron needs but few squadron commanders want. First class operators but individuals and non-conformists. Ideal people to be given dubious missions. They had been assembled from disparate locations and arrived at Charlie in a strange helicopter donated by one of the Arab Coalition members. They chose not to keep it at the airfield itself but hid it away from prying eyes in a nearby wadi. Of their mission they would say nothing, and rightly so, but they attached themselves to my imprest and asked if I had any Iraqi dinar!

Next day the Herc duly arrived and we departed once more to Oscar. This time we had to go via King Khalid Military City airfield, or KKMC as it became known, on the outskirts of Riyadh. KKMC had become the airhead for the larger aircraft of the war, the Galaxies, AWACS, KC-135 tankers and C-130s by the dozen. We taxied into a slot and the loadmaster announced that we would leave in about an hour. We had parked alongside some large concrete blast walls and, being naturally curious, I wandered off to see what was behind them. Turning the corner I came upon a sight that I had not expected. There in a neat row were five 'Spectre' AC-130H gunships.

In Vietnam the Americans had developed the concept of a gunship by arming a Douglas Dakota DC-3 with a range of heavy guns and used it as a flying tank to suppress enemy fire whilst trying to insert or extract their own troops. It was known as 'Puff the Magic Dragon' and proved to be a valuable asset. The 'Spectre' was the logical progression and had been given into the keeping of No 16 Special Operations Squadron. Four of the aircraft were closed up with no obvious signs of life but there was movement just inside the door of the fifth. Expecting to be challenged by a guard at any moment I made my way towards the manned aircraft, but no challenge came. As I got to the door a large black face appeared with a huge grin on it.

"Saw you coming. I was 'bout to lock up. You want to look 'round?" The voice belonged to a burly six foot black warrant officer.

"Yes please. " I said seizing the opportunity, knowing that it might never come my way again. From the outside the 'Spectre' looks very much like any other C-130, but inside it is very different. Aft of the cockpit this aircraft is devoted to the art of the aerial gunner and smelt of oil and cordite. The armament comprised two 20mm Vulcan gatling guns, capable of firing 6000 rounds per minute, a 40mm cannon and a 105mm howitzer. All the guns were positioned on the port side, a gatling gun in each doorway, the 40mm cannon amidships and the howitzer in the tail, just forward of the ramp. The weaponry is impressive enough but what makes this particular gunship truly awesome is its magazine. Every conceivable space is occupied with ammunition. In a conventional fighter you are limited to the odd three or four second burst because your total ammunition load is counted in hundreds, if you are lucky. (Possibly the origin of the expression 'giving [him] the whole nine yards' derives from the fact that in several aircraft gun systems, the ammunition belts were 27 ft (9 yds) long and so, if you give the whole nine yards, you give everything.) In the 'Spectre' you run out of fuel before you expend all the bullets. Well, almost.

"All these guns have IR (infra-red) and LLTV (low light television) sights," said my guide, "And the pictures from them are displayed on a HUD (head up display) in front of the pilot, so's he can see what the gunners are aiming at as he circles the target. The Vulcans and the 40 mil cannon are fed automatically," he continued as though he was taking a party of tourists round a theme park. "But the 105 is hand loaded."

"What rate of fire can you achieve with that?" I asked.

"Well," he said, "When we're on song, at 10,000ft you can get two shells in the air and a third in the spout."

"How accurate is it?"

"Darndest thing I ever saw was pickin' off individuals as they ran out of buildings in Grenada." was the reply. It seemed rather like using a sledge hammer to crack a nut but it answered my question. "It's s'posed to be recoilless," he continued, "But it still knocks the tail of this ship six feet sideways each time she fires." The stress on the airframe does not bear thinking about.

A few days later one of these 'Spectres' was lost. It was returning from a mission just off shore from Kuwait when it disappeared. No trace was found of it and it is assumed that a missile had hit the magazine.

Back at Oscar life continued its tedious way. A brief diversion was provided by a small wooden box that I found. It was about six inches square and three deep, with a round hole in one end. This looked like the ideal candidate for a jape, so I painted the words "Bat Box" on the side in white 'Tippex' and hung it up just outside the office door under the eves. It remained there without comment for three days and then one evening an Army Major came into the Ops room and said, "I see you've got a bat box. I didn't know there were any round here."

"Oh yes," I said, "They come in and out of the office all the time."

"What, at night?" he asked.

"No." I replied, "We get bats in and out of here all hours of the day." I am not sure he saw the joke. I think he may still believe there are bats at Oscar. There may well be now, for when we finally left, the bat box remained 'in situ' and for all I know may still be there.

A minor triumph of the Oscar escape committee was the discovery of the 'Brit Club' down in Abu Dhabi. It was built at a time when Britain held sway over this part of the world and the UAE was known as the Trucial States. It was tucked away at the quieter end of town on one side of a bay overlooking the main conurbation and had all the facilities you would expect in a British club; reading room and library, dining room, bar and a splendid outdoor swimming pool. In its heyday membership was exclusively British but with the ceding of the territory to the Sultan this had been extended to include local worthies. The name of the club had also been altered to reflect this change in circumstances and was now simply known as 'The Club'.

It had been the custom that any visiting British serviceman could become a temporary member of the 'Brit Club' upon the presentation of his ID card (identification papers - in the RAF these are officially known as Forms 1250 but are usually simply referred to as a '1250') and the rumour was that this prerogative still pertained in 'The Club'. With the general restriction of movement in and out of Oscar it was not easy to test this theory but, abusing my position as quartermaster and using some pretext of necessity to go down town, I managed to escape one Saturday morning. I concluded my business in town and turned off the main road down the drive to The Club. At the end of the drive was a barrier and security box. Prepared for some bluffing and explaining I wound down the window of my car and proffered my 1250. The security guard did not even take it. He just saluted smartly, raised the barrier and waved me through. I parked in a convenient slot and went to make myself known to the club manager. "Of course you are welcome." he said, "All the club facilities are at your disposal. I ask only that you settle all bills in cash." This was a small price to pay for the exclusive use of an oasis.

And oasis it was. For an hour or two it was possible to relax, forget about the war and have a civilised beer. The other great asset was the telephone. At Oscar, all private telephone calls were strictly 'verboten' and rightly so. Not, primarily, from the point of view of giving away secrets but more from a fear of giving away the location, for the source of telephone calls are easy to trace. However, here at The Club the public (but secluded) phones were an unlikely target for tapping or tracing. They were linked to the club switchboard and could, therefore, be paid for after the call had been made thus negating the need for a mountain of small denomination coins that must be shovelled into a public 'phone box faster than you can talk.

I used this opportunity to ring my wife and assure her that all was well. She had not been expecting a 'phone call and was very surprised to hear my voice. We had corresponded by letter almost daily but there is nothing like a real conversation. Not that I could afford a prolonged discourse, even at The Club's realistic rates. Until this time I had told no one at home of my whereabouts. In the early days I had written to friends and relatives explaining that I was unable to disclose my exact location. However, I had stuck samples of sand to the letters with Selotape and told them to try and guess where I was from the geological clues provided. Most guessed correctly, that I was in the desert! However, in answer to her question "Where ever are you?" I felt that I was not breaching any security by replying, "Abu Dhabi". This was sufficient and although it was still a rather nebulous answer, in the minds of my nearest and dearest it served to fix me in space, well away from the front line.

As I said earlier, The Club was an oasis, a hand hold on reality and I wish to thank the staff for their hospitality. But back to the war.

We had reached that time of the month when the earth's shadow blots out the light from the moon and the nights are dark. Living in the UK I had forgotten what a dark night was. There is so much cultural lighting from street lamps etc. that light pollution is reaching serious levels. Only in the remoter parts of Scotland do you start to approach natural darkness but even there it is beginning to be eroded and at astronomical levels some of the fainter stars are no longer visible. In the towns of southern England you are lucky if you can make out the main constellations. At the other end of the scale, here in the desert, it was equally difficult to make out the constellations because it was so dark and the air unpolluted that the sky was full of stars. One consequence of all this darkness was that it severely limited the night time operations of the Chinook and Hercules crews. NVGs (night vision goggles) are very good but they work according to the laws of physics and not magic. They are, after all is said and done, nothing but photo-multiplyers and if there is no light they cannot multiply it. 10 X 0 still equals 0! Not being slow on the uptake, the aircrew decided to put this 'down' time to good use. The Herc crews at Oscar announced that, as things were rather slack, they were going to catch up on some basic training and fly a few circuits at Dubai. It turned out that there were one or two ulterior motives to these training sorties.

"We might just stop off in the desert and take a few photos," said Dave, one of the pilots "And then pop into the duty free shop at Dubai airport. Are you interested?"

"Too right." I said, "Just give me time to collect my camera and credit card and I'll be with you."

We flew out over the desert towards Dubai. Having been authorised to practice desert landings, the captain selected a broad strip of relatively flat sand and, after a couple of tentative approaches, eased the aircraft down.

"OK." he said, over the intercom, "The photographic party can get out, and don't forget the shovels."

Half a dozen of us got out, two of the party carrying spades and two large plastic bags which looked rather heavy.

"What's in the bags?" I asked, once we were clear of the aircraft."

"Empties." was the reply. "We have accumulated rather a lot of - er - 'bottles' and the're not the sort you can ask your local Muslim dustman to take away. So we're going to bury them."

And they did.

Meanwhile, the Herc had taxied to the far end of the sandy strip, turned, and, in a dust storm of its own making, took off. It disappeared at low level over the sand dunes and all was quiet. After a few minutes, our mobile radio crackled into life. "OK. Coming in for the first pass. See how it looks." All was still quiet then suddenly, from the direction in which it had disappeared, the Herc re-appeared, no more than 50ft above the ground, wheels up and travelling at speed. Well it was fast for a Herc. I never cease to be amazed how, externally, the Herc can be so quiet. For such a large aeroplane it is almost silent until it is right on top of you, ideal for clandestine work. Certainly we had heard nothing of it until it had crested the dunes at the far end of the wide shallow depression in which we were standing. I think the designers must have found some way of channelling all the noise inside. Cameras clicked, and the great bird roared overhead, climbed slightly and banked for a return run. Even though we could now see it, at a mile distant it was not what you would call noisy. After several more passes at various speeds and attitudes, Dave called it back to earth. "That will do for the Squadron scrap book." he said, "We might even get the odd one in the flying mags back home and help boost the funds."

With wheels and flaps down, the aircraft executed a 'short' landing and seemed to have stopped almost as soon as it touched down. Such is its STOL (short take off and landing) capability that it is possible to operate a Herc from some of the larger American aircraft carriers! We battled our way through the sand storm at the rear of the aircraft to the ramp and climbed on board. "Right." said the captain, "We'll go and shoot a few circuits at Dubai and then stop for a spot of shopping."

Shooting circuits is part of what is known as instrument flying and instrument flying is what commercial aircrew do for most of their lives. It involves flying accurately at prescribed speeds and heights using radio navigation aids and ground radar control. A 'must' if you are trying to obtain a civilian pilot's licence but very boring. After about 40 minutes the captain declared that "Enough was enough and it was time to visit the Duty Free."

The duty free shop at Dubai International Airport is renowned as THE duty free shop in the world. Nowhere else have I come across such a selection of goods at such attractive prices. It is the only duty free shop where I have seen a range of sports cars for sale. I am not quite sure how you get your Porsche Carrera into the overhead locker of a Jumbo jet, but at the prices they were asking it was worth a try. However, business was bad. The Gulf War had all but wiped out international traffic and those carriers still operating seemed to be from countries with austere religious backgrounds or where the inhabitants had no disposable income. The shop was therefore empty and we were pounced upon by the staff and personally escorted through the Aladdin's cave.

It was debatable whether or not we were actually entitled to duty free goods. Nevertheless, we argued that in our extended journey from the UK and eventually back to the UK, any cigarettes or drink would be consumed 'in transit' and any hardware would be declared at our point of entry upon our eventual return. The vendors did not care two hoots for our moral dilemma and all but dragged us inside. I have to admit that I spent some time fondling a bottle of Booth's best dry gin but eventually my conscience got the better of me and I put it back on the shelf. Oscar and Charlie were supposed to be 'dry' camps but if you looked hard enough, finding a drink was not impossible. Fortunately my need for alcohol was not such that I needed a clandestine supply and, apart from two minor lapses (literally two single drinks), I did not consume any alcohol from the time I arrived at Oscar until the cease fire was announced - I just became addicted to coffee instead.

My particular interest was the hi-fi department. There I found what the whole of Abu Dhabi, including the souk, could not supply; the little Sony portable radio that I had coveted ever since I had seen Smithy's. Even at duty free prices it was still £110 but that was £40 less than the UK price and as I could not get one from any other source I was not going to argue. I was back in touch with the real world. I put it on the credit card with a mental note to tell the keeper of the king's purse (my wife) the next time I wrote.

The other aspect of the 'no moon' phase was that the Chinook crews up at Charlie took it into their heads to embark on some R&R (rest and relaxation) and, on our return to Oscar I discovered a message saying that the first group would be arriving that evening, for a 'few' days. This posed something of a problem. To begin with there had been no hint of this taking place and since their departure the rest of us had spread out and it would take some delicate negotiating to reclaim their bed spaces. There was also the problem of what to do with them. New empires had been established during their absence and where they had once ruled the roost others now held sway. It was clear from the message that they would also want to spend some time 'down town'. In view of the strict access control that still prevailed at Oscar this was not going to be easy.

I went to Colonel Sid with the problem and we decided the best solution was to ship them to a hotel in Abu Dhabi as soon as possible with the strict injunction to keep their heads down and not to return until they were due to go back to Charlie. In the event this worked quite well and for the next two weeks I turned my talents to running a travel agency. My clients were only too glad to disappear into the local flesh pots and wanted nothing whatsoever to do with the running of Oscar. They took this opportunity to find the whereabouts of the local Interflora agent and, having collected the appropriate monies, ordered single red roses to be sent to all our respective wives and sweethearts etc. on St Valentine's day. Chivalry and romance are not quite dead.

The arrival of one of these 'Thomas Cook' tours was rather irregular and bears the telling. As I said earlier, the fabric of Oscar was incomplete as we had taken over the site before such niceties as Air Traffic Control facilities had been installed. There were not even any runway lights and we had had to position temporary 'glims' at intervals along the runway edges. These glims were no more than ordinary domestic light bulbs powered by a rather old and temperamental mobile generator which was also situated by the runway's edge. All they provided was a sketchy outline of the runway and as there was still a need to maintain as covert a posture as possible, were only illuminated for the shortest necessary time. It was our practice to wait until the incoming aircraft called up on the radio that we had established in Ops, race out to the runway in a Landrover and crank the generator into life. This meant that the strip was usually lit up about five minutes before the arrival of the aircraft and the lights extinguished as soon as it left the runway and taxied onto the taxiway.

On this particular occasion the generator refused to take any meaningful part in the operation. No amount of cranking, and it was hand cranked, cursing or pleading could persuade it into life. The aircraft made a low approach, overshot and asked if there was a problem. We explained the situation and said we were doing our best. After a further five minutes of frenzied inactivity, on the part of the generator, the pilot said, that if we could illuminate the touch down point with vehicle headlights he would land using NVGs. He elected not to use the aircraft lights as these only gave a narrow field of view and would wipe out the NVGs' ability to pick up peripheral queues. So, assuming he knew what he was doing, we duly positioned two 'Rovers either side of the touchdown point with their headlights pointing obliquely down the runway and hoped.

The red and green wingtip lights of the Herc appeared out of the darkness over the sand dunes behind us and suddenly we were engulfed in the roar of the engines. The dark shape of the aircraft passed briefly through the pool of light thrown out by the vehicles and disappeared into the blackness beyond. A sudden crescendo of noise heralded the application of reverse thrust and then all was quiet. Slowly the aspect of the red and green navigation lights changed to indicate that the aircraft had turned round at the other end of the strip and was back-tracking towards us. About halfway along it turned to the right and parked in the nearest available pan. The pilot seemed unperturbed by the experience and said that it was easier than some of the 'field' landings he had been asked to undertake. It was yet another example of the versatility and flexibility required of military personnel.

For the record, the generator started first time half an hour later and gave no further trouble. An ample example of the perversity of inanimate objects.

Round about the middle of February, one of the Land Cruisers that we had hired from Avis started to give some trouble and as it coincided with the monthly payment of rent for our vehicles I thought it an ideal opportunity to 'escape' for the day. However, it was only just before I set off, that I discovered they had not been hired from the Abu Dhabi office but from Dubai. I hurriedly acquired a map of the area and a street map of Dubai together with rough instructions on how to get there from one of the airmen who had visited the town before the squadron's move to Oscar, and set off. From Oscar to Dubai was about two hours drive, much of it on dual carriage road but through featureless desert. On reflection however, that is not true. The landscape was not featureless it is just that to the stranger's eyes there are few distinct features. Fortunately the map I had acquired had been used for local low level night flying exercises and all the tall radio/tv masts and similar obstructions obstructions had been highlighted. Equally fortunately there happened to be a mast at most of the significant turning points on my journey and so all I had to do was head off in the general direction of my destination and count the masts.

The street map proved to be uncannily accurate and I found the Avis office without any trouble at all. The manager, Hillary Llewellyn, made me very welcome. The war had devastated the tourist trade and she was pleased to see any customers, however bizarre or unlikely. Her only concern was that we did not drive the vehicles outside the UAE, apparently the vehicle insurance was only valid within the Emirates. I thought it politic not to mention the fact that at least half of them had been bundled into the back of a Herc and were now in the far Northwest of Saudi Arabia and, for all I knew, in Iraq itself. The consequences emanating from an accident between one of our vehicles and a man on a donkey on the road to Damascus did not bear thinking about. So I simply paid the rent and explained about the problems with the Land Cruiser

I had brought with me. Replacement was immediate. The new vehicle was a 'top of the range' model and possessed every conceivable mod-con, even an altimeter!

Note 16 Feb.: Put newly acquired HF radio to good use. Listened to five nation's rugby match on BBC World Service. England beat Scotland 21-12!

By the middle of February the weather had started to get warmer. We still had the odd rainy period but in general the daytime temperatures were up in the low eighties. One result of this was a proliferation of short hair cuts. The army has always been noted for its 'short back and sides' but the RAF has traditionally leant towards the smart but not severe. However, with all the dust and heat, long hair was a positive nuisance. One of the airmen on the aircraft refuelling section claimed to be a barber of sorts, well he cut his own children's hair, and had a set of hairdressing scissors and hand clippers, so with a certain amount of trepidation I booked an appointment.

For 50p he did a practical job. There was not a great deal of style to it and the result bore a close resemblance to a startled hedgehog, what my father would have referred to as a 'tup'ny all off'[1], rather like a field of stubble but without the poppies, nevertheless, a daily wipe with a flannel was all that was needed to keep it clean and it was dry almost instantly. The prospect of summer was, however, not viewed with relish. In June, July and August, the temperature in Riyadh regularly exceeds 40°C and the thought of fighting in NBC suits and gas masks in the confined environment of a helicopter cockpit gave a whole new meaning to 'boil in a bag' and 'oven ready'.

The onset of the warmer weather was but one of the many problems facing the powers that be.   The ideal solution was to end the fighting by the middle of March and there were at least three reasons for this. Firstly, as I have just mentioned, the very real problems associated with extremes of temperature, both to men and machines. Secondly, the 17th of March was scheduled as the start of Ramadan, a Muslim holy month when fasting and abstinence are practised by the faithful. Although provision is made in the Koran for the strict observances to be modified in the light of dire peril it was thought not prudent to risk putting it to the test. Thirdly, it was uncertain if the general public (and therefore the politicians) of the Coalition partners would continue to back a lengthy campaign. A short sharp skirmish was one thing but, damn it all, it was supposed to be over by Christmas!

[1] This derives from the days when a barber would trim your hair for 1 penny (1d), give you a short back and sides for a penny-ha'penny (1½ pence) and remove the lot for tu'pence (two pence).

There was also the problem of achieving the planned figure of 50% reduction in the effectiveness of the Iraqi ground forces before commencing Coalition ground operations. The air raids appeared to be going well but there was a small flaw in the plan. The commanders did not know for certain how well. In the early stages of planning it was assumed that technology would reign supreme; air reconnaissance was to be kept to a minimum and damage inflicted upon the enemy closely monitored by satellite. But the planners had reckoned without the weather. Throughout late January and early February the weather had been very poor with a great deal of rain and low cloud covering the target areas. It was not bad enough to keep out the low level strike aircraft but it proved a severe restriction to the satellites orbiting 250 miles above the earth's surface. Eventually when it was considered that sufficient air strikes had been launched to achieve the 50% attrition target, a series of recce sorties were sent in. Their reports proved to be sensational. Instead of 50% damage it was estimated that almost 80% of the Iraqi ground power had been either destroyed or seriously disrupted!

An ultimatum was therefore presented to Saddam Hussein. Get out of Kuwait by mid-day (Washington time) on 23 of February or suffer the consequences of a land assault.

Despite all these high affairs of state were unfolding, life at Oscar continued its uneventful way as the entries in my diary revealed:

16 Feb: The Wing Commander paid a flying visit (pun not intended) and asked me to take him down town in order to buy a camcorder. This, he assured me, was to record the activities of the squadron and therefore should be funded out of the imprest. I found myself in no position to argue. We took the opportunity to visit The Club and have a curry. I think my stomach must have shrunk; perhaps I should eat more than one meal a day.

17 Feb: Took my sand wedge out onto what, in less arid conditions, would pass for an airfield and spent nearly an hour practising bunker shots from one sand dune to the next just outside the gates of the compound .

18 Feb: Have just censored a letter from one of the airmen to his wife where he refers to Saddam Hussein as the Mad Mufti (sic). Well I knew what he meant, I hope she does.

19 Feb: Very warm. Several swallows appeared so it must be summer. There are certainly enough flies for them to feed on.

20 Feb: Went to Charlie to pay out allowances. There are signs of boredom as the 'no moon' phase drags to an end but also an air of expectation that something big is going to happen soon.

21 and 22 Feb: Much the same as before. Getting warmer.

And so we waited. Mid-day of the 23rd came and went with not the slightest hint of an Iraqi withdrawal. Therefore, as promised, at 0100 hrs (local time) on the 24th Operation Desert Sabre was launched and the long awaited final phase of the Gulf War, to liberate Kuwait, swung into action.

8 - DESERT SABRE   24/28 Feb '91

By the beginning of January, Iraq's ground forces in and around Kuwait were estimated to comprise in the region of 90 brigades which the Coalition planners equated to approximately 600,000 men. However, subsequent intelligence analysis shows that due to undermanning, desertion and casualties resulting from Coalition air strikes the actual number of effective soldiers at the commencement of the ground war may have been as few as 200,000, some say even less.

The forward elements of these troops, found from ordinary soldiers and conscripts, were ranged along the coast of Kuwait to its southern border with Saudi Arabia and then in two lines, stretching 150 miles into the desert along the Kuwait/Saudi and Iraq/Saudi frontier. Behind these lines were units of the elite Republican Guard carefully placed 'in strategic reserve' along the north-western Iraq/Kuwait border. Officially they were to back up the ordinary troops in the 'unlikely' event that they should need aid. Unofficially they seemed ideally placed to swoop in and take the glory if victory looked imminent or secure a line of retreat (for themselves) should things not go according to plan. Not that they were no good. Quite the reverse in fact. However, the very fact that they were Saddam's crack troops meant that he was hardly likely to launch them on a suicide mission.

The Coalition had mustered a total of approximately 770,000 troops; the US providing almost two thirds with Saudi Arabia, Britain and France making up the bulk of the rest. Out of this strength a force of almost half a million men were committed to the ground phase of the liberation of Kuwait.

Intelligence reports and the disposition of his forces suggested that Saddam Hussein expected a frontal assault from the South with possible attempts at a seaborne invasion from the Gulf itself. So that, after much careful planning and consultation between the main protagonists, was the basis of what the Coalition provided. In broad terms, the strategy comprised the following elements:

US and UK naval elements bombarded enemy installations on the coast and the islands close to it while a contingent of US Marines launched a mock attack on the beaches. However, as a contingency, this feint was to be upgraded to an actual amphibious landing if it looked as though it might prove to be successful.

The Arab elements of the Coalition Force made a northern thrust at the Kuwaiti border along the coastal strip whilst further inland the US Marine Corps engaged the Iraqis in a major diversionary battle.

To the west of the Marines, but staying within the borders of Kuwait, Egyptian and Syrian soldiers pushed north and then swung east to attack the positions in Kuwait city from the west.

That was the plan that Saddam expected and that was what he got. However, the Coalition planners also had a couple of surprises up their sleeves!

Far out to the west, beyond the flanks of the Iraqi troops, the main allied assault was poised. The first group, comprising US and UK armour, described a curving left hook, cutting off the supply lines to the enemy's front and engaging the Republican Guard before it had time to either re-enforce or retreat. Meanwhile, even farther west, US and French units performed a similar but wider left hook, deep into Iraq, to cut off any retreat from Kuwait up the Euphrates valley towards Baghdad. It was hoped that these attacks upon the Republican Guard from the side and rear would have a crushing effect upon the morale of the front line elements and force an early surrender.

The first indication at Oscar that the ground war had started was a news blackout on CNN. Throughout the air campaign reporters for this American television news network had regaled the world with pictures and reports that sometimes made you wonder if there was such a thing as secrecy, but that is one of the penalties of modern technology. Gone are the times when the only way a general could communicate with his commanders was by messenger on foot or horse back, or the civilian population came to hear the outcome of a battle only weeks, months or even years after it had taken place. With satellite communication it is now possible to relay events to any corner of the world as they happen. There are advantages and disadvantages in this. The people of the world are kept better informed and this may go some way to act as a restraint on the combatants, however, the constant bombardment of tragedy and war that makes up so much of our newspaper, radio and, especially, TV reports tend to trivialise the events and make us immune to their horror.

Prompt reporting can also have disastrous results on the armies taking part as the commanders in the Falklands campaign discovered to their cost. Time and again, British troop movements were reported before their objectives had been achieved. To the Argentinians this was better than having agents in the enemy camp. But in the Gulf the lesson seemed to have been learnt and for twenty four hours all the news networks had to broadcast was library footage and speculation.

Another sign that the ground war had started was the succession of red sunsets. The movement of large numbers of tanks and other assorted vehicles stirred up the dust of the desert over a vast area and the very fine particles were carried aloft by the wind. As Oscar was positioned to the Southeast of the battle zone the setting sun, viewed through all the haze, appeared as an enormous red ball. Each dust particle in the air diffracts the light from the sun just a little bit and the combined effects of millions of particles is sufficient not only to make it appear red but also to form a 'Fresnel' lens effect and thus magnify it. For a good half an hour each evening the setting sun could be observed with the naked eye and numerous sun spots seen quite clearly.

Coincidental with the start of the ground war, another humorous piece of prose, Murphy's Laws of Combat Operations, found its way along the grapevine. In true Murphy tradition it proved to be uncannily accurate.

1. If you are short of everything except enemy, you are in a Combat Zone.

2. If your attack is going really well, it's an ambush.

3. If the enemy is in range, so are you.

4. If it's stupid but works, it is not stupid.

5. Incoming fire has a right of way.

6. Don't look conspicuous ... it draws fire.

7. When in doubt, empty the magazine.

8. The easy route is always mined.

9. Professionals are predictable. Amateurs are dangerous.

10. No combat ready unit ever passed inspection.

11. The diversion you are ignoring will turn out to be the main attack.

12. Never draw fire ... it irritates everyone else around you.

13. A large element of warfare is based on deception. Fool the enemy, not yourself.

14. Make it impossible for the enemy to get in and you won't be able to get out.

15.Never share a trench with anyone braver than yourself.

16.Despite what your commander may think, you are not Superman.

17.No battle plan survives contact with the enemy.

18.Communications will always fail the moment you need support.

19.Your personal weapon was made by the apprentice.

20.Recoil-less rifles ... aren't.

21.Suppressive fire ... isn't.

22.Automatic weapons ... aren't.

23.There is only one thing more accurate than incoming enemy fire ... incoming friendly fire!

24.If you are forward of your position your artillery will always drop short.

The last two items were unfortunately prophetic. The Coalition air attacks had been so devastating on the morale of the Iraqis that in the early stages the ground forces encountered no more than token resistance. Consequently, they raced forward unopposed often far ahead of schedule. In one instance this was to have deadly results. An American air patrol, seeing armour heading northwards in an area far forward of any expected Coalition Forces, assumed it to be retreating Iraqi troops and attacked accordingly. By the time they realised their mistake it was too late; nine British soldiers were killed and eleven injured. I believe it was a genuine accident and, although subsequently the blame was apportioned to the attacking aircrew, it seems to me that, if looked at dispassionately, it was the inevitable result of an over successful campaign.

The start of the ground war proper heralded the end of the SF involvement. Now that conventional tactics were being employed the unconventional and clandestine exploits of the SFs were no longer appropriate. Two SAS squadrons were withdrawn back to Oscar leaving just one, D Sqn, and the Chinooks at Charlie. True these troops were given jobs to do but they were more of an administrative nature than is usually associated with SFs. Several of the Chinook crews made it to Kuwait amidst the black smoke from the burning oil wells and other devastation that Saddam's retreating army had wrought. One pilot likened it to the description of Mordor from Tolkein's Lord of the Rings, but at Oscar there was a general feeling of 'we've done our bit, now send us home'.

A sign that everything was going better than expected was the arrival of a signal on the 27th of February outlining a programme for the withdrawal and repatriation of the SF units starting six days later! We could hardly believe it, and it never happened, but it galvanised us into action and we embarked upon a 'practice pack'. There was a general foraging for cardboard boxes and other suitable containers, and items which we hoped were of no further use were packed up 'in anticipation'.

'The End of the War is Nigh'

By 0800hrs on the 28th of February, almost exactly 100 hours after the start of the ground war, it was over. In the face of overwhelming odds the Iraqi government acceded to UN Resolution No 660. It is likely that this sudden capitulation was brought about, not by the liberation of Kuwait itself, but by the annihilation of those sections of the army making its disordered retreat up the Northern highway. Carrying all the loot and plunder they could they ran into the Coalition's surprise, its two left hooks, and were then finished off from the air. The size of the Iraqi defeat may be judged by the numbers of casualties. The Coalition suffered 223 dead and 697 wounded; the Iraqis, 9000 and 17000 respectively. In addition somewhere in the region of 90,000 Iraqi prisoners were taken of whom over 14,000 refused subsequent repatriation. However, over 100,000 avoided the Coalition net, escaping up the Euphrates valley, and Saddam Hussein remained at large.

The BBC World Service informed the world of the end of the war in its matter of fact way and, for me, it triggered an unexpected feeling. Although I had not been at the forefront of the conflict I suddenly felt that I was no longer at risk; all the tension, which I had not consciously been aware of, was suddenly released. When you are attached to the SF, if even very loosely, you never quite know what is waiting for you around the next corner and this inevitably plays upon your mind. It was like the conclusion of a daring stunt at the circus where you suddenly realise that you have been holding your breath. That feeling still returns whenever I hear the tune Lillibularo and I am sure it will haunt my dreams.

Apparently, the Voice of America commissioned a survey to discover which of all the international radio broadcasting services, including itself, was thought to have given the most truthful account of news items and least likely to broadcast propaganda. The BBC World Service won hands down. When asked why this was so, an Asian listener replied, "Any radio station that takes the trouble to broadcast the names of the winners of the Chelsea Flower Show to the whole world is hardly likely to lie about anything."

This general feeling of release pervaded the whole of Oscar. There were no great celebrations, no air of euphoria, just a sudden awareness that it was all over. After dinner someone produced a bottle of port and those who assembled in the Ops room partook of a measure. I must admit that port loses something when drunk from a red melamine mug, but not much. I consumed my second sugar mouse, a pink one, and wondered how long it would be before we got the order to return home and I could eat the last one.

Already Oscar appeared in a different light. For the past few months it had become 'home'. It was the place where you existed and where you took your being. Your wife, family and all that was back in the UK had become figments of the imagination because they were unobtainable. Now, all of a sudden and almost unexpectedly, they were back within your grasp and Oscar took on the guise of an impediment, like being stranded in an airport in the middle of a journey. But in our hearts we knew that it was not going to be as easy as catching the next 'plane. We were still subject to military discipline and would have to wait, who knew how long, until the powers that be saw fit to release us.

9 - GOING HOME 28 Feb / 27 Mar '91

The news of the Iraqi surrender was not 4 hours old when an Army Air Corps helicopter pilot, Dave Kirby serving with the SAS as a parachute jump instructor, came into the office.

"I've brought the free fall tandem rig with me." he said, "If I can organise an aeroplane, would anyone like to jump?"

Very early in my military career I had chickened out of a ride in an F-104 Starfighter and have regretted it ever since. Subsequently, I have accepted all such offers on the basis that they may never come my way again. "Yes," I said, "I'll have a go." Everyone else in the office chose that moment to disappear.

"OK," he said, "I'll let you know when I've set it up." and left. I promptly forgot about the offer.

Two more visitors in the shape of photo-copier service engineers turned up and said that regular servicing was part of the deal for the copiers we had bought. I had seen no reference to this in any of the paper work I had inherited and wanted to know how much it would cost. "This service is free." one of them said, "Because you have thrown out Saddam Hussein, and please may I have your autograph." This request rather took me by surprise. I had never been asked for my autograph before, and have not subsequently. It suddenly occurred to me the profound effect Saddam's invasion of Kuwait and the threat of further expansionist exploits had had on the local people. Let us not kid ourselves, the nations of the West were not embroiled in this campaign for any altruistic purpose. They were up to their necks in sand in order to secure the continued supply of oil for the peace and stability of their own economies. The Saudis have been well aware of this fact for a long time and it is for that reason that they have never signed peace treaties and allowed foreign troops to be stationed in the Kingdom. The philosophy has always been this: "If Saudi Arabia is in trouble and that trouble threatens the oil, then the West will give aid. If it does not, they will probably not come. In that situation what use is a treaty. It will only serve as an embarrassment." And they are correct.

Almost as soon as the cease-fire was announced it started to rain and it continued to rain on and off for a week. It gave one the feeling of being on a miserable summer holiday from which you cannot wait to get home. It was a very odd coincidence, but I happened to open one of the BFPO 3000 letters from a someone who had only signed the letter with an initial and surname and therefore gave no hint as to sex or status. The contents of the letter, however, made it very clear that the writer had been in a very similar situation as it said, "Now comes the hardest part of all, the waiting to go home. It will test your patience to the extreme." It proved to be prophetic but, in a way, provided some comfort because it made me realise that we were not the first to experience this situation.

For the SF, the next few days were a period of much confusion. To the local commanders, the commencement of the ground war by conventional forces had signalled an end of SF involvement and therefore they started to initiate their own plans for withdrawal. This, however, did not coincide with the view of those at HQ. We at Oscar could see no earthly reason why one SAS squadron, and therefore the Chinook and Herc support, had to be retained at Charlie. It was mooted that perhaps they were staying to cover the peace negotiations. However, the talks, scheduled for the 3rd of March, were to be held a Safwan, a small air strip just to the north of Kuwait in Iraq itself a long way from Charlie and outside their effective range.

Going Home

Then came the announcement that Norman Schwartzkopf wished to say a personal thank you to all the members of the SF who had taken part in the campaign. He intended to grace them with his presence on the morning of the 4th and that as many as possible were to assemble at Arar, a remote airfield near the Saudi/Iraq 80 miles North of Charlie. This meant the transportation of more than a few people back from Oscar and delayed the repatriation plan by several days. In the end, Stormin' Norman cancelled his visit but insisted that the SF should be properly thanked. They were, therefore, to re-assemble at Oscar on the 7th when the DDSF (Deputy Director of Special Forces) would speak to them. The assembled masses made their weary way back to Oscar only to learn that someone in Whitehall had suddenly become aware of the plan for an unseemly rush back to Blighty and ordered A Sqn back to Charlie, "just in case!" As a result, when DDSF arrived more than half the SF were not present and those that were, were in a less than receptive mood. To add to the misery, his address was not particularly inspiring. I got the distinct impression that this visit was a chore and his "Thank you", "well done" and "we can all learn from the experience" rather forced.

It turned out that there may have been some purpose in A Sqn's recall to Charlie as on the 6th, John Major, the British Prime Minister, paid a visit and was taken to Kuwait to see things for himself. I know that security is of paramount importance but there are times when the men 'need to know' something and just a hint of purpose to the seeming mayhem would have done a great deal for the maintenance of morale at this time. It is a fact, often forgotten by commanders, that if you insist on treating the troops as unthinking automatons then you should not be surprised when they unthinkingly get grumpy or rebel.

After DDSF's visit the plan changed again and all the SF personnel were once more recalled to Oscar. The first Herc load, which comprised a mixed bag of SAS and aircrew, arrived at about 2200 hrs on the night of the 7th but, although I had resurrected my tour operators hat and prepared to receive the returning troops as best I could, accommodation was very tight and none too palatial. The mood of the Chinook guys was such that Squadron Leader Fields, their flight commander who had returned with them, declared that next day they would decamp to a hotel down town. And so they did. The remaining members of the squadron returned 24 hours later. It was dark when they arrived and, standing out on the pan directing them to the waiting minibuses, it was often difficult to see exactly who was who. In the midst of this organised chaos an airman came up to me and said, "I understand you like a gin and tonic, sir".

"Yes." I said, rather taken off my guard.

He thrust two water bottles in my hand. "Have this drink on us." he said, "For all your help." He then disappeared into the darkness and to this day I am not absolutely sure who it was. I opened the water bottles. One was full of gin, the other full of tonic, still fizzy. Where it had come from I could not imagine but that gesture of thanks did a great deal to restore my faith in mankind.

Wing Commander Irwin was not particularly pleased to learn that the first contingent had gone off to the flesh pots of Abu Dhabi without his blessing but, as I pointed out, there was little I could do about it and at least it had relieved the overcrowding problem. By the next morning he too had had a change of heart and by the middle of the day almost the entire Chinook squadron was billeted in the luxury of Abu Dhabi's Gulf Hotel.

For the time being I remained at Oscar and started winding up our tenancy in the vain hope that we would not be remaining for much longer. I managed to contact Doug Steers, an ex-pat who had set himself up in the plant hire business at the beginning of the war and from whom most of the plant and portacabins had been acquired upon our arrival, and opened negotiations for disposal of the same. He was only too pleased buy them back but, by the time we had paid for cranes and transport, there was little surplus cash. However, in the end, it probably cost us no more than if we had rented in the first place. Nevertheless, I was still uncertain how the accountants back in the UK would view the transactions.

On Monday 11th we received good news and bad news. The good news was that the main body of the SF would leave for home on or about the 13th. The bad news was that one sqn of SAS would remain to cover the signing of the peace treaty which, it was estimated, would not take place before the 1st of April at the earliest. They would obviously require helicopter support and a skeleton crew had to remain. As I was tasked to switch off the lights and shut the door after their departure it meant that my sojourn was also extended. Gloom and despair descended upon me and I decided to join the others down at the Gulf for a few day's R&R. I arrived just in time for a beach Bar-B-Que and disco which certainly lifted my spirits for a few hours.

Next day, after a leisurely breakfast, I had to drive back up to Oscar to pick up some imprest paper work that I had omitted to take to the hotel. I was rootling about in my desk when a voice said,

"I've got the 'plane. Are you coming to jump?"

I looked up and there stood Dave Kirby. As I was too shocked to respond he repeated the question. I had completely forgotten about the rash promise I had made a few days earlier but from somewhere I plucked up my courage and said, "Yes."

"Right." he said, "Be down on the pan at 2 o'clock and we'll brief."

2 o'clock seemed to rush towards me like an express train. I had never made a parachute jump before, static line or free fall, and here I was about to do my first with the SAS. I hoped they would be gentle with me. I found Dave and another guy, whose face was vaguely familiar but whose name I knew not, surrounded by all manner of webbing and harness and what looked like brightly coloured, rolled up sleeping bags. "Those are the 'chutes." said Dave. "They're OK. I packed them myself." It was obvious that for the next hour or so I was going to have to trust this guy implicitly and it is an odd feeling when you realise that you have suddenly let go the rudder of your own destiny.

Dave explained that we each wore a separate harness but that they were both attached to the same, two man, parachute. For the free fall part of the drop we would be strapped securely to each other but once the canopy was opened he would separate us so that we would arrive on the ground as two people and not a tightly tied parcel. We had two 'chutes. The main one, attached to Dave's back, was a large, square (oblong actually), steerable canopy of a type similar to those you see the parachute display teams use. The second 'chute was also square but much smaller. This was attached to my front and was our reserve should the main one fail to open. "We will still hit the ground quite hard," Dave said, "Because it is only about half the size of the main one but it should prevent us from ending up resembling strawberry jam. If that fails, Pete here," and he pointed to the third member of the party, "Will clip himself to us and we will all descend on his 'chute. That will be a heavy landing." he added. Pete grinned and continued checking his rig.

"One further point." Dave continued. "When we actually leave the 'plane we will do it sideways." I looked at him quizzically. "Over the years I've tried various ways of trying to get people to jump out of aeroplanes." he said. "I've tried pushing them out and pulling them out but neither method is particularly satisfactory. If you give them too much time to think about it they chicken out." I could well believe him. "The best method I've found so far is to stand sideways on the edge of the ramp. When we get the OK to go I grip your shoulders, swing you inboard and then out, and you can't stop. You also generally end up heading in the right direction, face down and away from the aircraft." It all sounded very plausible to me so I nodded and laughed nervously. "Finally." Dave said, "When we've had enough, I'll pull the rip cord and deploy our 'chute. It is, in effect, a wing, an aerofoil shape that is inflated by our downward and forward motion and is fully steerable. To steer it you collapse one side or the other by means of control lines. The collapsed side produces less lift than the other and you turn in the direction of the collapse. Release the control line, the wing section re-inflates and you're back to straight and level again. Once it's deployed we'll have a go at flying it back

162

and forth and aiming it at the landing site, which is where we are standing now. About 50ft above the ground we'll turn it into wind and at about 2ft I will shout '3-2-1' and we both pull hard on the control lines at the back. This should arrest our descent and we should just step onto terra firma. OK? Any questions?"

"Just one." I said. "What height are we going to jump from?"

"Well." replied Dave. "It's an ideal day. Slight wind and no cloud whatsoever. Officially you are not supposed to jump above 8,000ft without oxygen, 10,000ft absolute maximum. We'll see what the pilot will give us."

The briefing complete, we each donned a one piece flying suit and canvass and leather helmet and put on our parachute harnesses. At each stage we checked each other's belts and buckles to make sure that we had done nothing incorrectly. The Herc, XV179 piloted by Flt Lt Alan Tribe, had already started and now taxied to where we were standing. We entered via the ramp into a hold, empty save for the Loadmaster. The aircraft taxied out, took off down the runway and then started a spiral climb to our jump height. We spent the time clipping ourselves to the main and reserve 'chutes and then to each other. We ended up with me at the front and Dave strapped tightly to my back. The only way we could walk was in strict unison, rather like a scene out of a Laurel and Hardy film. It seemed like no time at all when the Loadmaster gave us the 'thumbs up'. He shouted that the pilot had levelled out at 12,000ft! and was making his approach to the DZ (drop zone). Dave and I made our crab like way to the edge of the ramp and waited for the green light. I looked out and could see the pink earth far below. The runway appeared to be the length of a foot ruler and the buildings like well ordered match boxes. The red light came on and Dave grabbed my shoulders. Seconds later it was followed by the green. We swayed in towards the dark of the aircraft hold and then out into the blue of the sky and the golden sun, and were gone.

As we fell we turned one complete somersault. I caught a glimpse of the Herc disappearing over my left shoulder and I thought, "What am I doing here?". Then the earth came back into view and stayed there. Dave had obviously stabilised us by waving his arms and legs in the appropriate manner because I had done nothing. However, remembering his brief, I spread-eagled my arms and legs to help stabilise our position. The next thing I remember was Pete, floating into view just in front of us, still grinning. Falling through the air is something that you have to experience to really appreciate. At 12,000ft, apart from the rush of wind in your face, there is no sense of falling. The earth is too far away and its aspect does not appear to change, in fact it was only much later when we were under the canopy and at about 1500ft that there was any perception of descent. A body, free falling in the air reaches a terminal velocity

of about 120 mph and once you have achieved this you can direct the air flow
with your arms and legs and manoeuvre your position. It must be the closest
to natural flight that human beings ever achieve. We fell and flew and flew and
fell, slowly turning this way and that to view the world in all directions. I had
expected the experience to be over quickly but, on the contrary, it seemed to
go on for ever. Eventually there was a loud flapping, cracking noise, a sudden
jerk and Pete, who had been flying in formation, suddenly accelerated away
from us. We appeared to have come to an abrupt halt and looking up I saw this
bright red and blue roof over our heads. Our 'chute had opened. Dave had
pulled the rip cord at 4,000ft. We had fallen 8,000ft, that is just over 1.5 miles!
It had taken 45 seconds. No wonder it had seemed like forever. As soon as
Pete was happy that our canopy had deployed properly he too pulled his rip
chord and arrested his earthward plunge. Our descent was now much more
sedate and we drifted down at a mere 25mph. Dave released the straps which
had bound us securely to each other and, now that the noise of the rushing air
had subsided, described how to steer the parachute by pulling on the rigging
lines and partially collapsing one side of the wing aerofoil or the other.

A Soft Landing

We could see the DZ below and manoeuvred down wind. The ground now started rushing towards us and, with about 50ft to go, we turned into wind to make our approach to the landing point. I already had my hands on our 'brakes' and before Dave could finish saying "3-2-1-pull" had yanked on the two control lines. We came to a dead stop, both vertically and horizontally, about 18 inches above the ground and then started to drift very slowly backwards. By the time we touched the ground we were travelling at no more than walking pace but we were unable to keep our feet and I regret to say that I ended up sitting rather unceremoniously and heavily on my instructor. Pete, who had already landed and taken off his parachute harness, ran over and collapsed our billowing canopy to prevent it from dragging us across the sand. We stood up and unbuckled our own harnesses. It is hard to describe what I felt, euphoric comes to mind but it is hardly adequate. I spent the rest of the day on cloud nine and it still gives me a thrill to relive the experience. All I can say is that if you ever get the opportunity to do something similar, grab it with both hands. That evening I broke the rules and 'phoned home to recount my exploits I just had to tell someone.

The 13th of March dawned bright and clear. For the majority of our party this was the day they had been waiting for for nearly five months, their return home. Just before tea time two coaches arrived at the Gulf Hotel and were packed with men and kit in very short order. Unlike typical coach trips, no one was late. For those of us remaining it was a bittersweet moment. At least it heralded the end of our sojourn but we still had no definite departure date and the atmosphere at dinner was very subdued. The next day an air of resignation established itself and despite the luxurious surroundings of the hotel all we did was mooch about, even drinking beer became a chore. I finally managed to get the imprest to resemble an acceptable statement of accounts and this took my mind off our forced exile for a little while.

By late afternoon a group of us had foregathered in the bar for yet another beer. It was mutually agreed that we needed some sort of a lift and someone suggested a trip to the gold souk to spend some of our ill gotten gains. Trading gold in Arabia is an every day activity as it is still looked on as a tangible form of security. Paper money is all very well and a bank account is safe but gold is universally convertible and besides which you can flaunt it. All gold is traded by weight, even the jewellery. You select the object of your desire, the vendor weighs it and then quotes you a price. The price asked is a combination of the cost of the raw gold, the workmanship involved and the vendors mark up. The price of the gold content is based on the current price, not the price of it when the article was made. You very soon learn that in order to get a reasonable bargain it is also necessary for you to be aware of the current price of gold on the international market. Further, you also need to be sure of the gold content of the item you are trying to buy. Purity is measured in carats and pure gold is defined as 24 carats, it is, however, very soft and is impractical for use in jewellery. All jewellery is alloyed with a base metal, usually copper or silver, to make it hard wearing but when calculating the material price of a piece of jewellery the cost of the base metal is insignificant and therefore ignored. In the UK the assaying of the gold content is strictly governed and the ubiquitous 'hall mark' is a guarantee of its fineness. The most usual degrees of fineness for jewellery are 9, 18 and 22 carats, that is 9, 18 and 22 twenty-fourths or 37.5%, 75% or 91.6% of pure gold but in the Middle East this is not always the case and some strange degrees of fineness are to be found. Not that I found any blatant attempts to defraud. That comes under the heading of theft which is abjured by the Koran and for which the penalties are severe. However, if the buyer is too naive be aware of the system then that is his problem, particularly if he is an infidel!

The gold souk is just one part of the local market. It has its shops and stalls and is no different to those selling clothes or vegetables. It is, nevertheless, an amazing sight to see so much gold and with so little obvious security. We wandered with the rest of the crowd just trying to comprehend the vast amount of wealth that was on display but it soon became obvious that what was on show was almost invariably 9 carat, of inferior workmanship and therefore 'cheap'. However, if you did your sums of weight, fineness etc. you found that the prices asked were extortionate, the vendors mark up was obviously considerable. All enquiries as to the price of an item followed the same routine. We would be immediately quoted a price. Without even considering it, our response was, "We are British, so don't ask us American prices." This would halve the asking price. Requesting the object's weight and the production of a pocket calculator would elicit a similar price reduction. We now had an idea of its true cost and the ensuing haggle was only over the quality of workmanship and the dealer's profit. However, to make a true comparison with UK prices it was necessary to add 17.5% for VAT! Even so the odd bargain was struck.

Upon our return to the hotel we found a most unexpected message waiting for us. The next day, a Friday (15th), being the Muslim holy day a fete was to be held in the grounds of the British Embassy and we were invited to attend.

Friday started badly with an announcement by US President George Bush that Iraq's continued use of helicopter gunships in its northern states against the Kurdish population would place obstacles in the way of the peace plan. Any delay automatically meant our prolonged stay. Nevertheless, by lunch time the prospect of the fete had somewhat mollified us and at about one o'clock we duly trouped down to the Embassy.

The British Embassy stood in some quite considerable grounds surrounded by a high wall. The production of our 1250's at the gate ensured our admittance into what can only be described as a time warp. It was just like stepping onto a village green in the heart of rural England just after WWII. There were cake stalls, beer tents, bowling for a pig (though I am not sure how they had squared that with the local authorities) and even a Punch and Judy show. Everywhere was decked out in red, white and blue bunting and a brass band played suitably 'British' music from a makeshift bandstand in one corner of the enormous garden. It was peopled mainly by ex-pats who lived and worked in Abu Dhabi, many of whom were suitably dressed in slacks and white shirts with club ties or summery dresses that were the height of fashion in the UK 30 years earlier. I am still not sure if it was fancy dress or a bit of the old empire refusing to lie down and die. For the locals it was an undeniably jolly event but for me and several others of our party it only emphasised our enforced exile and made the longing to return home even stronger.

With the imminent approach of Ramadan, the Muslim holy month of fasting and abstinence, it was decided to decamp to the International Hotel in Dubai. Whilst Abu Dhabi is not what you would call zealous in its prosecution of the religious laws detailed in the Koran, it does insist on banning the sale of alcohol, even from private hotel bars, for the whole month. Dubai, on the other hand, is rather more liberal, and discrete consumption of the odd beer is tolerated.

According to my diary, the start of Ramadan and St Patrick's day co-incided. Is this a portent? The start of Ramadan is regulated by the clear sighting of the new moon and in 1991 there was some debate as to when this occurred. Some authorities said it happened on the 17th others, that it had not happened until the 18th. If this is not Pagan then I don't know what is. But we as Christians are no better as we use similar lunar criteria to fix Easter. My faith has always been shaky; this does nothing to help it!

'Another week lumbers slowly along. We fill it with eating, drinking, sleeping and waiting. We have received a movement schedule dated 24th March with our names on it but as yet there is no sign of our being released.'

By this time most of the vehicles, rented from Avis, had been returned, more or less as received. We explained that a small detachment were remaining for the foreseeable future and hinted that, as we had been such good customers, they might see their way to upgrading our remaining transport. They said they would see what they could do and next day fronted up with a Rolls Royce. This has to be taken into context. We were living in a land of extreme oil wealth where Rollers are not exactly rare and even the humble 4X4 (four wheel drive) 'jeeps' took on luxurious forms. The most exotic that I saw was a bright red Maserati with a price tag of about £160,000. 4X4's have become a way of life with the Arabs. Many of the desert dwellers no longer embrace the nomadic life, following their herds of goats and camels from one area of pasture to the next, but have taken to staying put in one location and using the 4X4 to fetch the fodder to the animals. Unfortunately within a day the Rolls Royce developed gearbox trouble. It was replaced with a large and very luxurious Mercedes but it was not quite the same.

Each day there was rumour of a decision regarding our departure and each day it came to nothing. The 24th was approaching with unseemly haste and with it the prospect of having to cancel the scheduled aircraft. On the evening of the 21st we were informed that there would be a definite ruling on our immediate future by mid-day the next day. It did not sound very promising and gloom descended upon us once again. The next morning was, as usual, sunny and hot. By mid-morning, after a late breakfast, all the company had assembled by the hotel swimming pool to await the news. At about 1130 the squadron leader appeared clutching a piece of paper. He did not have to say anything, the look on his face spoke volumes. We had been released; the order to go home received!

The immediate reaction was for everyone to jump off the high board and 'dive bomb' into the pool, causing the other residents a certain amount of consternation, and swim to the poolside bar for a celebration. The sense of relief was overwhelming. We went around, shaking each other's hands and trying to reassure ourselves that it was true. After a spirited lunch, I retired to my room and ceremoniously ate my third and final sugar mouse and then sat down and mapped out my own escape plan. As you will remember, it was my task to be the last one to leave, to make sure all the bills were paid and that we left nothing behind but our good will and thanks. The evening was spent in quiet euphoria, eight of us went down town and found a small curry house in the back streets of Dubai where the locals ate. The whole meal, and it was enormous, cost less than a dinner for one back at the hotel.

By 0930 on the 24th we had said our goodbyes to the International Hotel, settled the bill, something else that I hoped would not be too difficult to explain when I handed in the imprest, and boarded a fleet of mini-buses bound, for the last time, for Oscar. At mid-day a VC10 arrived and, in almost less time than it takes to tell, turned round and departed with the main party, bound for the UK. Only half a dozen or so of the Chinook detachment now remained but as soon as they had finished loading equipment and tri-walls onto a Herc they too disappeared with a faint trail of engine exhaust into the setting sun.

I now had to set about making my own way home. If it was humanly possible I wanted to be back in the UK by the 27th, the date of Jonathan's (my eldest son) girlfriend's 21st birthday. Also it would be Jonathan's 21st birthday on the 2nd of April. The official arrangements for my repatriation were obscure to say the least. My name did not appear on any of John the Mover's lists and there were no more aircraft scheduled into Oscar. There was still a small contingent of SAS remaining at the base but they were staying on to 'set up a training scheme for the local security forces'. Even John the Mover was decamping to Dubai. There had been vague rumours of a seat on a Herc out of Bahrain but that was nearly 300 miles away and I did not relish the thought of 17 hours in all that noise on a canvas seat especially as an old back injury, the result of spending too many hours hunched in the doorway of a Puma helicopter cabin (height 4ft 8ins!), had started to play up and was, at times, causing me considerable pain. Not only that, but rumours had drifted back that the Customs/Military Police at RAF Brize Norton and Lyneham were making thorough checks of all personnel and luggage returning from the Gulf in case any one tried to smuggle in an Iraqi tank or other similar undesirable item. The flight was bound to arrive in the early hours of a cold and damp morning and the thought of several more hours spent waiting whilst 100 squaddies argued the toss over whether a Kalashnikov was dangerous or not, or that the 14 kilos of gold hidden in the bottom of their hold-all was really a present for mum and therefore exempt from import tax, filled me with despair. I was, therefore, inclined to make my own arrangements.

I had already decided that, although I still had one or two things to wrap up at Oscar, I too would ship out of Dubai and return to Abu Dhabi for the remainder of my stay and take up temporary residence at the Sheraton Hotel. It was situated close to a British Airways office, my first port of call upon arrival.

"I am a war veteran. Take me home." I announced to the bemused girl behind the desk.

"All flights are suspended." she said. "We do not envisage starting up again until the end of April."

So much for BA. Next door was the local travel agent. "No trouble sir." said the very helpful man. "There is an Air Lanka (Srilankan Airways) flight leaving at 0730 on the 27th and arriving Heathrow at about 1600".

"How much?"

"Three thousand eight hundred and thirty Dirhams," he said, "and ten Dirhams airport tax."

"I'll take it."

"There is one slight problem."

"Ye-es?"

"You must change flights at Schiphol in the Netherlands and continue with KLM to the UK. But it is all transferred and there will be no problems." He ended assuringly.

"If it goes via Timbuktu I'll still take it." I said.

"Oh no." he replied, "But it is diverted over Saudi Arabia and Egypt. Normally it would fly direct across Iraq. That is why it takes so long. It is the war you know?"

A Ticket Home

I said I knew and offered him my VISA card and Passport. The latter caused him some concern.

"You have no entry visa for the UAE." he said.

"No." I replied, and loosely explained the mode of my arrival.

"But you cannot leave," he said, "Unless you have arrived. I think it is a matter for your Ambassador. I cannot issue the ticket until your papers are in order. But I will make the reservation." he added. For which I gave him my thanks.

Now here was a fine mess. I was, in effect, an illegal immigrant. Back at the hotel I rang the embassy. To them it was not a problem. They had dealt with several such cases over the past few days. If I called in tomorrow they would sort it. Great! I had also arranged for the removal of the portacabins the next day at 1030. Again, no problem there would be someone at the embassy who could help me at 0730.

At 0730, on the dot, I presented myself at the embassy gates and was directed to the appropriate office. A very helpful gentleman told me that he had arranged for me to meet an officer of the UAE Immigration Department at 10 o'clock the next morning at Bateen airfield on the outskirts of the town where they would issue the necessary stamp for my passport. I was, however not to reveal the true purpose of my visit and say that I had arrived by military transport only a few days earlier. This all sounded a bit dubious to me, but he assured me that all would be well nevertheless, I was still rather apprehensive and my limited experience of Arab bureaucracy did nothing to allay my concern. He wasn't the one desperately trying to get away to a tight deadline.

I drove straight from the embassy to Oscar where, promptly at 1030 a large mobile crane and 10 articulated lorries presented themselves at the main gate of the camp. The guards were naturally suspicious as I had carefully forgotten to inform them of the arrival of this convoy, but after the obligatory cup of coffee and only a little hand waving they let them through. Within two hours the site was bare. The only evidence of our sojourn was the trampled sand around what had been our offices and accommodation and a few gusts of wind soon obliterate even that. It was as though we had never even been there; our passing all but forgotten.

As I prepared to leave Oscar for the last time I saw two soldiers loading what looked like rugs into a rubbish skip. I went to see what they were doing and found that they were throwing away the posteens (the woollen overcoats) that the SAS had worn for warmth and disguise out in the desert. Upon inquiry, I was informed that they were now surplus to requirement and if I wanted one to help myself. Despite their bulk, these were souvenirs not to be passed up. Most were in fact very dirty and in a rather sad state of repair but I managed to find two that were recognisable as coats and, after a good shake which removed the surface dust and goat droppings, threw them into the boot of the Merc.

Back in the hotel I suddenly realised that it was not only the posteens that were shabby, I was still wearing the same slacks, shirt and bush boots that I had so hurriedly packed 3 months earlier. Yes, they had been washed but they were not as smart as they could be. I desperately needed some new clothes, especially if I was to impress the UAE Immigration Department. The town was just beginning to wake up after the afternoon siesta and the shops were still almost empty so it did not take long to acquire my new ensemble. I bought two of the most gaudy floral design shirts in heavy Italian cotton, a pair of fawn/grey drain pipe Chino's and some grey silk socks. For shoes I chose green and brown 'yachting' shoes. Not my usual style at all but they were new, clean and I felt great in them. I was now ready for anything. But I had reckoned without the UAE Immigration Department.

I had been to Bateen airfield several times before and so knew my way. I even found the right office without too much trouble. It was the approach of the Immigration officers that threw me. Firstly they invited me into an office and offered me coffee. We then talked about the weather, the war and a host of other things for about half an hour. And then straight out of the blue came the questions, "How long have you been in our country? Where did you enter? Why did you not gain an entry stamp?" I managed to tell the lies I had arranged at the British Embassy but I am not sure I was wholly convincing. I thought the best tactic was to adopt a subservient attitude and apologised profusely pointing out that as part of the Coalition force and operating under military regulations it had not been possible to observe the usual civilian niceties. This seemed to work and my passport was stamped but I was dismissed with the injunction that I would not be allowed the privilege again.

I suppose it was all part of a face saving exercise on the part of the UAE authorities who felt that they had to be seen as retaining some modicum of control. But I did not care, I had the key to my escape and drove straight to the travel agents where my ticket was promptly issued. I had already settled the Avis account and had arranged to leave their Merc in the Airport carpark early the next morning. The only outstanding task was to close the bank account which I did with due ceremony and many thanks for their help and services to an unusual client.

I returned to the hotel to pack my bags. I had already despatched most of my military kit in the faithful tri-wall which had been loaded on the Herc and which, I hoped, would eventually catch up with me back in the UK. However, I still had a considerable amount of odds and ends and my hotel room looked rather like a rummage sale. It was obvious that I was not going to get it all into my rucksack, the two posteens alone more than filled it and I was forced down town once more to look for a suitcase. Again, the souk came up trumps and I managed to buy a large Samsonite Oyster suitcase for about half the UK price. This proved to be a veritable bottomless pit but even so I had to stand on it to get it shut.

I also took this opportunity to buy souvenirs for friends and relations back home. My immediate family had already been catered for with gold necklaces, earrings and brooches from the gold souk, but I felt that I ought to take a token for all those who had supported me with letters and 'red cross' parcels. I have always found difficulty in choosing this category of gift. You do not wish to spend a fortune but you do not want to buy tat. Usually you spend hours of fruitless search and still never find anything suitable. But today the gods must have been looking my way for inspiration struck. I would take home camels! The idea came when I happened upon a shop full of *objects d'art* which included boxes of small camels carved from bone; cheap and cheerful but apropos. Camels were the answer. The smokers of my acquaintance would get cigarettes similarly named.

I slept well that night but woke before the alarm clock went off. The reprieved man ate a hearty breakfast and loaded his cases into the boot of the Merc. I cannot remember what my airline baggage allowance was but I must have exceeded it by a considerable margin, I could hardly lift the Samsonite Oyster and was more than glad that the designers had seen fit to add wheels to it. If there was any argument I would just pay for excess.

The drive to the airport was uneventful but I almost forgot to leave the Merc key at the Avis desk. I had already passed through Emigration and it was only when I was emptying my pockets to go through the metal detector when I remembered it. Even though there appeared to be no other passengers, the security people were unwilling to let me back through the gate in order to return it. It would probably have meant another immigration stamp in my passport. Eventually, with a suitable amount of 'baksheesh' I managed to persuade one of the baggage handlers to return it for me. However, my problems were still not over. As I passed through the metal detector and body search I was met by an official who was holding my small hold-all and had a very dour expression on his face.

"Why are you carrying a gun?" he asked.

I have to admit that I was genuinely surprised at this question. I had relinquished my SA-80 when the cease fire was announced and apart from a couple of empty A-10 gatling gun shell cases as souvenirs I had no weapons at all. I had even remembered to put my Swiss Army pen knife in my case. "What gun?" I asked incredulously.

"The X-ray shows that you have a gun in this bag." he said. "Open it please."

I suddenly remembered what it was. In the unseemly rush to leave Oscar the movers had left a packing case strapping applicator in the hangar and on my final sweep round I had found it and thrown it into my bag. Packing cases used to be secured with steel banding but it has been largely replaced with a nylon/plastic substitute. This has several advantages. It is lighter, costs less and does not sever your hands when you try to remove it. It is also easy to apply. You simply take the strapping from the supply reel, pass it through the fixing applicator, wrap it around the case and feed the end back into the applicator. This applicator is multi-purpose and with one pull of its trigger tightens, joins and cuts the strapping to length all in one action. Unfortunately for me the applicator design resembles that of a pistol.

I cheerfully produced it from my hold-all but as I did so I noticed the security guard take half a step backward and start to fumble with his pistol holster. I reversed it and handed it to him butt first, explaining what it was. He did not seem to understand. Fortunately there was a strapped case standing on the adjacent baggage conveyor and I employed it as an impromptu aid to my presentation. After prolonged examination he finally acknowledged that there was nowhere to insert ammunition and that it was not a firearm, but he would not return it. At this point I volunteered to surrender it and leave the country without it but that only seemed to make things worse. He could not take responsibility for it, it must go with me. Eventually it was agreed that, with the addition of a large yellow and black security label and the aircraft captain's permission, it could accompany me in the secure part of the aircraft hold. I'm not quite sure what he thought I was going to do with it. Perhaps he envisaged me hijacking the aircraft and binding all the crew to their seats. In reality, I think it was yet another case of face saving. Having confronted me with, what was after all, a genuine query, he was unable to admit his mistake and just pass the incident off. It had to be played to the end with him being seen to have maintained face in the presence of an infidel. For me, it exposed another facet of the Arab psyche, and provided twenty minutes entertainment.

The aircraft was on time and we left without further incident. Only about half full, most of the passengers having boarded at previous locations, I was pleased to be able to stretch out as my back was now really painful, probably as a result of wrestling with my case. Sitting confined in one seat for the next six hours would have been a trial indeed. I could have done with a gin, but the aircraft, originating from Muslim sources was dry. Nevertheless, the coffee was hot and strong, the stewardesses much prettier than the average Herc loadmaster and at last I was on my way home!

10 - BACK IN THE OLD ROUTINE - 27th MAR .....

Despite the detour around Iraq and Turkey, the aircraft taking me home arrived at Schipol Airport on time. In the same way that leaving Western culture and setting foot in the Middle East had been a shock to the system so was returning to the European way of life. I had got used to the sunshine, the sand and the smells. I had obviously also got used to the bureaucracy because it quite took me by surprise when the immigration official just waved me through passport control without even a second look. With that hurdle cleared, my next concern was my luggage. Having stood at the baggage carousel until everyone else had gone it suddenly dawned on me that I was in the hands of civilians and that I was not expected to hump my own kit from one aircraft to another. I was back in the real world where a transfer flight was just what it said it was. Nevertheless, I checked with the ground staff just to make sure that my luggage had been directed to the Heathrow flight. One thing that was not mentioned was the packing case strapping 'gun' and I thought it prudent not to stir up the mud in that particular pool. If it followed me, all well and good. If not, so what?

Having located my departure gate I found that I had about 40 minutes to kill. I felt I needed a beer so I made my way to the lounge bar. Despite the notice which, although in Dutch seemed to indicate that foreign currencies were accepted, the barman greeted my proffered Dirhams with a sceptical shake of the head. He explained, in almost perfect English, that, because of the Gulf War, European banks had suspended trading Middle Eastern currencies and therefore he could not tell me what the exchange rate was or even pay the note into the bank should we come to some mutually acceptable figure. I told him that I had just escaped from that particular conflict but, whilst he seemed impressed he still declined to take my cash. I wondered how many other people returning from the Gulf had been similarly caught out. The banks in the Middle East had been only too eager to take pounds and dollars but nowhere had I seen or been told that I would have a problem changing the money back again on my return. What had happened to all the Arabs who had decided to leave their homes and take a short holiday in the West until the mess had been cleaned up? Whatever the answer it did not help me. I was faced with the classic dilemma. I had ordered a beer with the honest conviction that I could pay for it. The beer stood golden and foaming in the glass in front of me but I now discovered that I lacked the means. It was impossible to say "I don't want it after all. Put it back in the bottle." and clearly the accounts had to be balanced.

I was rescued by a fellow traveller, a German I think, who offered to buy the drink for me. I thanked him graciously and gave him a five Dirham note.

He tried to refuse it but I insisted that he keep it, as a souvenir, if nothing else. On reflection, I realised the note was only worth about 65 pence so both our honours were left more or less intact. I had not had a beer for several days, because of the particular way in which the inhabitants of Abu Dhabi interpret Ramadan, and this one went down extremely well. There was, however, no time for a second beer even if I could have found another mug to buy me one. No sooner had I consumed it, than the departure of my flight was announced. I picked up my hand baggage, made my way to the gate and boarded a KLM Boeing 737.

The flight to Heathrow took all of 40 minutes, hardly enough time to climb to cruising height let alone break out the duty free. In no time at all we were back on the ground and I had returned home. My bags having been loaded first, because I was a transfer passenger, inevitably appeared almost last on the carousel. However, even though I waited for all of 30 seconds after retrieving my luggage the 'gun' did not appear so I left. It is probably still bumping round a carousel somewhere, probably Cairo.

I decided to go through the RED customs channel. Not because I had vast quantities of contraband that I felt I ought to declare but because of the large sums of foreign cash I had about my person. I have always found the Customs men amicable if you don't try to put one over on them. In fact they often seem totally uninterested if you voluntarily dump vast piles of service equipment on their desk. From the questions he asked, my Customs man seemed more interested in my past exploits rather than in any contraband that I might be trying to sneak in. He waved the not inconsiderable quantity of gold jewellery through as gifts, which they were, but felt compelled to charge me import duty on my SONY radio which left the honours about even. I did not feel too aggrieved; the radio had still cost me less than the UK price and all my presents had come in free. We parted friends and I emerged into the airport arrivals concourse.

I was greeted by a great shout and there to meet me were my wife and two sons, those who had bid me a subdued farewell some 75 days previously. Was that really all it was? 10 weeks and 5 days - 2½ months! It had seemed like forever. The reunion was perhaps even more tearful than the departure. Janet's opening comment was "God! You look starved." In truth I had lost just over a stone in weight and, with my close cropped hair, I have to admit I did look a bit gaunt. Jonathan and Matthew gave me a great hug and dutifully relieved me of my bags. Now, as a family, we are not known for overtly expressing emotion but we must have left the rest of Heathrow in no doubt that a special meeting had just taken place.

The journey home down the M3 to RAF Odiham was full of questions; as many from me, wanting to know what had happened since I had been away, as from Janet and the boys, wanting to know the truth behind the guarded comments I had written in my letters. In fact it took many months to re-tell my adventures and even now, occasionally when we are sat around the dinner table with a glass of port, some small detail which I have never told them before comes back to the forefront of my memory. This book is, in its own way, a session on the psychiatrist's couch, as the marshalling of my thoughts and the setting down of the words has triggered several memories which had been submerged in my unconscious.

There was, however, no time to gather my thoughts on my arrival home. As I have said, one of the reasons for making a rapid departure from the Gulf was to celebrate two twenty first birthdays. The first, Lara's, (my eldest son's girl friend) was that very day and in extremely short order we were back on the road heading towards Basingstoke and an up market Chinese restaurant in order to celebrate the event. It was all rather surreal. It was not my place to be in the lime light but circumstances decreed that it should be so. I had assumed the aura of hero although in my own eyes this could not have been further from the truth. However, after the initial declamations I suddenly realised that that was what my friends and family wanted so I played along, modestly I hope. In reality, all I wanted to do was go home, have a quiet drink and be with my wife. That came in due course but I had to wait for it. The dinner was, however, a great success and I took the opportunity to distribute some of the presents I had brought with me; gold jewellery for some, 'camels' for the others.

The next morning (Thursday), after a leisurely breakfast, it occurred to me that I ought to tell someone that I had returned home. My participation in the Gulf War as a whole had been rather ephemeral. True I had had an official signal attaching me to 7 Sqn's SF Flight but my comings and goings had been, to a large extent, of my own doing. However, I was now back in Blighty where some form of normality reigned, or so I hoped. I rang my Desk Officer.

"I'm back." I said, expecting some sort of reaction. Nothing. The welcome back was almost as brief as the original posting instruction. He made only very general enquiries as to my health and well being, no reference at all to where I had been or what I had done and showed no surprise at all that I was back in the UK without having passed through any part of the military system.

"Take a months leave," was his short answer to my question as to what I was to do next, "Everyone else is."

"Then what?"

"Back to your compass base surveys. Life carries on where you left off."
And that was that.

The 'phone went dead and I looked rather blankly at the receiver. I assume he was busy with more important things like trying to maintain a viable air force with half of it on leave. But, even so, I felt, not quite abandoned, but rather as though my experiences of the last three months counted for nothing. Perhaps as far as the rest of the world was concerned it was not important but it was not quite the reaction I had expected or needed and I suddenly felt let down. On reflection I suppose it was quite natural. For the last quarter of a year I had been living in an unreal world and it had a profound effect on me, however, it was a world that very few other people even knew of, let alone had any cognisance, and therefore they could not maintain my euphoria even if they had wanted to.

My immediate future, however, was mapped out for me. As soon as Janet had been sure of my arrival she had contacted one of our long time friends, Dave Cheesewright, and organised a game of golf. And so, at 10.30 on the morning after my return from war, the three of us tee'd off for nine holes at the Army Course, Aldershot. Considering that I had not played since before Christmas I was not too rusty and my bunker shots showed definite signs of improvement but the pain in my back was getting worse and I was beginning to wonder if I had sustained a more serious injury.

On Friday (29th) the Boots the Chemists' '1 hour develop and print' offer lived up to its claim and the photographs I had taken whilst away were soon ready for viewing. They brought back a great flood of memories. Even though I had only just returned, I had forgotten many of the details of my exploits and the pictures served as reminders. I therefore proceeded to regale my family with yet more war stories. Fortunately, they were not yet bored and allowed me to talk and talk. It was undoubtedly very therapeutic for both sides.

Saturday (30th) brought Jonathan and Lara's combined 21st birthday party. This time the celebration was much bigger than the family get-together that greeted me Wednesday evening as it included many of their friends and work associates. It was held in the canteen of the local Sony factory where Lara's father worked. Again I unintentionally usurped the centre of attraction and, realising it, tried to fade into the background as it was Jon and Lara's day but everyone wanted to know what had happened in the Gulf. It is was difficult for me to come to terms with the degree of concern that the general public back in the UK had felt for us out in the Gulf. Even though they had been fed an almost running commentary by the media there was nothing like a first hand report, although I am not sure that my account matched up to what they imagined it was 'really like'. Nevertheless, the party was a great success and we all got drunk, which seemed to relax my back just a little. However, I was still more comfortable standing up than sitting.

Next morning, Sunday (31st), we got up late. Not because of any hangover from the previous night's party but because we had forgotten to put the clocks forward! I wish they would leave them alone. Midday is when the sun is due south and at its highest altitude and it should not be messed about with.

Monday. Today, the 1st of April 1991, is the 73rd anniversary of the formation of the RAF and no one has yet seen the joke!

We had arranged to visit my parents who live in Dunstable (Beds), about 80 miles north of Odiham. The drive did nothing to help my back and when we arrived I found that it had almost locked up. However, by lying on the pavement and relaxing the muscles I managed to get some sort of mobility back into it. I did this covertly, trying not to cause my parents too much concern and mumbled something about looking for a noise under the car!

The house was festooned with banners, both inside and out, my father shook me by the hand, a thing he did not usually do and my mother hugged me as though I were a child. I suppose I still am in her eyes. My brother and his family were also in attendance and greeted me with unusual warmth. As I said before, we are a family not known for its outward displays of emotion, or even affection, and this welcome overwhelmed me. That is not to say there is any coldness or animosity between us, quite the reverse, we are in fact quite a close unit, it is just that we usually don't show it. I began to find it faintly embarrassing as several of the neighbours had also gathered and behaved as though I had played a major part in the conflict. Other relatives arrived and I repeated the stories. I should have videoed the first rendition. I do not mean this to sound flippant or for you to get the idea that I was not immensely proud of the court paid to me. It is just that I found it difficult to cope with. Failure I can handle; praise is outside my usual experience.

As usual, my mother had prepared far too much food and my self imposed diet of the last three months prevented me from doing justice to it. Nevertheless, Jonathan and Matthew made up for my deficiency. I could not face the drive home and relinquished the task to Matthew, who should have taken his driving test the day of my return. For some reason or other he postponed it! He drove very well, perhaps too positively and confidently for a driving examiner, but we shall see.

Tuesday (2nd) Jonathan's birthday - My back had got so bad that I could not put off the inevitable any longer, but it was still with certain misgivings, that I eventually rang RAF Odiham's Medical Centre to make an appointment to see the Doc. Aircrew are always wary about officially declaring that anything is wrong with them for it is all too easy to be declared 'unfit' and thereby lose your aircrew category and hence your job and the significant bonus of flying pay. One of the high points of stress in any aircrew's life is the annual medical. No wonder we all apparently suffer from high blood pressure; the only time it is taken is when your future career is potentially on the line. Nevertheless I had to do something. If you have never suffered from back pain it is impossible to describe the disability it causes. The pain is with you all the time and even lying flat on the floor only reduces the scale of it. Sitting on anything other than a hard upright chair is truly uncomfortable and bending is out of the question. You know you are in a bad way when you cannot even bend far enough to put on your own socks or trousers and I had just about reached that point. The most annoying aspect of the whole thing is that there is nothing to show for your trouble. If you lose an arm or a leg the injury is obvious but the source of back pain is invisible and therefore engenders little or no sympathy. Its effect, however, is quite debilitating and capable of reducing fit, hard men to tears and its constancy gnaws at the soul and reduces you to utter misery. But life goes on and you can always take another couple of aspirins! The receptionist told me that if I came in straight away the Doc would be able to fit me in between the airmen's sick parade and their wives' pre-natal clinic. I declined to ask if there was any connection but said I would be there as soon as I could.

The Medical Centre waiting room was full of the usual collection of coughs, colds and sports injuries. I often think it would be an interesting exercise to work out just how much time is lost to sports injuries, and not just in the services. I am sure that it accounts for a great deal of time and money. However, I am also certain that the benefits of exercise outweigh the costs, but don't tell the accountants! After a relatively short wait, I was summoned to the Doctor's office and hobbled stiffly towards the door only to find an unfamiliar civilian, dressed in a dark suit, sitting behind the desk.

"Hello." he said, "The Squadron Leader is away on leave and I'm the locum. What's the problem?"

I explained that my back had first given me trouble some two weeks before my departure from the Gulf and that it had got steadily worse.

"Hm." he said, after having given me a thorough examination. "You've not slipped a disc but you appear to have dislocated one of the vertebrae in your lower back."

"How serious is that?" I asked with some alarm.

"Not as bad as you might think." he said seeing my concern. "They quite often pop out. The muscles then go into tension and stop the spine from collapsing and you from falling over. Often by just lying on the floor for 48 hours the muscles in the back relax sufficiently to allow the bones to re-align of their own accord. But if, as you say, you have been carrying this injury for several weeks, then by this time the muscles will have become so tight as to not allow the bones to re-seat without a certain amount of manipulation. The best thing you can do is find a good osteopath."

This was a revelation. Many doctors are still old fashioned enough to consider osteopathy as quackery and will only prescribe pills to dull the pain or the surgeon's knife *in extremis*, and operating on the back is still an uncertain affair. In between the two, conventional medicine has little to offer. Patients are therefore condemned to prolonged and often acute suffering because the medical profession is unwilling to accept that someone who has not taken the Hippocratic oath may just have something worthwhile to offer. Fortunately, more and more doctors are taking an enlightened view and I had been lucky enough to fall into the hands of one of them. Even so, because osteopathy is not a recognised medical practice it was up to me to find my own practitioner. When I got back home I searched the 'Yellow Pages' for an osteopath and found one in Alton, a small market town about ten miles to the south of Odiham. Miss Gore, an inappropriate name I thought, made sympathetic noises but said she was unable to see me until the following morning. I said that I thought I could last that long, put the 'phone down and gritted my teeth.

Wednesday (3rd) - The Osteopath was a rather small woman in her early 30s(?) and did not look strong enough to un-dislocate a finger. She examined me, more by feel than by sight, and asked me to lay face down on the couch. After about 20 minutes of massaging my spine, just above my right hip joint, she asked me to lay on my side, placed my left leg over my right shoulder and pulled; at least that is what it seemed like. There was a loud 'click' from my back and I wondered if she would ever be able to untie me let alone stand me upright again.

"Oh ye of little faith!!"

The result was only just this side of a miracle and the most meaningful demonstration of the principle of the lever that I have ever witnessed. It was as though someone has just taken a great physical weight from off my shoulders. The sharp cutting pain was gone and I was able, tentatively, to touch my toes when she asked me to. My back was still very sore and she said it would get worse before it got better but that it was only the muscles re-aligning themselves. I walked out onto Alton High Street a new man. It was the best £18 I have ever spent.

The next several days were spent finalising the imprest. Although I was happy with the daily accounts and had got them to more or less balance there was still some lose ends to tie up. The first task was to rid myself of the quantity of UAE Dirhams and Saudi Arabian Ryals that I had brought back. I was not quite sure what to do with them and so rang the cashier at RAF Odiham for guidance. Suddenly I was back in the un-real world of peace time service life. The cashier was horrified that I should have public money in my quarter. She recited the section and verse from the accountants AP (air publication) which stated that public money was to be kept secure at all times and added that if I did not have a safe of my own then I was to surrender it to her at once and she would issue me with an appropriate receipt. I somehow didn't have the courage to tell her of the insecure places I had kept it in over the past three months, I was sure she would not believe me anyway. So I took it out of the vanity case which has served me well as a strong box, put it in an envelope and made my way to the Accounts Section in Station Headquarters, fondly known as Handbrake House.

But my dilemma was not over. I handed over 11,250 Dirhams and 2,800 Ryals and nearly caused the cashier to have an apoplectic fit. She had assumed that I had just a few pounds worth of currency to hand in but when she had finished calculating the total value came to £2,264 . 13p, at the last known exchange rates. And that was one of the problems. Because dealing in Middle Eastern currency had been suspended and not yet resumed, she had no idea of the exact exchange rates. She started to lecture me on the irresponsibility of drawing such large sums of cash when they were not for immediate issue. I felt like being very rude but realised that it would have got me nowhere, so I just grinned inanely and mumbled something about war and difficult and unusual circumstances. Eventually, after consultation with the Chief Accounts Officer, she reluctantly decided to take it. I did point out she had two choices but the humour of the remark was lost in a tide of righteous indignation. Nevertheless, I got my receipts.

Back at home my next task was to fill in sheaves of RAF Form No 6663, known as 'treble six threes'. 6663's are supposed to detail the movements of the people covered by the imprest and list, day by day, where they took their meals and were accommodated. The reason for all this paper work is to highlight anything over and above normal service fare so that individuals may be reimbursed at the appropriate rates. There was, however, yet another problem. The 6663's are designed to contend with a group of people that have followed the same itinerary and, for ease of accounting, should be filled out periodically, once a week say. In my case not one of these forms had been completed since the departure of the original group in mid November, 4 months ago. The problem was exacerbated by the fact that the remainder of the party was sent out to the Gulf in several discreet packets throughout November, December and January and not always by the same route. Some of the men were allowed to return to the UK over the Christmas and New Year holidays, not all together but in staggered shifts, and returned in an equally rag-bag fashion.

It took me nearly two weeks to piece together who did what and when, and out of the 90 odd people that made up the detachment, the largest number to follow identical itineraries was a group of six. Many of the others required individual record sheets. Not only that, but there were also gaps in the record which, for reasons I am sure you can guess, I was unable to get answers to. At the end of the day I had to make up some of the details and take as realistic a stab at the truth as I could. The whole imprest was unusual, to say the least, and I thought it prudent to write a narrative to explain some of the more bizarre items in the fond hope that it might save time later. When I had finished, this narrative covered four pages of closely typed A4 paper! I rang Command Accounts and explained that the paperwork for the imprest was complete and requested my next course of action.

"Oh, just put it in an envelope and send it to us." was the reply.

"You don't understand," I said, "I have two cardboard boxes full of assorted paperwork and I would like to come and explain it to you."

There was a long pause. "Well, if you feel you must, we can fit you in tomorrow afternoon, say about 2.30."

That was what I wanted and at the appointed time I once more presented myself at the guard room at RAF Strike Command, High Wycombe. There had been some changes since my first visit back in early January. The portacabins which had housed the temporary security staff were still in the car park but were now locked and showed no sign of habitation and the armed guards were no longer obvious. The police corporal at the guard room, having checked my ID directed me to my destination and off I went. There was a definite air of peace time normality about the place. At Station Headquarters I was directed to two more portacabins at the back of the building, told to knock and go in. Inside the 'cabin, seated at a desk covered with forms and papers were two officers, a Flight Lieutenant and Squadron Leader. The Squadron Leader looked up with an air of resignation.

"Can we help?" he said.

I explained the purpose of the visit.

"Ah yes," he said, "You rang yesterday. "Well what have you got for us?"

Using my typed narrative as a script I spent the next several minutes explaining why I felt it necessary to see them in person. "As I see it, I said, "There are two alternatives. Either you accept this imprest in good faith or I stamp SECRET on every last receipt and document."

The Squadron Leader smiled and shrugged his shoulders, rose and motioned me to follow him. He led me to the adjoining portacabin and opened the door. It was stacked from floor to ceiling with buff envelopes and boxes.

"I can see that your imprest has some special peculiarities," he said, "but this is the size of our problem." and he waved his arm over the contents of the room. "Leave yours with us and I doubt if you will hear any more about it."

I left feeling relieved but still wondering if there would be any awkward questions when they got their teeth into the details. After all this time the only comeback I had was about 2 weeks later when I received a small white form informing me that there £400 was due to me to cover the expenses of living in a hotel at the end of my detachment. It was quite unexpected but I did not refuse.

About three weeks after my return I received a 'phone call to say that my faithful tri-wall had arrived safe and sound and was awaiting collection from 7 Sqn's hangar. There had been rumours that the customs men had been through all returning kit with a fine tooth comb. But my box appeared to be as I had despatched it. Even the American camp bed which I had swapped for a 24 hour COMPO food pack was still there together with a great deal of dirty washing.

It proved to be much easier to hand equipment back than it had been trying to get it out of stores in the first place and there were no arguments over lost kit whether real or imaginary. There was a similar instance at the end of the Falklands Conflict. One day, right out of the blue, forms appeared with instructions for any equipment lost with the sinking of the Atlantic Conveyor to be listed. This form ended with the statement, 'Items so listed will be written off'. This was an unheard of act of generosity by the MoD and ,shall we say, 'a few', extra items were added to cover past and future 'losses'. If the Atlantic Conveyor had been loaded with all the kit listed against it, it would have sunk in harbour never mind on the wrong end of an Exocet missile 8000 miles away in the Southern Atlantic. It was obviously well insured!

Eventually it was time to go back to the ACO and resume the work I had left in such unseemly haste. I was received like a conquering hero. Boffins don't often get the opportunity to go to war or see the fruits of all their work in action. I was the sole member of the ACO to go to the Gulf and therefore assumed the role of their representative in the conflict even though I had not done anything remotely connected with their research work. Nevertheless, it behove me to regale them with all the details. It was the practice at the ACO, once a month on a Friday afternoon, for a member of the establishment to give a presentation on the work that he or his department had been engaged in. That way everyone was kept up to date and it provided an opportunity for cross-fertilisation between the various disciplines. A revolutionary idea which, no doubt, has been stamped on subsequently. These seminars usually lasted between 30 and 40 minutes and the Senior Scientific Officer suggested that this would be an ideal vehicle for me to 'tell all'.

I duly prepared my lecture and it was advertised on the notice board. I collected together what slides and mementoes I thought would interest them, dressed up in my desert cam and wore one of the SAS' discarded posteens. It was an awesome occasion. Never before, or since, have I addressed an audience of such rapt attention and it gave me a glimpse of the power that great actors possess. After what seemed like no time at all I looked at my watch and found that just over one and a half hours had elapsed and no one seemed bored.

In retrospect it was my official debrief. It allowed me to marshal my thoughts and rehabilitate myself in the real world of ordinary people and I am very thankful for the opportunity. But I was not the same. I had tasted a different way of life and even the freedom of compass base surveys began to pall. I needed a change and that change came one day in November. Norrie and I were out on a compass base when an airman came out to say that there was a telephone call from my desk officer. With a very strong feeling of *deja vu* I picked up the phone and a voice said, "We are putting together a training course for navigators in support helicopters and would like you to become an instructor."

"You must be desperate." I said.

"Yes." he said.

I went anyway.

But that was not the end of my Gulf experiences. When the announcement of the award of the Gulf War medal was made I duly waited for my name to be called but it did not happen. Upon inquiry I found that those concerned with issuing medals had no knowledge of my involvement. I know my duties had been covert but this was ridiculous. Subsequently I discovered that because I had only been loosely attached to 7 Sqn I had somehow fallen through the cracks of the list. The error was, nevertheless, soon resolved and the medal now hangs in a show case on the wall of my study.

Apart from the Gulf War medal, which was awarded to all who participated, a smattering of decorations also found their way to the Chinook SF contingent. Contrary to popular belief, not all those who deserve awards for bravery receive them. There is, believe it or not, a quota system. To my mind all the aircrew deserved something as did many of the ground crew. Simply getting airborne in a Chinook is an act of bravery but to take one clandestinely into enemy territory at night and at very low level is 'above and beyond the call of duty'. Nevertheless, the resulting awards were almost a lottery and it left a certain amount of ill feeling, especially when quite prestigious decorations were handed out to some who had strayed no further than the edge of their desks. I know that planning and support are important but it does not warrant that form of recognition. Promotion? Perhaps. An MBE? Maybe.

When the honours and awards list was finally published in the London Gazette the names of those SF members who had been honoured were excluded in order to preserve their anonymity. The entries simply said,

"DSO ... Major Bloggs, 1st Mounted Foot, etc. and three others".

Collectively, the Chinook SF unit picked up a DSO, a DFC and a handful of MiDs (mention in dispatches). Subsequently, in the New Year Honours list, a couple of MBEs also found their way to ground support members who had played their part. But that was it. Out of almost 100 men who had made up the unit less than 10% were recognised for the exceptional courage and devotion to duty shown by all of them.

You may counter this by saying 'that that is what they are paid to do', but consider the following. All military personnel are 'on duty' 24 hours a day, 365 days a year. There is no such thing as overtime, no such thing as 'stand by pay' and, contrary to popular belief, they pay the same tax as anyone else and rent for the quarters in which we live. Add to this that they can be, and are, called upon to place their lives on the line at a moment's notice. For this, a specialist aircrew flight lieutenant (equivalent to an army major) is paid in the region of £38,500 per annum; less than £4.50 per hour! Part time office cleaners are paid more. Roll on the minimum wage! It was rumoured that the Saudi authorities had offered to pay £1,000 bounty to all UK military personnel who had taken part in the war but that this had been declined by the British government who did not want the Soldiers of the Queen to appear to the world as mercenaries. It would probably have been taxable anyway!

Eventually, everyone who received the Gulf War medal also received campaign medals from the Saudi Arabian and Kuwait governments. These were, by British standards, a little gaudy and seen by some as almost an insult. Nevertheless, they were given with the best intentions and most of us were proud to receive them. However, it was decreed that, as a British campaign medal had been authorised for the conflict these 'foreign decorations' could not be worn by serving personnel on their uniforms but could be retained as a 'keepsake'.

I have dined well off stories of my Gulf War experiences but the dinners are now becoming less and less frequent. However, my sons still do not tire of telling friends, at every opportunity, of when their father went to war with the SAS. I hope that this account, in some part, sets the record straight.

Printed in Great Britain
by Amazon

79672718R00109